# Through The Years
## Memoirs: Volume II

*By*
*Patt Abrahamson-Besse*

Sand Point Publishing
Escanaba, Michigan

**PATT ABRAHAMSON BESSE**
Pattabe@charter.net

Printed in the United States of America.
This book is printed on acid-free paper.

# Memories

*Memories:* They are what sustain us in our "Golden Years." We thrive on memories created *Through The Years.*

*Memories:* Of our childhood, of our family, of our town, of local history, of historical events and of personal relationships.

*Memories:* Happy memories with laughter, sad memories with tears. We have them all. They define who we are.

*Memories* are our legacy - proof that we have been here. The generations before us have touched our lives - just as we will touch the lives of the generations to follow... with Memories.

*Patt Abrahamson-Besse*

# Dedication

I am dedicating the second edition of "Through The Years" to my beloved son, Gary Abrahamson Jr. who passed away on August 18, 2012. A mother should not survive a child - That's not the way it is suppose to be. I cared for Gary for twenty-five years after his brain-injury and his death has been devastating. He missed his father, Gary Sr. who died sixteen months previously. My hope is that they are together. Still I will miss my beautiful son every day of my life.

The following is his obituary and a great tribute to the man he was.

## Gary Charles Abrahamson Jr.
## Obituary

On August 18th my beloved son, Gary Abrahamson Jr. died peacefully in his sleep. I have to believe that. I turned off the TV and shut off his lights at 11pm and we went through our usual bedtime ritual. Lots of kisses and telling one another "I love you." The same way we ended our days for over twenty-four years. Earlier in the evening he sang Happy Birthday to his step-father, John Besse while we celebrated his 86th birthday.

Gary was born in Chicago on October 7, 1950. In 1987 he died while jogging. Faith, God and technology brought him back to spend 25 more years with us. We were so blessed. No, he wasn't the same Gary: his memory was severely impaired and he needed 24 hour care. His dad, Gary Sr. who died just over a year ago always said, "Gary's tragedy affected me more deeply than anything else in my entire life. I am truly grateful to God for allowing me to love and care for my son, Gary, in my old age."

Gary's tragedy changed all of his family of origin. We cried, laughed and loved together. Gary's life and tragedy taught us so much. The community loved Gary too and showed much compassion. He was a regular visitor to the Civic Center.

Gary was special. He attracted friends like a magnet. He loved humor and had the most infectious laugh. He really loved life.

Music was a huge part of his life. He knew every Beatles song and sang along with them on his CD. We had tickets to take Gary to see the Fab Four at the Casino in October. I hope he is listening in Heaven.

He loved playing pool since he was a kid. Years ago he won second place in the Wisconsin State doubles tournament. He loved to jog and won many 10 K races.

He loved the Packers, the Chicago Bears, the White Sox, the Cubs and coaching young kid's baseball. He was an all-around athlete. He excelled in hockey, played in many international tournaments in the Sault and was top scorer in the league two years. And dancing! He was a terrific dancer and music, always his great love, helped him through the years he lived after his tragedy.

Gary cared about people and was generous to a fault. His sister, Vicki, talked about how his charisma was the core of who he was and said he had a magnetic personality.

His brother Jeff commented, "Although Gary's life became tragic almost 25 years ago, he was blessed to have parents that took his tragedy and turned it into a labor of love. Though Gary's life wasn't what he or any of us hoped it would be, it was -- after his brain injury -- as good as it could be under the loving care of my parents."

Peggy Bryson, former editor of the Daily Press writes, "I am so sorry. I loved Gary. We did several articles in the Daily Press about his struggle and I so much admire the family devotion to him. RIP Gary. If ever a demonstration of parental love was to be witnessed it was here...with the Abrahamsons."

His sister Vicki's thoughts: Gary Charles Abrahamson – my precious big brother. Oh how I will miss your wonderful smile

*Gary with his sister Vicki.*

and your warm heart. Those that knew the "old" Gary, the one before the brain injury, would have known a kind, sweet sincere man. He was a tall, handsome, classy guy with beautiful blue eyes just like his Dad. Gary was a person who loved life to its fullest and a man who experienced life and people the way many are afraid to venture. He was a rebel and saint. He believed in peace and harmony and love for all with an open hand and a big heart. My brother Gary smiled and laughed a lot in his post injury days and his love for music outshined any brain injury that he had suffered. He always remembered the words to his favorite tunes from the Beatles to James Taylor. I remember Gary as a perfectionist, from the way he dressed, to the way he danced, to the way he embraced professional life, and the way he dedicated himself to sports. He could still figure out the balance in your checkbook before you could add two and two. He was an avid speller and would occasionally gently correct your grammar. Gary would still make

us laugh on many occasions and taught us all to take life a little less serious.

Gary received an Associate's Degree from Great Bend Kansas Community College and was continuing his education in a nursing program to become a nurse anesthesiologist when he was struck by tragedy in 1987.

God Bless Him for his Journey and all he taught us along the way. May his sweet soul go to Heaven and may he finally be in peace. We will miss him with all our hearts ... he was such a good man, father, son, and brother. He suffered for us all ... and brought out more compassion than we all knew we had. MAY GOD REST HIS SOUL.

Gary is the son of Patt Besse and the late Gary Abrahamson. He will be sadly missed by his sister Vicki (Dave) Cass of Fox Point, WI and brother Jeffery Abrahamson of Alexandria, VA., his step-father, John Besse. Gary will be missed by nieces, Heather, Mary Pat, Kelly, Gabrielle, Audriana and nephews, Graham, Zachary, Noah, Tony, Mathias and Jaden. So many people made a difference along the way in Gary's life. Charlene Carlson, who brought him communion every week for many years, was one of those people. Gary also had many special caregivers including Brenda Milkovich, who sang his favorite Beatles songs with him. Gary will be missed by many others who loved him, both family and friends. A special scholarship is being established in Gary's name.

# *Contents*

# Acknowledgements

First and most importantly my humble and deepest gratitude goes out to Rick Rudden, Editor of the Escanaba Daily Press for recognizing my writing, my style and possibly what a senior writer with wealth of experiences could contribute as a columnist. Without Rick's belief in me as a writer and without his thumbs-up for me to write a weekly column - this book would not be happening.

My husband Gary, has been very supportive and instrumental in selecting topics of interest and supplementing me with his vast knowledge of local and national history. He is always there for me - to garner his opinions, his critic and his praise - when he exclaims, "Yes, Patt that's it." I go with it.

Laced throughout the book are photos provided by the Delta County Historical Society Archives. Their diligent effort to preserve local history has also served to enhance my book.

My readers have become a huge part of my life. Their head nodding takes many forms: phone calls, letters, E-mails and approaching me in the community to affirm their appreciation of my column and the subjects I write about. So a huge THANK-YOU to all of my readers!

This book was a combined effort with the folks at Richards Printing: Jeff Richards, Ray Richards and Tre Ballo. I worked daily with their graphic artist, Chris Keenan. Between us we came up with the cover design, photo placement and text format. His knowledge, unique style and help were invaluable.

Cherish Yesterday

Dream of Tomorrow

Live for Today

## FORMER RESIDENTS CREATE WINERY
**Friday, August 17, 2007**

A variety of subjects pique my writing interest: local and national history, local sports, World War 11, politics and nostalgic stories relevant to seniors. However, nothing delights me more than doing a story about a person born and raised in Escanaba that has soared like an Eagle to phenomenal heights of accomplishments.

Gus and Phyllis Anderson are a great example. Gus, born and raised in Escanaba, graduated from Escanaba High School in 1948. While attending Augustana College in Illinois, Gus met his future wife, Phyllis.

Phyllis was from the Chicago area and they married when she finished her nurse's training. Gus continued his education at Northwestern where he attained his degree in dentistry becoming an orthodontist.

Upon graduation Gus went directly into the US Air Force where he practiced dentistry. While in service the Anderson's spent time in California where eventually Gus opened his dental practice. After a trauma accident Gus lost the vision in one eye and not knowing if he could continue his dentistry they moved to northern Delta County where they owned a farm.

Fortunately, Gus was able to continue dentistry and after a few years of practicing in Gwinn, they moved to Menominee where he practiced from 1969 to 1972. A couple of severe winters motivated them to move to Northern California—where he eventually retired from his dentistry career in 1991.

In 1981 Gus and Phyllis came across a beautiful valley with open hayfields and grazing horses. Gus says, "Unfortunately the property was not for sale. After locating the owner on the county records and with months of negotiating, we were able to purchase 40 acres in 1983. Along with our son Todd and his wife, we began the development of Conn Valley Vineyards."

Literally, from bare hands, Gus and his son built the caves, the winery, the home and the vineyards. Gus says, "The vineyards are the beginning of great wine. You don't make it in the winery."

The vines are densely planted with as many as 2,640 vines to an acre. The rows are planted north and south which allows the morning sun on the east side of the vines and the afternoon sun on the west. Leaves are removed on the east side of the vines to allow sun exposure on the fruit in the morning. Gus relates, "We remove little or none of the leaves on the west side so the fruit is shaded from the hot afternoon sun."

Lake Hennessey is located just three miles south of the vineyard. Each afternoon in the summer a breeze funnels up from the lake at 3 o'clock in the afternoon. It continues until 7 o'clock in the evening cooling the vines and allowing the grapes to mature more slowly.

"All great wines have a sense of place. The French call it *terroir* – the site, the soil and the climate," says Gus. "Our vineyards indeed give our wines a true sense of place!"

Over the next 23 years the vineyards produced some of the Napa Valley's most successful Bourdeaux styled wines; wines that received accolades from wine consumers, wine reviewers and journalists.

Their son, Todd, a geologist, and his wife, Ronnie took over the operation of the Conn Valley winery; Gus concentrated on running the vineyards, but in less than a year Gus realized he loved wine making too much to not continue making wine. "At a time when most men my age were retired Phyllis and I founded Eagles Trace, a winery dedicated to making small lots of wine."

According to Gus, "Eagles Trace, the name chosen for our wine, refers to two significant historical themes of the United States. The Eagle became the official National emblem in 1782 when the great seal of the United States was adopted and signified the new country's freedom, strength and expansion into the future.

As the early pioneers expanded westward through the Appalachian Mountains, they found a "trace" or wilderness path through the mountains. Not unlike those early Americans, I set about on a wilderness path to find a way to create one of the world's great wines."

Gus' hobby and passion was destined to become yet another successful enterprise. "Eagles Trace is an extension of the passion I developed for winemaking over more that 35 years as a home winemaker and later after studying grape growing and winemaking in the early 1980's at the University of California at Davis," relates Gus.

Recently, at a Delta County Historical Society fundraiser, the Andersons donated a bottle of their prized wine, Eagles Trace, for the silent auction. The lucky bidders were Dean and Ann Shipman.

The Anderson's vineyards are located in Conn Valley, within Napa Valley, where five wineries existed long before 1900. Gus explained, "Those early immigrants knew from experience in Europe where the best grapes would grow. Unfortunately, three of those wineries went out of existence during the phylloxera epidemic of the late 1880's and the last two succumbed to prohibition."

The Andersons have an interesting web-site www.eaglestrace.com that includes the winery's complete history and from which wines can be ordered and shipped to your home. Their Key to the Cellar Club features Merlot in May, Cabernet Sauvignon in September and Latitude 38 in November. They offer complimentary private tours and wine tasting when you visit the Napa valley. Their wine is sold all over the world.

Gus and Phyllis are like many former residents: Escanaba will always hold a special affinity for them. Three years ago the Andersons purchased a home with 400 feet of lake frontage near Fuller Park and spend the summer months where roots were planted many decades ago. Gus remarked that "Escanaba has always been home." Phyllis agreed "I really enjoy it here—it feels like home and Gus has many family members here."

❧❦❧

## FAMILY CAREGIVERS NEED CARE TOO!
## Friday, August 24, 2007

Respite: It is quite a simple concept. It means an interval of relief from something distressing or trying. And God knows those that provide care for a loved one need respite time to re-energize and relax. The idea sounds simple enough—but is it?

It is not a simple task to obtain the help of others so that caregivers can take a break from all of their care giving responsibilities. Caregivers need that time-out for rest and renewal and the numbers of care givers are mounting with people living longer.

Funding is a huge problem and many families cannot afford private pay. Often the caregiver of a family member ends up ill from the mental and physical stress caused from the overwhelming 24/7 duties of care giving.

Another problem: Some people, we found out, shouldn't be in the business of health care. It requires special people with empathy, respect for the person they are providing services for, and above all—realizing that even if a person needs care for their activities of daily living—they should be treated with the utmost dignity.

We have had some great caregivers over a period of 19 years— and we have experienced some horrible situations. Our son, Gary, is unable to remember and tell us if he has been abused in any way. That means we have to be especially vigilant.

An example: Years ago we discovered new black and blue marks on Gary's body while showering him. The marks were multiplying and it took us a while to realize what was happening. Gary had a habit of poking people for attention. Apparently this particular aide sent from an agency would poke him back very hard on his torso. We confronted her and fired her on the spot.

Another caregiver in Florida left him in a car without air conditioning in 90 degree weather. He came home overheated and lethargic. Yet, another agency sent a black person that could not speak English.

One local caregiver drove around paying his bills and "lost" Gary. Gary, sitting in the car and apparently tired of waiting, got out of the car and disappeared. The police finally found him. That same caregiver took him to the golf course. We provided funds for both to play, but found out later that the caregiver played and Gary just road on the cart. He kept Gary's money.

One caregiver stole money from our house. Shortly, thereafter she was dismissed from the agency. Over the years, we have experienced some bad situations.  Thank goodness, for the most part, the majority of people we have employed were caring people.

Presently, we have a young gentleman, Nick, that spends two hours every day with Gary.  They play pool, air-hockey and chess. Nick also does stretching exercises provided by a physical therapist and monitors Gary on the treadmill.  Nick has been with us for 8 years.  He works through Community Action.  He has empathy, treats Gary with respect and has been a God-sent for us.

The problem we have had trying to get funding is age related. There are programs out there for the elderly—that is, over sixty. Gary doesn't qualify for most programs.  He falls through the cracks.

In fact, 16 bills have been introduced on Capitol Hill between January and May of this year.  Most of these bills don't have a chance to become law because of political and budgetary reasons; but the fact that they have been introduced represents a "stake in the ground" in support of care giving families.

The proposed legislation includes social security tax credits for those leaving the work force to care for a loved one, tax credits for family caregivers and care coordination for Medicare beneficiaries who have multiple chronic conditions and more.

The National Family Caregiver Support Program is an example of legislation that is helping family caregivers.  It provides services through Area Agencies on Aging and is the first legislation that is helping family caregivers.

Over 3000 adult day centers nationwide are providing recreational and socialization opportunities to both younger and older adults who live with cognitive or physical impairment.  Many adult programs offer sliding fees and some offer free care. Medicaid often provides coverage for adult day services.

So what is the future of Respite Care?  In December 2006, Congress passed the Lifespan Respite Care Act which was created to increase availability of both planned and emergency respite services regardless of the age of the care recipient.

There again, the bill promises relief to family caregivers, but it will be some time before caregivers find an improvement in local services since the act requires an allocation of $289 million over a five year period.  Presently, congress is being urged to provide necessary funding to support this critical legislation.

I have contacted our Congressman Bart Stupak regarding the bills before congress. Bart assured me he recognizes the needs of family caregivers and also of his commitment of a yes vote for any legislation being introduced to facilitate family care givers.

Some states respond in-kind better than others. Oregon, Nebraska and Wisconsin have already passed and implemented their own Lifespan Respite legislation. These states will serve as models for how respite care will be organized and delivered throughout the country in the future.

What Lifespan Respite legislation promises is a coordinated statewide respite service with a single point of access. The encouraging news is that whether respite services are ultimately provided at the state or national level; the importance of respite for family caregivers and their loved ones is finally receiving the recognition it deserves.

If you or a family member is a caregiver there may be help available for you. Check with Community Action or the Area Agency on Aging. And continue to check these agencies for programs that may become available. Caregivers NEED care too to stay strong and continue their loving work. Finally, legislators on Capitol Hill are beginning to look at this problem seriously!

## DANCING YOUR WAY THROUGH LIFE
**Friday, August 31, 2007**

I addressed 'dancing' in a previous article. I loved the book, *And never stop dancing* by Gordon Livingston, MD. And although I wrote about it previously there is so much more to 'dancing' and the effect it has on our life and attitude.

For starters: Dance really does lighten the heart. It challenges the mind and strengthens the body. The music you dance to is invigorating and let's face it—those of us that love to dance know that "cutting a rug" brings much joy and happiness to our lives.

Dr. Cohen, M.D., Ph.D., director of the Center on Aging,

*Patt Abrahamson, Escanaba, and her son, Jeff,*
*dance at Jeff's wedding in 1986.*

Health and Humanities at George Washington University says, "Dancing tops the list of activities that promote physical and mental health. And interestingly, a 2003 study published in the *New England Journal of Medicine* found dancing may delay the onset of dementia for those at risk.

"Because dancing is done in a group setting, the social interaction is beneficial as well as the immune system enhancer." says Dr. Cohen. "Dancing is multilayered. It's physical activity, but it is also an art, involving two different art forms. There is the choreography of the dance and then there's the music. Art is special. Art is in the soul of the species."

I remember when we lived in Chicago and danced at the famous Aragon Ballroom. It was absolutely magical: The huge ballroom with its "star" lights cascading down from the blue velvet ceiling, watching the moves and grace of other dancers and oh! The big bands and their wonderful music!

A criterion to pick a gated community when we wintered in Florida for ten years were: the size of their dance floor and would they hold regular dances. The commonality we had with friends was our love of dance. Many couples engaged in ball room dancing lessons—we dappled in that.

Our love of dancing and music has rubbed off on our kids: Their vacations are Jazz cruises. Our youngest son, Jeff, really took it seriously and does it well. He "borrowed" some of our prized collection of big band albums and took dance lessons. He is fun to dance with and knows all of the more complicated dance steps.

Besides Swing, my husband and I Cha-Cha, Rumba, Tango and Waltz to our own moves and sense of rhythm. But we admire and love to watch accomplished dancers. We never missed an episode of *Dancing with the Stars*.

Many of us will remember the less complicated times of the 40s—when movies were wholesome and entertaining. Dance was 'huge' as stars such as Fred Astaire swirled across the silver screen. His partner, Ginger Rogers, did everything he did—but in high heels and backwards! How about Sammy Davis and Gene Kelly with their athletic dance moves? Then there was Ann Miller who tapped-danced her way into our hearts; also Shirley McClaine, the

Step-brothers and many more.

Just a sprinkling of songs that relate to dance are: *Dancing in the Dark; Dance of Love*; *Dance Ballerina Dance; Tennessee Waltz; Sway* and *The Waltz you Saved for Me.*

One man, David, from Sun City Center in Florida tells about when he was first married: His wife was an excellent dancer and watching her swirl around the dance floor with other partners really got to him. He thought, "I'm really missing the boat. I have got to learn to dance."

He claims he had two left feet. He took lessons for years, and practiced diligently. He says, "things started to progress." Today, at age 85, he is a prolific dance teacher. He has been teaching ballroom dancing for 20 years. He says music was what attracted him to dance. "The music is wonderful," he says. "And when you put steps to music, you really get a good feeling."

Cruise companies recruit older men who dance: They are allowed to take cruises free and some even provide a small stipend. The companies that feature dancing want the women to have partners. And older men that dance are rare and in demand. There are many specialty cruises: Big band cruises, Country Western and Jazz.

When we were in high school very few guys were able to dance the Jitterbug. My husband was one of them and really; dance is—what brought us together. Many relationships begin on the dance floor—an excuse for guys to hold someone they admire. In his class of 1949 there were maybe two or three guys who could Swing Dance and do it well. But the class of 1947 had several outstanding dancers.

Jack Coyne was one of them. My husband has kidded him: "Jack, you guys didn't have the greatest athletes in your class—but your class had All-State dancers!" Others in that class that were great dancers, besides Jack, were Leo 'Stooge' LaCrosse, Jim Piche, George Frazer and Rodger Coolman.

And many of us can remember Gunnar Beck and his wife, Ruth swirling around the dance floor at the House of Ludington or the Terrace Gardens. And there was Foy Arbor—wow! could he move! How we loved the huge dance floor at the Terrace! They packed the place with dancers as a carousel in the middle of the floor rotated with twinkling lights while the music played.

Some of the bands that come to mind in those days were Ivan Kobasic, Chet Marrier, Jerry Gunville and Wally Severinsen. And the duo of Gene Cote and Pat Henderson played regularly at the Ludington.

David from Sun City Center says, "It is never too late to learn to dance." He currently is teaching a couple in their 90s. And Dr. Cohen says, "You don't have to be a good at dancing to derive physical and mental effects. It's beneficial regardless of how successful you are. However, to benefit from dancing, you have to do it on a regular basis, at least once a week." So—put on your dancing shoes. *You Make Me Feel Like Dancing!*

**MEDAL OF HONOR RECIPIENTS:**
**AMERICAN HEROES**
**Friday, September 7, 2007**

Abraham Lincoln said: "Any nation that does not honor its heroes will not endure long." In 1862, President Abraham Lincoln signed the Act for the first Medal of Honor to recognize one's personal bravery and self-sacrifice, going above and beyond the call of duty. Of the more than 48 million Americans who have served in the U.S. Military, fewer than 3,500 have been awarded the Medal of Honor. Today there are 109 recipients living.

My husband, Gary (a true patriot) has always revered the Congressional Medal of Honor Recipients. A few years ago he purchased the book *The United States of Americas Medal of Honor Recipients.* He studied his heroes. He scrutinized them. He talked about them. His dream and aspiration was to meet, talk and shake hands one day with one of these uncommon heroes of valor and courage.

Over Labor Day week-end his dream was realized. He said, "Pack up; we're going to Green Bay. The Medal of Honor Society Convention will convene for the first time in Wisconsin and we're going to be there!" Last year it was held in Boston. So we packed the van and we were off and running! We spent three glorious days meeting Gary's heroes. 61 of the 109 living recipients attended.

He had the unique opportunity to speak with many of the recipients. He heard many of the heroic stories of courage—some of which I will relate. But rest assured these men would have you believe they are not the heroes—rather their comrades, who died for their country—they say, "Are the real heroes."

*Gary Abrahamson, left, poses for a photo with Robert Howard, Alabama. The two attended the Medal of Honor Society Convention this week in Green Bay.*

JOHN WILLIAM FINN, California is the oldest living recipient. He celebrated his 98th birthday two weeks ago and was in attendance at the convention. On December 7, 1941 during the first attack by Japanese airplanes on the navel station, he secured and manned a machine gun on an exposed roof top under heavy machine-gun fire from Japanese air-craft. Suffering multiple wounds, he continued fighting until ordered to seek medical attention.

MARY EDWARDS WALKER, New York was the only female to ever receive the Medal of Honor. Walker was an assistant surgeon and received her award for valor during the Civil War. As a battlefield surgeon she operated and treated the severely wounded, even including the Confederate soldiers. She was a prisoner of war for four months.

JACKLYN LUCAS, North Carolina was considered a "baby marine." In 1942 he quit school in the 9th grade and was only 14 years old when he enlisted in the Marine Corps without his mother's consent. He reached his 17th birthday while at sea, six days before he earned the Medal of Honor. He is the youngest recipient.

Lucas, following the landing at Iwo Jima, crawled through a ravine with three other men of his rifle team when the Japanese opened a hand grenade attack on them. The men jumped into two shallow foxholes. Lucas pushed down a thrown hand grenade into the volcanic ash and covered that grenade along with another with his body. He was left for dead by his companions, although he was miraculously still alive. Severely wounded in the right arm and wrist, right leg and thigh, and chest, Pvt Lucas had saved his companions from serious injury and death.

Truly amazing; after the war he returned to the ninth grade to finish high school.

RONALD RAY, Georgia sat next to Gary at the Breakfast with the Heroes. They were equally amazed that both of their grandfathers came from Norway. Ray, First Lieutenant in the army received his citation in 1966 for valor during the Vietnam War.

Ray came to the aid of a patrol under heavy attack; he silenced three enemy positions, shielded two of his men from a grenade blast, suffering wounds to his feet and legs and wounds from a machine gun. Then he led his men from their surrounded position, preventing their annihilation.

ROBERT HOWARD, Alabama enlisted in the U.S. army in 1956 at age 17. He retired as a full Colonel in 1992 after 36 years of service. Howard served five tours in Vietnam and is the only soldier in our nation's history to be nominated for the Congressional Medal of Honor three times for separate actions within a thirteen month period. Although it can only be awarded once to an individual, men who served with him said he deserved all three.

His citation for actions of valor occurred in 1968. While on a rescue mission, his platoon was attacked by a superior force. Unable to walk and weaponless, he crawled through a hail of fire to retrieve the wounded platoon leader and crawled from position to position rendering aid and encouragement and directing defensive fire, repulsing enemy attacks.

Gary shook hands and talked with the above male recipients. He said, "It was truly an honor to be in the presence of so many great American heroes." Four individuals from the U.P. have been awarded the Medal of Honor; Albert Smith, Calumet, Joseph Kemp, Sault Ste. Marie; Oscar Johnson, Foster City; Owen Hammerberg, Daggett.

The convention is ongoing throughout the week at the Radisson Hotel in Green Bay. The average age of the recipients is 74. Young men and women, Honor Guards, from all three branches of service are at the beckoned command of the recipients: Their presence is to facilitate and assure the heroes of their comfort in anyway they can. Cars, limousines and busses were lined up to take them to planned activities or wherever they wished to go.

A host of activities are planned through September 10th. A black tie dinner on Saturday evening will showcase the Medal of Honor Society distinguished awards to people who exemplify the ideals that make our country strong. Network news anchor Brian Williams, Brett and Deanna Farve are among this years award recipients.

The culmination will be at the Packer Game on Sunday. The Medal of Honor Recipients will stand as a group right on Lambeau Field and be introduced to the Green Bay Packers fans in a special pre-game tribute that will include a military flyover and paying tribute to the Medal of Honor Recipients and the men and women serving in our military today.

For each Medal of Honor Recipient the story of greatness is different; all incredible acts of bravery and heroism. For Gary, his dream of meeting Medal of Honor Heroes has come true!

## WHEN THERE'S A WILL  THERE'S A WAY!
## Friday, September 14, 2007

Remember Leona Helmsley tagged with the moniker, 'Queen of Mean?'

That name wasn't completely deserved, though. She gave millions to charity. Anyway, when I read about Helmsley's will I was consumed with thoughts of Escanaba's great benefactor: The Bonifases. More on them later.

Leona Helmsley was a billionaire real estate developer and gained some fame

*Leona Helmsley "Queen of Mean"*

internationally in the '80s when she was convicted of tax evasion and sentenced to prison for a short time. Yes, during her trial she had the audacity to say, "Only the little people pay taxes." The quote and other trial testimony described her as a tyrant boss, hence the tag, 'Queen of Mean.'

Helmsley's will was released recently—some pretty weird stuff. It has been said that even death could not stop her from exerting control from the grave.

Her dog, Trouble, was favored over flesh and blood relatives. Can you believe she left $12 million for the care of her 8 year-old Maltese—yet, passed over two grandchildren with nothing—zip—zero. No explanation other than "reasons which are known to them."

The other two grandchildren received $10 million each—but forewarned they'll lose half the money unless they visit their father's grave at least once a year. The will also states that they will have to prove their visit by signing a guest book.

Her brother got $15 million and Trouble will continue his pampered existence with him. But when white-haired Trouble dies he will be laid to rest next to Helmsley.

Donald Trump, Helmsley's real estate rival in New York said, "The dog is the only thing that loved her and deserves every penny of it."

In fairness to her, she bequeathed most of her $400 billion estate to charitable causes: religious or educational causes, groups that work to protect children among other charities.

At first I thought leaving three million for the task of acid-washing or steam-cleaning her mausoleum stone at least once a year seemed "over the top."

Hold that thought—it is what brings me to the Bonifas'.

First—many people that live in this community today are unaware of the Bonifas' rags to riches story or are unaware of their generosity to our community. We should celebrate their memory and their community contributions with a Bonifas Day or perhaps Lincoln Road should have been named Bonifas Road—much more meaningful to our community.

Some background information on the Bonifases and how they ended up in Escanaba with an opulent home on Lake Shore Drive is in order. Bill Bonifas was born in the 1860s and came to be known as the "Timber King." He came up the hard way and knew how to pinch a penny.

Born in Luxembourg, he came to the United States arriving in New York with only a few dollars to his name and wearing a suit that was much too small for him. He planned to work in the wheat fields of South Dakota but got on the wrong train and ended up in Green Bay. Lucky for us!

He came to Escanaba and went to work cutting timber into railroad ties and fence posts. He saved enough to send to Luxembourg for his seven brothers and sisters. He bought up land for 65 cents an acre. He was known as "Big Bill" to the hundreds of men that he employed in the lumber camps.

He died in the 1930s. His fortune at that time was over $20 million—at least 200 million in today's money. He left the bulk of his fortune to his wife Catherine. Catherine, like her husband, was an immigrant from Ireland. She was hired as a maid in the Garden Lumber camp.

She was very shy, a homebody, who scrubbed her own floors – even with millions. They never had children. She was almost embarrassed by the size of their fortune. Yes—she even darned their socks and packed a lunch for "Big Bill" when he went on overnight business trips.

When colleges, churches, neighbors and friends hounded her for donations she looked to John Lemmer for help. Lemmer, a respected Delta County School Superintendent became the Lumber Queen's financial advisor.

Many gifts for education are evident of Lemmer's influence. She funded a technical school, a new public elementary school in Garden, a Catholic high school, a public senior high school, a junior college and a school for handicapped children.

The Bonifas fortune helped to build a combined city hall, county courthouse and recreational facilities in Escanaba. When she died, in 1948, her will left $2.5 million to many charities, members of her family, the city and schools, and Catholic churches.

Their name and legacy will always be synonymous with "doing great things" for Escanaba and Delta County. And now, for the thought I asked you to hold. The Bonifases have been laid to rest in Holy Cross Cemetery in a Mausoleum. I recalled how Leona Helmsley provided for her mausoleum to be maintained.

Apparently there was no such provision made in the Bonifas will—we don't exactly have a multitude of mausoleums is the area—to my knowledge that is the only one. And it is quite possible upkeep of stone wasn't even a figment of thought at that time.

Curiously, I peeked in there several years ago. The two burial vaults lined both sides; the walls appeared to be in dire disrepair with tumbled marble stones. It was eerie—downright haunting.

I returned last week to again check the Bonifas' resting site for this story. Disgusting is the best I can say! The building is covered with black mold—now the glass on the front entrance door has been frosted. Dale, an employee of Holy Cross Cemetery, says the frosted glass was added to hide the unsightliness. Droppings from animals are all over. And although their names are on the building—-their birth and death dates are absent.

Considering all that they have given to this community they deserve better. The building should at the very least be pressure washed or acid cleaned. The dates should be added and possibly some landscaping—perhaps a plaque commemorating their community contributions and a fund for some decorative pots with flowers every year. Perhaps a short walk way to the mausoleum with a stone bench would also be a nice addition.

Any ideas how we, as a community, could rectify this? Is there an organization willing to undertake this project? The Bonifases left their fingerprints all over the community. It's time for our community to step up to the plate.

## WIN ONE FOR THE GIPPER!
### Friday, September 21, 2007

Football season is in full-swing and many armchair quarterbacks will be pounding on the sofa, stomping their feet, shaking their fists, clapping, yelling and screaming at the TV either in ecstasy—or rage depending on whether the "play" was great or a "stupid" mistake. My husband joins the fray with millions every Sunday. So—some football talk is in order.

One of the great football heroes from our neck of the woods was George Gipp (born in 1895) whose life was cut short. He died at age 25.

Paul Hornung, former Green Bay Packer great and Notre Dame graduate said, "George Gipp was, perhaps, the greatest football hero who ever played for the University of Notre Dame. While much of his life was portrayed in the movie, *Knute Rockne - All American,* little is known of how Gipp actually was. Ronald Reagan's performance as the Gipper did not reveal the real Gipp, either on or off the field."

Michigan's Upper Peninsula can lay claim to George Gipp: He was born in Laurium and attended school in Calumet. Gipp spent a good part of his youth at the Calumet Y.M.C.A. He learned swimming and basketball at the 'Y' and also received an introduction to billiards. But from age 10, baseball was his sport.

In 1908, Gipp won the Laurium annual foot race. Basketball

*U.P. football legend George Gipp, who was born in 1895 and died at age 25.*

was also a sport where Gipp thrived. In 1910 he became a starter on the Calumet High basketball team that won 24 games in a row.

Gipp was unwilling to bring his grades up to participate in organized sports. Consequently, his career as a high school athlete was cut short. Two weeks before graduation he was expelled for smoking in the hallway. In fact, there is no record at Calumet High School of him graduating.

He was preoccupied with gambling; his great love. As a teen, he liked to play cards and shoot pool more than going to school. During his career at Notre Dame, Gipp would find a way to place bets on every game. Coach Rockne despised gambling and was unable to prevent Gipp from having a relationship with every bookie in town.

But, I am getting ahead of the "Gipper's" story.

Wilber Gray, a Calumet native and graduate of Notre Dame met Gipp on the street one day and suggested with his ability he could get a scholarship from Notre Dame. When summer ended in 1916, Gipp got an offer to go to Notre Dame and play baseball.

A fund-raising drive raised money for Gipp's train fare. Gipp was depressed at Notre Dame: The atmosphere was confining and he wanted to recapture some of the fun he had in Laurium. But he decided to stick it out.

One day he was fooling around kicking a football with his friends. Coach Rockne spotted Gipp's style and grace and watched him for about 10 minutes. Rochne said, "This rather tall lad, slid the ball to the ground and dropped-kicked with perfect ease—fifty yards. When he strolled from the field as if bored I stopped him."

"What's your name?" Rockne asked. "Gipp," he said. "George Gipp. I come from Laurium, Michigan."

"Played high school football?" Rockne asked. "No," said Gipp. "I don't particularly like football. Baseball is my game."

"Put on a football suit tomorrow," Rockne invited, "and come out with the freshman scrubs. I think you'll make a football player."

The next day Gipp came to the practice field. The very first time Gipp touched the ball he blazed through the freshman line for a touchdown.

Gipp was good at everything; but undisciplined: He smoked, gambled, drank and had a "devil may care" attitude. He reminded my

*Ronald Reagan played "The Gipper" in Knute Rockne: All American (1940)*

husband of a great athlete from Menominee in the '40s: Mike Shatusky. Mike also was great at everything.

Gary reminisced about a track meet at Menominee in the spring of '48. In the broad-jump event, you are given three trys: the longest one is your official mark. Shatusky announced, "I'm doing only one try and that's it!" Before he did his jump he disappeared behind the bushes and lit up a cigarette—then won the event hands-down with one try!

Shatusky was cocky too—just like Gipp. He played with

teammate Menominee's legendary Billy Wells, who was voted the most valuable player in the 1954 Rose Bowl game. Shatusky went on to the U of M and captained the football team. Later he became a coach. Menominee has had many outstanding athletes.

Gipp became a legendary hero at Notre Dame and was named their first All-American in 1920. At the time of his death he was scheduled to sign a contract with the Chicago Cubs.

In November 1920, he developed a tickle in his throat, then tonsillitis. He also had an injured shoulder and continued to play with fans screaming for him. He was hospitalized in December.

He rallied for a few days—then succumbed on December 15th to pneumonia. Coach Rockne visited him the day before he died. Gipp whispered to Rockne, "I've got to go, Rock. It's all right. I'm not afraid. Sometime, Rock, when things are going wrong and the breaks are beating the boys—tell them to go in there with all they've got and *win one for the Gipper*. I don't know where I will be then, Rock, but I'll know about it and I'll be happy."

His fellow team mate, Hunk Anderson, also from the U.P. eulogized Gipp: "George was without a doubt one of the greatest players of all time. The way he could punt, drop kick, and run the ball was more than brilliant...His magnetic leadership, his genius as an open field runner, his spine-tingling dashes and his matchless morale endeared him to thousands and made football history."

Gipp has been enshrined in the National Football and Michigan Halls of Fame. George Gipp, Hunk Anderson and Billy Wells were among the charter members inducted into the U.P. Sports Hall of Fame in 1972. Mike Shatusky was inducted ten years later in 1982.

## The Genie Has Been Left Out of the Bottle!
## Friday, September 28, 2007

My husband, Gary, is a real news hound: he watches the nightly news and several opinion type talk shows—many on the

Fox News Channel. You see, he is an ultra conservative. Recently he exclaimed:

"The Genie has been left out of the bottle!"

Oh, oh, beware; he's on his soap box again! "Explain that," I said, wondering if this is the beginning of yet another difference of opinion. It makes for anything but dull conversation.

"Look how society has deteriorated. Think of different civilizations; the Romans, the Greeks and the Egyptians among others that became so decadent they ceased to exist. Look at the negative changes in our society that began in the sixties. Morality standards have hit the basement and we are on a collision path to self-destruction!"

"Now anything goes!" he continued, after viewing the Hardee ad that has already been pulled. "To think I would buy a hamburger because some woman on a TV ad is acting provocative or buy a new car because a woman is sprawled out with cleavage, batting her eyelashes and flirting with the car. Does the advertisement industry really think we are that simple-minded?"

"For example, look at the way people dress today! Look at the provocative garb women wear; skimpy with bellies and much more exposed! Look at the way people dress to go to church: jeans, T-shirts with disgusting slogans or images; hats on backwards; look at the tattoos on *body* parts; the earrings on lips, in their nose, on their eye brows and boys wearing earrings."

"And how about the language that is acceptable today: The F word and the P——- Off. Even woman today use the filthy language; unheard of when we were young." Guess the more innocent times are from another era. Remember the film, *Gone with the Wind,* when Clark Gable said 'Frankly, my dear, I don't give a damn.' That was considered outrageous and it was censored.

Gary rambles on. "There was more gallantry and respect in our day. Men opened up doors for women; they walked on the outside when escorting a woman or they gave their seat to a woman standing on a subway or bus. Society as a whole was more respectful—more courteous."

I think to myself, how can I argue that? He has a valid point! I, too, have witnessed the changes. But then I thought about the young mother at Penny's Salon that cuts my hair: Kathy Kobasic. Her 16 year old son called during my evening appointment and asked permission to go out and get some ice cream. "No," she said. "I will bring some home."

She mentioned he had homework to do. I said, "Isn't it great with the computer; kids don't even have to go to the library." She quickly added, "Oh, we don't subscribe to the internet. I don't want my kids exposed to some of those chat rooms I have heard about. And when we are not home I want to know they are 'safe' from some of the bad elements on the internet that kids get involved in.

She added her plans for the week-end. "I am having my son choose a recipe he would like to make. First, he will make a grocery list and I will accompany him to shop for the items. He will proceed to make his chosen specialty at home while I oversee it. All of the Kobasic men have a specialty dish they make. When we have family get-togethers each brings their specialty dish."

Wow! How refreshing! Talk about a throw-back to more innocent times! That is not to say all of today's youth are on a collision path with descending morals. We have met and are aware of many young people who are wholesome and headed in the right direction. Thank goodness for the positive direction from parents; for the most part our area doesn't mirror the national image.

However, when Gary rants about politics; we can engage in a real debate! As a rule we have a *real* difference of opinion.

Take the war for example. I felt from the beginning we shouldn't have been involved in a war in the Middle East. Those people have been engaged in controversy for centuries; they're teaching their kids hate; their belief system is off-the-wall as far as I am concerned. It is widely believed that Muslim martyrs will enjoy rich sensual rewards when reaching paradise. Who in this country thinks that if they sacrifice themselves (blow themselves up) they will go to Heaven and will enjoy 70 virgins? What a put down to women!

I wondered how the Muslim women perceive that! Some of them are blowing themselves up in the name of Allah. Will they be rewarded with 70 virgin men in paradise? Such ludicrous thinking!

To put it mildly I am not happy with President Bush's policies. Now we are involved in a civil war. When will it end or will it ever? Will we have troops there for the next fifty years? Why do we have to be the policemen of the world? We've had troops in Korea for almost 60 years. Presently, we have troops stationed in Bosnia. We also had occupation troops in Germany and Japan for a long time.

Gary's take on the war is opposite of mine. "I think we were justified to invade Iraq, based on the reports we received from the intelligence community; that they had weapons of mass destruction and ultimately would distribute them to terrorists. The difference is, after we beat their army, I thought our troops should have been pulled out instead of occupying the country."

We agree on one thing. This isn't working and our thinking is in line with more than three-quarters of the country that feel the same way: We would like to see our troops come home!

Even so, with all of society's detriments, we still live in the best country in the world. And we live in the best part of it: The Upper Peninsula of Michigan.

## ARE YOUR FRIENDSHIPS BENEFICIAL OR HURTFUL?
### Friday, October 5, 2007

Friendships come and go on our journey through life—and for a variety of reasons. What basic elements hold a friendship together for years and what causes them to fall by the wayside after a short time? The reasons are many and varied.

Friendships as a rule are an important social relationship. Researchers have found that even one close friend could extend someone's life, and even increase the likelihood that someone would recover from a heart attack or cancer.

By the same token, friendships can be deadly: they can cause stress that may make you ill—or at the very least, unhappy. So do you try and fix it or cut the ties? *When Friendship Hurts* is a great book by Jan Yager, Ph.D. It's tells how to deal with friends who betray, abandon or hurt you.

Yager defines the four basic elements of what is a friend:

• It is between at least two persons who are unrelated by blood.
• It is optional or voluntary.
• It is not based on a legal contract.
• It is reciprocal.

A friendship should entail trust, empathy, honesty commonality, care, confidentiality and respect. But, most crucial of all a friend is someone you like and who likes you and with whom you share a positive chemical reaction.

Friendships can wax and wane for no apparent reason and then again the reason can be devastating causing as much stress as the relationship. So much has been written on the value of friendships in our life—not much has been said about friends who betray, wound and abandon you.

Remember Linda Tripp and her betrayal of Monica Lewinsky? In an interview by *George* magazine Tripp explained her view of the betrayal:

"I didn't betray Monica Lewinsky. I figured that whatever happened would be better for her than the callous abuse she was suffering at the hands of the president. Getting the truth out would end her obsession. Besides, privacy wasn't Monica's concern; she had already told 14 people."

Jealousy and envy is a key factor on relationships that can be described as negative or destructive. Even close friends can be green with envy or perhaps jealousy enters the relationship. Jealousy stems from what your example or success stirs up and in turn causes the friend to have the need to make you feel bad.

How does she retaliate? She pulls away from you, ignores you, devalues your accomplishments and withholds praise—anything to make you feel bad about yourself. And make no mistake about it—jealousy is very common. You need to decide if the jealousy is isolated. Or if it is a constant conflict, maybe terminating the friendship is in order.

Yager says, "Few of us are taught how to express anger. Instead we are "taught" that anger should be avoided, pushed down, swallowed, denied, and ignored. Instead of owning the anger and working it out with the people with whom one is angry, betrayal occurs. The action then becomes a substitute for the anger; it is still not a direct expression of the anger but a substitute for it."

Changes can occur in a relationship to alter the dynamics. Sometimes a weight loss or weight gain can challenge a friendship—especially if the friend is still overweight, resents it and is jealous.

Yager defines hubris as excessive ego and boasting. We have all known people like that and how much you can take or stand that person is a personal thing. "Hubris sets someone up for betrayal and retaliation because it makes him a likely target for contempt," relates Yager. "Once hubris is detected, friends will often desert in droves rather than stay around a puffed-up friend." Nobody cares to tolerate a braggart.

I found it curious that Yager mentions the male when talking about being puffed-up and an excessive ego; and the female when discussing jealousy and envy. Could these be gender-related traits?

Personally I have found that mutual respect and tact are important elements in a friendship. Joan, one friend of mine since first grade, has lived in California for years. Over the years we have maintained a great friendship. Two years ago she moved back to the area and our friendship is as strong as ever.

The only "words" or disagreement I can ever remember probably had to do with a boy in high school. If my memory serves me right, I let a guy she liked hold my hand and walk me home. Guess that could count for a betrayal.

In regard to couples: Sometime a friend can marry someone that your chemistry clashes with. Remember in a foursome all parties have to enjoy one another's company. You have four distinct personalities—so is it any wonder that finding the right mix and commonality in two couples is rare.

Friendships can be beneficial or hurtful. You need to decide if a friendship hurts. Yager says, "If your friendships are consistently less than what you had hoped they would be, a Band-Aid approach to changing that situation is doomed to long term failure."

Then again a friendship just wanes for no reason; you just quit communicating. Perhaps you are juggling a career and family that leave little time for close friendships. Over a lifetime friends wander in and out of our lives just as casual acquaintances do.

I have found that technology (the internet) has broadened my friendships. E-mail connections have many advantages. They are available any time of the day or night. E-mail friendships can connect you with people who share the same interests. They keep you "in touch" more than letter writing or even phone calls because it is instant.

My observation of a friendship is this: Whether it is hurtful or beneficial can only be decided by you. If the friendship is beneficial, embrace it, respect it, treasure it and it will continue to blossom. If it is hurtful, stressful, or causes you undue mental anguish and you can see no light in the tunnel —then for health's sake and peace of mind dump it—get out of it.

## MEMORIES SUSTAIN US IN OUR "GOLDEN YEARS."
**Friday, October 12, 2007**

We all have memories of our childhood, of our family, of local history, of historical events and of personal relationships. Happy memories with laughter, sad memories with tears; they define who we are.

It is truly amazing what can trigger a memory from 50 or 60 years ago. In my newly released book, *Through the Years,* which is a compilation of 18 months of my columns plus writings never before published, most memories are of the collective variety— memories we can all relate to.

Indulge me now because I am going to attempt to humor you with some very personal memories.

The trigger for the first one was an article I read recently about head lice; yes, that's right—head lice. I remembered my school years at the old Washington School. The school nurse, Miss Sheehan, visited all of the grade schools.

Apparently having head lice was of epidemic proportion back then. The nurse would line up the kids one by one with long tooth picks or some such thing and pick through our heads. When the nurse discovered lice she would stand you aside. Even though almost half the class was in the "louse" group it was embarrassing to a child.

I remember the day I was sent home with a note from the nurse stating that I had head lice. My mother literally went "nuts." She reacted as if I had purposely set out to catch lice. Anyway, the whole family got infected. My mother was fit to be tied!

She tried concoctions like vinegar and kerosene on my sister and me with the longer hair—then fine tooth-combed our hair twice a day. When that didn't work she took my sister and I down the basement and told us to keep a towel over our face. The dangers of chemicals in the '40s were unknown then. Can you believe she sprayed us with DDT? We were all choking and gagging. The treatment got rid of the lice and came darn near getting rid of us!

I thought about the time my brother and I were playing house along side of the garage. My mother gave me an old pan to pretend I was cooking like her. Franny and I picked some weeds and broke them up in the pan; kind of like cooking green beans.

Then he said he knew where there were some matches to make a real fire for me. Kids are innocent and don't realize consequences. The neighbor saw flames shooting in the air, yelled at us and we ran away. From across the alley we watched the fire department put out the fire. We didn't come home until supper time.

My mother was waiting with a big stick. She had never spanked us—just pinched my arm on previous occasions. Down the basement again! I suppose she didn't want the neighbors to hear our screams. It was my first and last "licking."

Here's a sad memory but one firmly etched in my mind. Somewhere around 1940 during the Infantile Paralysis (Polio epidemic) my friend, the former Joan DeGrand, myself and several other kids were quarantined when Carol Richter was diagnosed with Polio. We had all been roller skating together. Carol ended up completely paralyzed and in an iron lung for some time. I remember the picture in the press of this huge machine breathing for Carol. In front of her was a large mirror so she could see people.

Eventually she came home from the hospital in Marquette when she could breathe on her own; but was still paralyzed. Joan and I went to the Richer home every day to see Carol. She had a bed cart that we used to take out her for rides. In the spring of 1943, at age ten, we arrived to visit Carol as Dr. Mall was leaving. Carol had a cold. He bluntly told us Carol had just died and led us in the bedroom to see her. That horrible memory has never left either Joan or I. To see a childhood friend die was so scary; something most kids don't deal with.

I want to share two e-mails I received in the last couple of days—about memories.

My column has reached former residents and classmates all over the country. This one is from the former Rosemary Erickson, a classmate and friend that I haven't heard from since school days who now lives in Apache Junction near Phoenix.

Dear Patt, Congratulations on writing wonderful articles in the Escanaba Daily Press, bringing fond memories and information to so many people near and far. I'm blessed receiving some of your articles from an Escanaba childhood friend who gets them from her brother, both who live in Milwaukee...

When you mentioned bringing pasties to your son in D.C. I chuckled. This would be one of the first things I'd order during a visit to the U.P. The second thing would be a good fish fry which I can't find here. Our cabbage, strawberries and tomatoes don't taste good either.

My old friend has also sent me Esky press pictures (column 6-8-2007) of Main Street in the 20's and circa '49 which were fun to see....Where did those years go!!

My husband passed away in 1999 and I have since rekindled a relationship with an old flame from 50 years ago...class of 1949. We are both disabled and find great comfort in caring for one another and having a good companionship.

We are looking forward to your new book and want to thank you very much for all of the effort you put into such fine writing. Blessings to you and yours. Best Wishes. Mary

This e-mail was heart-warming too!

Congratulations Patt. How exciting for you. I am going to purchase a couple copies of your new book; one for my parents Jack and Mickey Coyne. They also love your column.

This past September, I accompanied my Dad to his 60th class reunion and I overheard many of his classmates talking about your column on the dancing talents of the class of 1947. I felt honored to be with him while my mom was recovering from knee surgery. Your generation certainly was the best! Best Regards, Mickey Wieciech.

I feel so blessed every day hearing from so many readers and friends. I will be at Book World (tomorrow) Saturday 13th for a book signing from 12 to 3 P.M. Hope to see you there!

# BACK TO THE GOLDEN YEARS...AGAIN
## Friday, October 19, 2007

Well, here I go again! (I sound like Ronald Reagan; that was one of his favorite expressions). More talk about the "Golden Years!" Everyday I experience the reality of changes that occur as a result of aging. Not just the little forgetful things; like not being able to pull up on the radar screen a name of someone I know well, but other changes: some funny, some frustrating, some disappointing and some devastating.

My husband, Gary, went to Doctor's Park for his periodic blood test. He came home all smiles (he used to hate having blood drawn.) Now he recounts the advantages and views it as a social outing. While waiting his turn he met Jim Hirn, former EHS teacher, and school-mate. "Gee, it's great to go over there, I always meet friends and have good discussions." (even if they are mostly health related).

"I also get special attention because my veins are difficult to draw blood from—so Debbie, the nurse takes care of me. Wow! They all know me and treat me with such kindness. Being older has its advantages; she helps me with my sweater and my jacket – just like when I was a kid!"

A few years ago, when George Ruwitch (former EHS coach and educator) was living, he visited Howard Perron and Gary in Florida. He stayed with Howard and Howard mentioned he had to help George put on his socks in the morning.

Help with socks? That was puzzling at the time. Well, at a much younger age than George was; Gary is *there* now. "Hey Patt, come here, I need help with my socks—I have an early morning appointment at the clinic."

Gary called our son in Washington on his cell phone; of course he doesn't own a "land phone," as they call it. When he didn't return the call for three days we became very concerned. Apparently he had left his cell phone at work over the week-end. "What's the urgency and big deal about getting a hold of me?" Jeff said.

"First, I was worried about you and secondly, I had to know if you got those tickets from a broker to the Navy game when I come to visit you," said Gary, as if a game is the next most important thing in the world. (He is happy as a lark to be attending the Navy/Wake Forest game tomorrow in Annapolis).

When Gary sleeps beyond 7 A.M. I check his chest to see if he is still breathing—is his chest rising up and down, or did he die during the night? He does the same for me. You see, these little rituals come with age!

And when I go to the grocery store on several occasions I have been asked if I need help out to the car. I wonder; is it my platinum hair that is the tip-off? Platinum, yes, I absolutely refuse to call it gray.

I love this one. I was shopping for a birthday card for my son, Jeff's October birthday. Ah-hah, I found a gem! On the front of the card there was a drawing of a hand holding a stinky diaper by two fingers and it said: Son, after changing thousands of your poopy diapers...Open the card up and it said...just looking forward to you returning the favor! Priceless! But hey, it could become a reality!

Or back a few months ago my husband said, "Patt, I have to pay to have the yard maintained and the driveway plowed. You need to get some help with the housework. We can't rat-hole so the kids can have a few more dollars." Uh-huh. He was right, although he worried that I would clean for the cleaning lady. I finally relented and now have someone clean every two weeks. I have more time for my son and hours to indulge in my favorite pastime: writing.

The "Golden Years" for some folks also bring with it disillusionment, disappointment, desperation and devastation. I will share an excerpt of an e-mail I received from a reader who put it into words more succinctly that I could.

She writes: "What's with the present generation anyway? So many people our age are hurting because of lack of respect, appreciation, and total disregard for us who have given to them endlessly. More times than I can count I lovingly put my life on hold and sacrificed to help my family physically, mentally, and financially.

Where are they now that I really need them in my old age even though I've asked nothing of them? Can't they take a few minutes of their time once in a while to at least call and see how we are? And we're not alone in this respect. We hear many others in the same situation, aching to hear from their family and spending long hours just waiting alone for death to ease their pain."

That is a sad commentary on the "Golden Years," but apparently reflects the suffering of many of the aged at the hands of their offspring. It is no secret that the aged in the U.S. are not revered like they are in the Asian culture where respect of the elderly and their wisdom reign supreme! What happened to the forth Commandment? Honor your Father and Mother!

## CONTRASTING THE '40s WITH TODAY
**Friday, October 26, 2007**

High school days as a female in the '40s were comparable to being on a different planet today. Take organized high school sports for example: We didn't have the same opportunities as high school girls today. They play basketball, softball, golf, soccer, run track, etc.

I remember playing intramural volley ball in school—that's it! Oh yes, I played volley ball at the beach in the summer. Those were flirtatious years. I didn't care about the game as much as who was playing.

I was so naïve about football. I attended the games as a majorette. Watching the action from the sidelines I didn't have the foggiest idea what the "downs" meant. I just joined everyone else and screamed and jumped up and down when our "Eskymo's" scored a touchdown. Basketball was a little easier to follow.

My perception then of girls playing sports would have been: "not cool, not feminine." Nothing I would have been interested in. The mind-set in the era I came from was that only "tomboys engaged in sports." Tennis was different. I did play that.

And golf! The only thing I remember about golf was that it was a game for the wealthy. Both my brother and husband caddied at the Escanaba Country Club for local members of what was then thought of as "High Society." The caddies made a quarter for 9 holes.

Naivety didn't end with lack of knowledge regarding sports. One reader just wrote about beliefs she had during our era in school. She thought babies came from kissing! And believe me; our thinking has come a long way from our parents.

My mother told me when she was expecting me (her first child) she spent many days over at her parent's home rocking on their front enclosed porch. As her belly grew she wondered how I would exit from her body and was afraid to ask. Obviously, she knew how I got there though. (Chuckle, chuckle).

Contrast those times with today: Eleven-year olds getting the "pill" or a "patch" or a condom in middle-school? Without their parents consent! YIKES! What is this country coming to?

We brought our own spoons to school. Kids lined up daily to be given cod liver oil and U.S. surpluses like prunes or raisins. We would have thought the pill was a vitamin—or that a condom might have been a new brand of candy bar or bubble gum. Yes, we were innocent! Too bad today's kids couldn't stay kids and enjoy those young innocent years.

Fast forward:

My boys played hockey in the Sault during the 10 years (1955-1965) we lived there. After a less than normal interest in sports I became addicted to hockey; attending all of their games and also the older guys games. I watched hockey on TV. I had favorites like Gordie Howe and Boom Boom Jefferion. We traveled with the teams to tournaments in Canada. It became a huge part of our life.

Clarence (Taffy) Abel lived in the Sault during the years we lived there. He played in the NHL; three years with the New York Rangers and five with the Chicago Black hawks. He won a silver medal in the 1924 Winter Olympics prior to even playing his first NHL game. Nine years after his death in 1964 Taffy was inducted into the U.S. Hockey Hall of Fame.

Taffy owned a nightclub on the St. Mary's River in the Sault that we frequented to dine and dance. One night in the late fifties Taffy, in a rare appearance, came on stage to sing a few bars. He was rather inebriated. He must have loosened his pants belt during dinner and to everyone's shock and surprise his pants fell down while he was singing! He continued singing oblivious that his pants were draped around his ankles; boxer shorts exposed. Two of his employees rushed on stage and pulled up his pants and buckled up his belt. I doubt he was even aware they had fallen down! He just kept right on singing.

I guess what really surprises me about sports is how 60 years later guys can remember a game play by play—and still talk about it. I never knew how affected boys were from playing competitive sports or how their experiences (both positive and negative) are engrained in their psyche decades later.

Larry Ebsch, Editor for years of the Herald Leader, (Menominee) is now retired but he still contributes a weekly column called ByeLines. He wrote an article (a few weeks ago) about the 1948 football game Esky lost to Menominee by one point; their only loss that season. Larry was in the class of '49 in Menominee and remembered the plays verbatim.

Gary, my husband and Larry talked on the phone endlessly reliving that game: the plays and the guys. They reminisced in general about those wonderful years.

They talked about Billy Wells who played for Menominee and Michigan State and was MVP in the 1954 Rose Bowl. Billy moved to California and organized a band called, Billy and the Playboys. He dated Debbie Reynolds several times when she was at the height of her career—before she married Eddie Fisher.

Then there was the Dome in Marinette or the Silver Dome as it came to be called. Young people could drink in Wisconsin at age 18. Kids came from the Escanaba area in droves. Larry remembers many of them who really knew how to hoist a few. He wondered how they ever made it back to Escanaba safely being in such a drunken state.

I am sure there are many stories of the Dome that some of the readers have tucked away. I never went there—I was too young and by the time I was eighteen I lived in Chicago. I would have only been interested in the dancing anyway.

Like I have mentioned before—memories become more paramount as the years pass by and it is really strange the silly little things that jog our brain-matter. What a magnificent creation the human brain; our personal computer!  Who can ever think we humans arose out of the sea?  The human being—God's glorious creation!!  Rising out of the sea?  No way!

## A TRIP TO REMEMBER TO THE NATIONS CAPITAL
## Friday, November 2, 2007

Each year my husband and I take separate vacations.  We are not as flexible as we once were so taking our son Gary, in a wheelchair is becoming more difficult.  This past summer I went to Washington to help my youngest son, Jeff, get settled in his new home and to help him with decorating choices.  I was in my element—decorating without picking up the tab!

My husband's recent trip took on a different flair.  He wasn't pulled aside and padded down like I was TWICE at the airports—but then he doesn't wear jewelry like I do.  Arriving in D.C. Jeff took him to a favorite restaurant:  Great exotic choices, sophisticated servers and cosmopolitan clientele.  Some had turbans; Muslim woman had their native shawls and long dresses; truly a melting pot of different cultures and nationalities.

While at the restaurant Jeff left the table and went to the men's room providing Gary with a clear view of a young couple dining at the next table.  The man looked Italian; tall, dark and handsome and very well-dressed.  Suddenly the man got up from the table and got down on his knees next to his lady friend.  He looked up into her eyes, said something to her, they embraced and they kissed several times.

When he got up, Gary asked him, "Did she say yes?"  He smiled, winked and said 'Oh yes!'

After an exotic dinner, Gary asked for a "doggy bag."  The server looked baffled that he should ask for such a thing and responded.  "We don't provide such things here."  I guess this is sophisticated Washington —not Escanaba where doggy bags are popular.

The next day they went to the Town Square in Alexandria. The place was a unique deli: A combination bakery with home-made soups and sandwiches stacked on fresh bakery bread. All of the servers were from foreign countries and struggled with English. You brought your food outside to a humongous area a block long dotted with tables. In the center was a place where different musicians could do their thing; spontaneously one appeared to play his guitar and sing. Kids and adults alike dropped coins and bills in his container.

Kids brought their scooters and made friends. The parents watched them while soaking up the sun and atmosphere. Many worked on lap-tops while drinking their lattes; and people of all ages laughing, chatting, relaxing and talking on cell-phones completed the scene.

Mary Pat, our 17-year-old granddaughter was attending the Homecoming Dance that evening. What an evening to remember! The young couples congregate at one home for photo shoots. The parents are invited to partake in the photo session and witness all of the young people in their finery.

Gary was taken aback as they approached a long winding driveway to a magnificent mansion undoubtedly worth several million. The girls looked like movie stars—they were incredibly beautiful; dressed to the nines in their cocktail dresses and displaying a definite air of city sophistication beyond their years. The parents, obviously filled with pride, took multitudes of photos.

The next day Jeff took his youngest daughter Kelly, age 6, and his dad to his office in the Treasury Department where he has a panoramic view of the Capital Building from his huge office window.

Security is ultra-tight in Washington. Two ladies, the security guards, had trouble admitting unauthorized guests due to a new complicated program. The Black ladies called the men, Mr. Gary and Mr. Jeff and were visibly frustrated and apologetic for the half-hour delay.

Gary, with his bizarre brand of humor suddenly outstretched his arms and began a little song and dance routine to cheer the ladies up. As he sang, *When You're Smiling* the ladies said, "You sure are 'somethin' Mr. Gary!" I doubt they had ever encountered anyone quite like him.

His brand of humor continued when they arrived home. His foolish routines had Kelly laughing at first—then she looked at her Grandpa and declared, "Popser, people are not laughing with you; they are laughing at you!" Can you believe that statement from the mind of a six-year old? Still, that didn't deter him; he continued with his antics as she tried not to laugh.

A great highlight was attending the Navy/Lake Forest football game in Annapolis before a standing room only crowd of 40,000 people. Gary related the scene. "The ceremony before the game was awesome. 1400 midshipman in their navy-blue uniforms and white caps marched on to the field in perfect unison. They filled the entire football field and you could see that people, including me, were filled with pride and admiration. The emotional ceremony brought tears to my eyes."

Gary wore his orange and black polo shirt with the Eskymo logo to the game. During the half Jeff was purchasing hot dogs while Gary stood in the concession area people watching. Lo and behold a lady from the Manistique area recognized the Eskymo shirt and excitedly exclaimed, "Hey, I'm from Manistique!" 40,000 people and up pops someone from our remote area in the U.P.! And ironically, she also worked for the Treasury Department.

The culmination of his trip was a delightful sunny day attending a brunch at the home of Paul and Ruth Dufresne, former Escanaba residents and classmates who live in Maryland. Ruth's brother, Gil Bullock, also a former EHS graduate and retired professor was visiting from the state of Washington.

One last incident occurred on his return trip during his lay-over in Milwaukee when Gary used the airport restroom. While inhabiting the stall he noticed a roll of toilet paper on the floor; the adjacent stall was also occupied.

He couldn't help thinking about the recent scandalous happening in the Minnesota airport restroom involving Senator Craig from Idaho. Gary was sure to keep his feet contained in his stall and not mess with the toilet paper lying on the floor. No, he didn't want to give off any misinterpreted signals for fear it might be an entrapment situation! Need I say more?

Indeed, Gary called it, "A Trip to Remember!"

# WHATEVER HAPPENED TO POLIO?
**Friday, November 9, 2007**

Polio also known as infantile paralysis presented in 1940 with one of the worst epidemics the state of Michigan had ever experienced; 1220 residents of Michigan, mostly children, were stricken.

Escanaba did not escape the wrath of the virus. Polio is a communicable disease caused by infection with the poliovirus. It occurs by direct person to person contact. It enters through the

*"As of 1941 campaign for funds to aid infantile sufferers swings into action throughout MIchigan, a survey shows that Michigan has but 35 "iron lungs," scattered from Detroit to Marquette, with which to combat the disease. At least some of theses are home-made contraptions which were hastily but ingeniously put together last year when 122 residents of Michigan, mostly children, were stricken in one of the worst epidemics the state has experienced. There are five artificial lungs in the Detroit area. The cost of a full size iron lung, such as the one pictures above, is $1,450"*
*Detroit News pictorial from January 26, 1941*

mouth and nose and multiplies in the throat and intestinal tract.

Between 1840 and the 1950s, polio was a worldwide epidemic.

In 1940 Carol Richter, a childhood friend (we were both age 7) became a victim to the horrible disease. It was an extremely hot summer day and we roller skated in the basement of the Richter home. Joan DeGrand, Stuart Jensen, and me were quarantined by the Health Department after Carol was stricken. There may have been others.

Not too far from Carol's neighborhood, Paul Dufrense (age 10) and a childhood friend of my husband was also stricken with polio. Gary and another playmate, Gerald Dufour, was quarantined. The dreaded red warning sign was posted on the door of our homes.

Carol and Paul both had different outcomes. In Carol's case her infection was paralytic; Paul's was non-paralytic.

I received many phone calls and e-mails when I mentioned Carol Richter in a previous article; all who vividly remembered Carol, who were related to her or had photos of her.

I remember as a child how frightening the word Polio was. A cousin of Carol's and former resident, Annette Katerincic wrote: "My earliest memories of Carol were in the "iron lung"...I was always terrified of Polio and so glad when they (discovered) the vaccine."

In 1941, a survey revealed Michigan had only 35 "iron lungs" scattered from Detroit to Marquette to combat the disease. Carol's sister, Elaine Anderson, sadly recalls Carol's initial involvement with the "iron lung."

Carol was taken to Green Bay and placed in an older model "iron lung." My father was an engineer on the railroad and all of the railroad employees raised money for a newer model "iron lung." Carol was eventually transported to Marquette in a train box car that had direct currant to plug in the "iron lung." During the trip from Ishpeming to the Marquette Hospital, a technician from Emerson Co. (the "iron lung" manufacturer) manually had to operate the bellows for Carol to breathe. He literally sat on the tailgate of the truck."

My recollections of Carol are still vivid today. Joan DeGrand DeHaas and I spent time with Carol almost daily. Carol lay paralyzed in her bed wheel-cart. We played paper dolls and we were Carol's hands. We played Chinese checkers and we were Carol's hands. We played card games like Old Maid and we were Carol's hands.

We were there when the nurses wrapped steaming hot wet wool cloths around her arms and legs daily trying to stimulate life into her limbs. We witnessed her stifled need to cry out in pain and her gasping breath.

Carol attended my 10th birthday party in April, 1943 in her bed wheel-cart. Joan fed her birthday cake. Two days later on April 25, Easter Sunday, we had a photo taken with Carol after attending services at the old St. Annes Church.

A week or so later the Skerbeck's Carnival set up in Escanaba. Carol cried to attend with Joan and me. Her mother relented. It was windy and cold. Carol's blanket kept blowing off of her bed cart. It started to rain and we rushed to get Carol home.

Carol apparently caught cold. Only the left half of Carol's

diaphragm had escaped paralysis. We visited her home in early May shortly after lunch. I had an errand to run and Carol seemed agitated and didn't want us to leave. We told her we would be back to see her by 3P.M.

Dr. Mall was just leaving the house when we returned shortly after 3P.M. He shocked us with news that Carol had just died and led us into her bedroom. She lay there with her eyes open and Dr. Mall bent over and closed them. Her mother, father and aunt were engulfed in grief and wiping away tears. Later, Mrs. Richter gave Joan and me each one of Carol's dolls. Joan received the Nun doll and I was given Shirley Temple.

At the cemetery Carol's sister, Elaine Anderson, recalls the minister competing with the background sounds of the Merry-go-

round at the carnival. Today, we drive through the cemetery every couple of weeks in the summer. I pass her grave-site and the memories all flood back: Memories of Carol, of the fear of Polio, and of the trauma I experienced as a 10-year-old facing the death of a childhood friend.

Paul Dufrense spent months in the hospital in Marquette. His involvement didn't require the "iron lung;" although he missed a year of school. His larynx was affected and his only residual effect was his weakened voice.

The March of Dimes was founded as the "National Foundation

*Carol Richter is in her wheelcart surrounded by friends Patt Abrahamson, left, and Joan DeGrand DeHaas. Richter died of complications from polio, a disease that killed countless people until a vaccine was discovered in the 1950s.*

for Infantile Paralysis" on January 3, 1938 during the presidency of Franklin D. Roosevelt. Roosevelt, who was stricken with the dreaded disease in 1921, was portrayed on the U.S. dime after his death

We oldsters can all remember, as kids, saving our dimes in a card to fight polio. Those dimes helped support the research that brought about the discovery of the vaccine. The effort begin as a radio appeal: Everyone in the country was asked to contribute a dime (10 cents) to fight polio.

Many scientists were racing to discover a vaccine in the 50s—but virologist, Jonas Sauk got there first. He developed the first successful vaccine in 1952.

Until recently the last case of non-vaccine related polio in the U.S. was in 1979. However, in 2005, four children in an Amish community in Minnesota were diagnosed with polio. None had been vaccinated for polio which is now a routine measure in the U.S.

## MICHIGAN / OHIO RIVALRY AND THE "10 YEAR WAR"
**Friday, November 16, 2007**

Most people think of the Michigan-Ohio State football game when they hear the word rivalry in connection with the two states. But long before there was such a rivalry Michigan and Ohio were on the verge of armed conflict, sometimes referred to as the Toledo War.

First, let's look at the football rivalry. College football has the fewest games of any sport; therefore, every individual game takes on magnified importance. And historically, Michigan and Ohio dominate the Big Ten conference and play each other last. That game usually carries implications for the Big Ten championship.

Although Michigan and Ohio State have played over 100 times, most fans of both schools believe the rivalry is about the "10 year war." Remember the decade (1969-1978) when Michigan's, Bo Schembechler and Ohio State coach, Woody Hayes faced off? Bo had coached *under* Woody, thus making it another sub-plot of rivalry.

Not until 1975 was a Big Ten team allowed to play in a bowl game other than the Rose Bowl. It was winning and going to the Rose Bowl—or lose and spend the next 365 days preparing for revenge. Of course the rivalry still exists.

The Toledo War (1835-1836) also known as the Ohio-Michigan war was a boundary dispute between the U.S. state of Ohio and the adjoining territory of Michigan. The governments of Ohio and Michigan both claimed sovereignty over a 468 square mile region along the border now known as the Toledo Strip.

Then when Michigan pushed for statehood in the 1830's, it tried to include the disputed territory within its boundaries, but Ohio was able to stop Michigan's admission to the Union.

The governor of Ohio and Michigan's then 24-year-old "boy governor" Stevens T. Mason were unwilling to cede jurisdiction of the Strip, so they raised militias. Both militias were sent to positions on opposite sides of the Maumee River near Toledo, but the so-called war consisted of mutual taunting and shots being fired in the air.

In 1836, the Michigan territorial government gave up the land under pressure from then President, Andrew Jackson. Michigan gave up the Strip in exchange for its statehood and approximately three-quarters of the Upper Peninsula. At the time Michigan considered it a poor compromise; but the later discovery of copper and iron deposits plus the plentiful timber in the U.P. more than compensated for the loss of the Strip.

A special convention was held in Ann Arbor in September of 1836. At first, Michigan rejected the offer, partly because of pride and partly because the U.P. was considered a worthless remote wilderness. However, the war officially ended in December, 1836 when a second convention in Ann Arbor known as the "Frostbitten Convention" passed a resolution to accept the terms set by the Congress.

The Michigan Government was spurred to action by the realization that the U.S. Treasury Department was about to distribute $400,000 to the states, but not to territorial governments. At the time Michigan was in a deep financial crisis and nearly bankrupt because of the high militia expenses.

Back to the Michigan-Ohio football rivalry: The legendary Bo Schembechler and Woody Hayes were quite colorful, outspoken and ultra-successful coaches –surely embraced by the media; they made good copy. Schembechler was an assistant coach on Woody's staff at Ohio State when he was younger, thus, fueling their rivalry.

The firing of Coach Woody Hayes was shocking! Interested in the actual event that was his demise as a coach; I ordered a PBS documentary film. Yes, he was colorful and ruled with an iron fist—he was hot-tempered and known for his tantrums as much as his victories.

During practice he would beat his fists on the helmets and shoulder pads of players who displeased him; sometimes he became so frustrated he would throw his own eyeglasses and watch to the ground. When they played Michigan, Woody would never utter the word Michigan—it was that team from "up north." The rivalry was intense.

The incident recorded on the PBS film that got him fired and ended his career in disgrace seemed almost hilarious to me. It happened in the 1978 Gator Bowl against Clemson. With less than two minutes to go Ohio State was going for a touchdown late in the game. A pass by the Ohio State quarterback was intercepted by Clemson's Charlie Bauman.

Bauman ran out of bounds at the Ohio State bench. When Bauman got up after being tackled, the hot-headed Hayes ran out and slugged Bauman. Picture that! Unheard of for a coach to tackle a player from the opposing team! He had to be pulled off of Bauman by the Buckeye players. And all captured on film! The next day the Ohio State athletic director had no choice but to fire the legend.

It is a known fact that opposing fans, especially Michigan fans, get treated very badly in Columbus. They are cursed at and may have beer or urine thrown at them.

In fact, the behavior of Buckeye fans is so despicable that University of Michigan sent an e-mail to fans traveling to Columbus a couple of years ago. It almost reads like a State Department warning to tourists visiting a Third World Country.

Some of the advice:

Try carpooling to the game; if possible, drive a car with non-Michigan license plates.

Keep your Michigan gear to a minimum, or wait until you get inside of the stadium to display it. Stay with a group. Stay low-key; don't draw unnecessary attention to yourself. If verbally harassed by opposing fans, don't take the bait. Avoid High Street in Columbus.

The irony is that most Michigan fans respect Ohio State more than any other rival. Most root for OSU to win all of its games leading up to THE GAME and consider them a worthy foe. In general most Buckeye fans are nonviolent, sober and act nothing like that small outrageous minority.

Tomorrow's game (Wolverines and Buckeyes) is at U of M in Ann Arbor with heavy stakes... Whoever is the victor goes to the Rose Bowl! My husband, a Michigan fan since childhood and my son, Jeff, a U of M graduate are sure to be watching and rooting for Michigan. GO BLUE!

**READERS FEEDBACK: Comments and stories.**
**Friday, November 23, 2007**

I can't imagine life without a computer now. E-mails from readers has become a huge part of my day since I try to answer them all. The railroad stories about the Streamliner touched so many people—especially during the war years. My recent article, *Whatever Happened to Polio,* set off another firestorm of e-mails. I felt compelled to share some of their stories.

"Polio—remembering those times vividly. I was in school, lived in Newberry, MI. There was panic. People left town to go to relatives or their cottages. My family considered going to our hunting camp to get out of town! I knew several people who contracted the disease and spent years in the iron lung. Thank you for writing."

**Eleanore Beck, Escanaba**

"Polio! Well as far as I am concerned it's still around. I contracted polio at age 16 months when we lived in N. Y. My family moved to California because the weather was better for me. I still wear a leg brace below the knee. The leg is shorter and has now caused back problems. I get Health News about anything on polio—that's how I got your article. I sometimes don't feel I fit in with the polio people, because I am not as bad off as many, yet I don't fit in with the "regular" people either. I park in a handicapped space and the "regulars" give ya a look. Then I show them I am wearing a leg brace and thank them for looking out for the handicapped. It is interesting to find out there are so many of "us" still out there. I found your article interesting."

**Wendy Springstead, San Rafael, CA**

"We had just moved here from Ohio in 1947. My middle son came in and lay down on the floor saying he was sick. The doctor came and thought it was spinal meningitis. The next morning he came again and told David to walk. He said, Take him to Marquette, he has polio. He was there for 13 days and crying to come home. They informed me how to do Sister Kenny hot pack treatments. We moved our washer in front of the stove, boiled pieces of wool blankets, and then put them through the old fashioned ringer. I put them on both his legs and back. David was 7 years old...When we brought him back to Marquette they said we had done a better job than they could have...We are certainly grateful the Lord brought us through this time in our life. Another letter from 92 year old Dorothy Duca."

**Dorothy Duca**

"I try to read your columns on line each week. I particularly enjoy the ones that bring back the memories of the 40's and 50's. I graduated from EHS in '53 and my sister Gloria graduated in '49. If you ever decide to do anything additional regarding polio, you might mention the involvement of the Escanaba Rotary Club and its efforts to help improve the lives of the kids who suffered from the disease...

It was the Escanaba Rotary Club that funded the purchase of the equipment and the hiring of Clarence Moore, the therapist, who were located on the first floor of the Jr. High School. The club also donated the building of Camp Harstad, located on land donated by Rotarian Ole Harstad out on the shore near Ford River.

My dad, Erling Arntzen, was the president of the Rotary Club and was instrumental in getting labor and materials donated for that project. There were at least a couple of my classmates who were stricken by polio; Mary Lee Woodward, Fred Paulson, and Russell Buckland that I can remember for sure...For a small town (Escanaba) they really accomplished a lot at that time."

**Mert Arntzen, Neenah, WI**

I received many e-mails relevant to my article, *Win One for the Gipper,* but one in particular stands out.

In the article I mentioned Mike Shatusky, a 1948 graduate of Menominee High School. I compared his athletic prowess with George Gipp. Mike went on to star in football at the U of M. He met his wife, Jan, in college and coached in California. Ultimately they moved back to Ann Arbor.

Jan writes, "A relative recently sent us an article written by you which was published in the Escanaba Daily Press on Sept. 21— "Win One for the Gipper." In the article you mention my husband, Mike Shatusky. I thought you might like to know what he has been doing for the last 60 years so I am enclosing an article you might find interesting."

The article states Mike won the prestigious UFER award in 2001. It is presented each year to an individual for his or her outstanding service to the U of M Athletic Program. (Bo Schembechler won it in 1994.) A quote from the article: Recently Mike had a challenge of his own, when after quadruple by-pass...he suffered a devastating stoke. It was determination, strength, his spirit and constant support of his family and his extended Michigan family, including many "M" men and women that he has won the "hardest game he ever played."

Jan's letter continues, "However, one of his most inspirational accomplishments was achieved after this article was written. Five years ago, Mike and his rehabilitation doctor, David Steinberg, MD founded a golf outing, "Strokes for Strokes. Stroke survivors get together in mid-July for this remarkable outing—people who never thought they would get on a golf course again, get together (some even being pushed in wheelchairs) for a day of golf and fellowship.

All of his family and friends are so proud of him for his continuing leadership, inspirational talks, volunteer work, great attitude and spirit of giving. He continues to work at the U of M Golf course and the U of M Track building."

What a great inspirational example of a former "Yooper" making a huge difference. His grandchildren call him "Michigan Mike."

## MA AND PA KARAS AND THE IGLOO
## Friday, November 30, 2007

If there was ever two people and a place that would qualify as an "institution" in Escanaba it would be "Ma" and "Pa" Karas and their famous "Igloo." Anyone who attended the old Escanaba High School during the '30s and '40s will remember them with deep fondness. Their little store, the Igloo, was attached to their home on 11th Street near the old high school.

The high school students coined the name Igloo the very first year (1929) the Karas's opened their new store. The name coincided with their team, the Eskymos, and the fact that sometimes during the winter after a huge snow storm the store was often approachable only through a tunnel cut from kids traipsing through the deep, hard snow.

How these two beloved people from Bohemia eventually came to live in Escanaba is a heart-felt story in itself. Ma Karas was born Helena Topinka in the late 1880's in Koslany near Praque. Her father, a business man, was a wealthy brew master who leased and operated small breweries.

Pa Karas, his birth name Frantisek, lived in a near-by village.

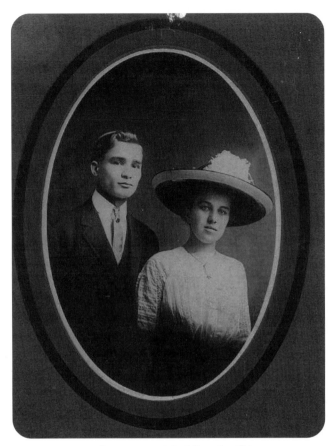

*Ma and Pa Karas Wedding in Chicago.*

His father, a poor farmer, owned two cows, a few acres and a little house, plus a trumpet which he played at local dances and weddings. No one could have ever dreamed of a union between Helena and Frantisek.

When Helena was around twelve she met Frantisek, but their early acquaintance was mostly a matter of nods acknowledging one another. Their social standings were miles apart.

Helena was sixteen when she and a younger brother, Alois gained their parents approval, after much hesitation, to come to America. A relative in Chicago made the arrangements.

Many Bohemian girls served as maids when they first arrived. Helena worked for seven years as a nurse for the three children of Mr. and Mrs. Levy. The Levy's called her Helen.

Meanwhile, Frantisek's father who had a natural passion for

*HIGHER LEARNING, Community College was organized in 1935 during The Depression through the efforts and cooperation of John Lemmer, then superintendent of schools, Charles Folio, U.P. representative for the University of Michigan, and Edward Edick, principal of Escanaba High School at the time. Alternating classes were held in four rooms of the old Senior High School on 8th Avenue. Those students completing a year satisfactorily received a freshman year's credit at an accredited college. Students who attended the college during the 1935-36 school year are pictured in this photograph furnished for publication by Clara (Karas) Embs of Gladstone, who is pictured in the second row at the far right. She has identified a number of the students as follows: from left front, Jean Wilson, Dorothy VanHorn, unidentified, Mary Alice Tobin, Charlotte Malloy, Lois Valentine, 'Phyllis Judson, Lucille Laviolette, unidentified, and Jane Baslien; second row, Dorothy Cox, Jane Hamilton, Helen Birmingham, unidentified, Helen O'Callahan, Vivian Gleisner, Helen Schmidt, Carol Crain and Clara Karas; third row, E.J. Fitzharris, Henry Nelson, Harry Nelson, Arthur Olson, Glen Hamilton, Glen Sandberg, Harold Snyder, and Bill Fitzharris; back row, Charles Folio, Chester Olson, Arvid Norlin, Sherman Hale, unidentified, Bertil Carisen and Mr. Acker. Anyone who has the identity of any of the unidentified persons is asked to call Mrs. Embs at 786-1729. Anyone with an interesting old photograph of local interest can submit it for publication. Although care will be taken with the historical item, the newspaper cannot guarantee their safety or return. It is recommended that a commercial copy of the print be made (not a photocopy). Send or drop off photos, including all information available about it, to: "Remember When?" Daily Press Lifestyles Department, 600 Ludington St., Escanaba, MI 49829.*

music wanted his oldest son to become a violinist. His mother sang folksongs while cooking and working in the fields. When their son was twelve, they found a man to give him free lessons for work as an apprentice file-maker. The arrangement lasted for almost four years.

American-born relatives in Chicago agreed to pay for the boy's passage to Chicago. His parents approved and he arrived in Chicago about the same time as Helen unaware of each other's presence. Frank became his American name.

He worked in a factory making $10.25 a week and thought he would eventually become a millionaire and organize an orchestra. During a machine industry strike, Frank took a job in a cleaners pressing pants. A young man brought in a suit to be cleaned; they recognized one another. He was Alois, Helen's brother. All three got together the following week.

Frank continued his music lessons. Upon seeing a poster: Wanted—Musicians for Army Bands, Frank joined the army. He talked with Helen. "Will you wait for me?" He was disappointed with the Army when he didn't get the music opportunities promised him. When he was discharged they married much to the chagrin of Helen's parents; he was a peasant's son. They were both 22 and so much in love.

In 1911, Frank resumed lessons both in violin and cornet with the best teachers in Chicago. He found a permanent position playing cornet for 36 dollars a week. In 1913 when hard times hit Chicago he lost his job. By now they had two children, William and Elsie. He read a want-ad that Menominee, Michigan needed a cornet soloist. No salary but guaranteed employment in a local factory with a wage of 15 dollars a week. After looking up Menominee on the map they moved to the town they thought ideal to raise a family.

Two more children were born; Frank and Clara. Frank became so overworked in Menominee that he suddenly decided to accept the job of orchestra leader after several offers from a movie theatre in Escanaba. All was fine until 1929 when the "talkies" caused musicians to lose their jobs all over the country.

For Mr. Karas it was a stroke of good luck. John Lemmer, superintendent of schools, suggested he qualify for an

*Ma and Pa Karas.*

appointment as a music teacher. He got the job and also became director of the Escanaba Municipal Band.

Mrs. Karas decided to go into business. They moved into a broken-down frame structure, made repairs, painted everything and opened for business in the fall of 1929. The youngsters heard Mrs. Karas's children calling her "Ma" and soon that became her name. They sold ice ream cones, candy, pencils, milk, pie, cakes, sandwiches and light groceries.

My husband was raised near the high school and remembers "Ma" Karas knitting a sweater when his sister was born in 1936. He also took violin lessons from Pa Karas. Later he remembers when Ma Karas gave the football players a scoop of ice cream for each touchdown and a scoop if they won the game. He was there when Don Wickholm, class of '46, collected a four scooper: three touchdowns and a winning game. By the time Gary, class of '49, finally would have won a three scooper the practice was discontinued.

Ma Karas was a pleasant woman with spectacles, a kind smile and always wore the typical housedress and apron. Ma knew a great many of the eight hundred high school kids that frequented the Igloo. Mr. Edick, the school principal, aware of her mentoring and closeness with the kids invited her to a pep assembly. She assumed she would sit in the audience, but to her surprise, he sat her on stage next to John Lemmer. She received the biggest hand anyone had ever received; an ovation that lasted several minutes.

Students wrote poems to her, they invited her to class reunions, student groups had dinners for her and the Daily Press sent a reporter to cover them.

Beloved Pa died in 1948 and beloved Ma died in 1951. They were cremated and their ashes were distributed throughout the community the loved.

Pa Karas was honored by the people of the community with donations to build the Karas band shell. Pa had taught thousands of students to play musical instruments. Last summer Harold and Mary Pearson, former Escanaba residents and summer visitors were impressed with the Wednesday band concerts and the small-town atmosphere in the park where families; children, parents and grandparents gather. Noting a need for upgrade of the band shell; painting, landscaping and electrical work, they donated $10,000 to cover cost of the renovations. Kudos to them!

Pa and Ma and Karas and the Igloo are an integral part of Escanaba history: A loving institution never to be forgotten.

**POLITICAL VIEWS**
**Friday, December 7, 2007**

Having a column on the opinion page almost gives me a license to—yes, voice my opinion! I talk to myself, oh well, argue with myself as I type fast and furious on the computer. When I need to bounce a political opinion off somebody I call in my husband, Gary. Believe me we have had our share of lively, colorful conversations. It makes for anything but a dull existence.

I have been both Democrat and Republican for different reasons—now I can go either way as an Independent. Gary, on the other hand, has always been a conservative...I think far to the right!

As the primary heats up with debates it appears like we are meeting more in the middle; we agree on more and argue about less—at least for now. It seems the American people are in a quandary about who is capable and who will lead our country.

The first time my husband ever voted was in Chicago in 1952. He voted for Dwight Eisenhower who ran against Adlai Stevenson, Governor of Illinois. I remember the Democratic precinct captain knocking on our door at all hours vying for our vote. Chicago was and has been controlled forever by the organized Democratic machine.

By the next election in 1956 I was old enough to vote. Again Eisenhower, as the incumbent was pitted against Stevenson. I followed my husband's lead being young and not politically savvy; however, as years past that would change. In more than one election we cancelled out each others vote. Guess we were always political from a young age.

To be sure there were many huge issues in presidential elections years ago. For example to name a few: In the 50's it was the Korean War, the cold war, and building up our defense capabilities. In the 60's it was the Cuban missal crisis, the Civil Rights Movement and the start of the Vietnam War. In the 70's the Vietnam War ended and the Impeachment proceedings of Nixon.

Today we face a myriad of huge issues. Heading the list is the unpopular Iraq War—in some ways reminiscent of the Vietnam War. Immigration issues have taken a front seat and no wonder: 6 million illegal immigrants have entered our country in the last seven years. Then there is the quandary over abortion and gay rights issues.

In my new book, *Through the Years,* I wrote an article about the three front runners in each party. At the time Romney was barely on the radar screen and I predicted him as the possible dark horse. His poll numbers have risen significantly.

*Theodore Roosevelt, 26th president of the USA (1858 - 1919)*

However, after seeing the last debate with more time given by the media to Mike Huckabee I liked him instantly.  He is a great speaker and debater.  And the very next day his numbers were on the rise. But his position on eliminating income tax in favor of a flat tax is far out.  He has many good points—but will have to modify some ideas if he moves ahead.  His campaign will need to play catch–up; hustle to raise money and organize state headquarters.  He has the least resources of the front runners.

Maybe he is the dark horse?  Presently, his motorcade has doubled in size—to two vehicles!

Indecision just a month before the Iowa caucuses underscores just how no GOP contender has satisfied the party majority.

And Hillary slipped after her last debate.  Obama is now squeaking ahead in the Iowa primary and has Oprah on his band wagon.  She is a dominating personality.  Still the pundits ultimately predict a nomination win for Hillary.

Remember the last election?  Howard Dean, the current Democratic National Chairman, was the frontrunner early on.  Kerry was way behind garnering only eight percent of the poll vote and ultimately won the nomination.  It's not over until it's over—the shifting sands will continue until the nomination.

A person cannot become president without the capabilities to raise huge amounts of money.

In my book, *Through the Years*, I listed Teddy Roosevelt's political thoughts from over 100 years ago.  Eerily, they resonate today.  His words follow:

A man who is good enough to shed blood for his country is good enough to be given a square deal afterwards.

Wars are, of course, to be avoided; but they are far better than certain kinds of peace.

Every immigrant who comes here should be required within five years to learn English or leave the country.

A typical vice of American politics is the avoidance of saying anything real on the issues.

Behind the ostensible government sits enthroned an invisible government owing no allegiance and acknowledging no responsibility to the people.

The only time you really live fully is from thirty to sixty.  The young are slaves to dreams; the old servants of regrets. Only the middle-aged have all their five senses in the keeping of their wits.

## MARIE OSMOND AND DANCING WITH THE STARS
## Friday, December 14, 2007

Of course by now most know that dancing is one of my favorite topics. My love of dance began at age seven with free tap-dancing lessons at Club 314 with Mr. Bill Pratt. I can still hear him call out; 'step-shuffle-back-step.' Is it any wonder I glued myself to the TV on Monday and Tuesday to watch that incredible show, *Dancing with the Stars.*

Marie Osmond, the giggly, bubbly, effervescent singing star and one of the contestants, again danced her way into the hearts of America. Her fan base kept her in the competition until the finals. Her last comment to the colorful judges was, "I don't care what you say; I can dance!" Trouper Marie gave it her best shot. Says Marie, "You know, you don't work 40 plus years in the business without knowing how to push yourself." And push herself she did!

Marie ended her stint in third place with the help of her fans and the whistling and cheering of her brothers, including Donny, in the audience. She competed against other star greats; Wayne Newton and Jane Seymour. Helio Castroneves, two-time winner of the Indianapolis 500 hoofed his way into first place and rightfully deserved. Spice Girl, Melanie Brown, took second place honors.

Marie displayed her staying power as she was plagued with tragedy during the competition: Her beloved father died; her son, age 16, was entered into a drug rehab program; and to top it off, at one point after completing a sassy Samba she fainted.

Talk about pressure! Marie was leaving on tour right after her stint on *Dancing with the Stars.* Locals will be treated to her Christmas Show at the Island Show Room on December 14-16. We purchased front row seats months ago for the show on the 15th and look forward to her performance.  Wonder if she plans on showing-off a few of her newly acquired dance steps?  For sure, she is pleased with the 30 pounds she dropped during the strenuous competition; another great by-product of vigorous dancing!

I remember Marie's debut on the Andy Williams show. The three- year- old sat on Andy's lap as he introduced her as, 'the youngest Osmond brother.'  Marie has eight brothers and is the only girl.  At age 13, Marie exploded on the country music charts with a #1 record, *Paper Roses*. It was also the first time in history a female debuted with a #1 record; then came follow ups, *In My Little Corner of the World* and *Who's Sorry Now"* Hopefully she will sing them at her, "The Magic of Christmas," show entwined with the usual Christmas standards.  Gosh, what a treat it will be to see her in person!

Marie starred with her brother in a weekly television variety show, "*The Donny and Marie Show* (1976-81).  In 1986 Marie married record producer, Brian Blosil.  The have eight children together; five of which are adopted.  They divorced in 2006 after 20 years of marriage.

Marie's charmed life has hit some low notes.  She struggled with post-partum depression and penned a book about it: *Beyond the Smile; My journey out of Post-Partum Depression*.  In 2006, she was hospitalized for a bad reaction to medication amidst denied reports she had attempted suicide.

Not only is Marie an international celebrity, but a savvy businesswoman.  In 1991 she launched her Marie Osmond Fine Porcelain Collector Dolls on QVC and at Disney Theme Parks.  In 1998 she reached quite an achievement by selling her millionth doll on QVC.

Marie, now 47, was born to George and Olive Osmond, who were practicing Mormons.   She was raised in a wholesome environment and turned down the starring role in the movie *Grease* (1978) on "moral grounds."

She starred in a touring production of *The Sound of Music* in the 1990's.  Of course I could go on and on of her credits and accomplishments.  But there is no question she reinvented herself in her recent stint as a competitor in *Dancing with the Stars*.

Marie was up to the challenge entertaining us every week with her bubbly, chatty personality, practiced dance steps, interactions with the judges and just being Marie!

Snagging third place in fierce competition says a lot about her popularity. 50% of the score was votes by the judges; 50% was call-in votes by the audience. Marie's huge fan base helped keep her afloat until the finals.

ABC will be capitalizing on the success of *Dancing with the Stars* with a new show called, *Dance War: Bruno vs. Carrie Ann* slated to begin in January. The two judges will each lead a team and serve as both coach and choreographer. Viewers will vote to decide which team did better. The losing coach will have to vote someone off their team in a loss. Sounds like another winner. We'll be there ringside!

Meanwhile the focus is on attending Marie Osmond's show, *The Magic of Christmas* at the Island Showroom. My two men, Gary and Gary JR in his wheelchair, will be there with me front row center. Ahh—-IT'S A GREAT LIFE!

## SPECIAL MEMORIES OF THE KARAS FAMILY
**Friday, December 21, 2007**

I wanted to write a Christmas story; one that tugged at your heart, one about memories, one about happy times and everyone knows in real life you can't escape the sad times. Then I thought about a follow-up article on the Karas family. Yes that's it!—one about memories; how they affect us and the footprints we leave behind.

If Pa and Ma Karas were living today they would be astounded how many people have such fond memories of them and their little store; the Igloo. Christmastime seems befitting to share more family stories and a few special e-mails from some of the folks whose lives were enriched by these two wonderful people.

Clara Karas Embs, the only living child of the Karas' four children, followed in her father's footsteps. Ultimately she became

*Clara Karas Embs and husband.*

the music director for the Escanaba Schools.

Clara is 91 years-young and lives in the area with Josi, her Scotty dog. Clara is an absolutely delightful, amazing woman. She is interesting and articulate.

She reminisced about her parents from the old-country; "Mother was determined that her children would be educated." All four children received degrees. "Mother and Dad would be very proud of their baby," says Clara. "Frank was an educator and coach at Ferris State and had a memorial field named after him. Elsie had a career in music at Muskegon Heights. Bill was an engineer and worked for the Delta County Road Commission."

Clara lived downstate when Mr. Lemmer, then Superintendent of schools called her and asked her to come back to Escanaba to teach strings. Her husband had died of kidney disease after five years of marriage—now her father had died. Clara and her son Tommy moved to Escanaba to be with 'Ma.' "I was grateful for the guidance at the time," says Clara. "The Lord said this is the path you should try." Clara, who found her niche in Escanaba, taught Junior High and Senior High orchestra and also music in the grade schools.

But life isn't always like the story book; happily ever after. Life would throw Clara a devastating curve. One summer she was preparing to go to graduate classes at Interlocken camp. "It would give Tommy a chance to be with boys his age at boy's camp at Interlocken," she relates. A trip to Doctor McInerney's office the day before they left revealed Tommy had kidney disease like his father. Tommy succumbed to the disease at age 14. Clara would never know an adult son nor experience grandchildren. Tommy's ashes are scattered behind the Karas Band shell –the memorial named for his grandfather.

Clara lives on with memories of her son, Tommy. She is resilient and remarked how wonderful it is to know how her parents are remembered with such fondness even today. "When you live in the moment," remarked Clara, "you are not really aware of the little things or the daily happenings that will affect lives for years to come." She keeps the article about her parents on a table and reads it over and over. The memories sustain her. She drives by the band shell every now and then and is so pleased it will be painted and updated.

## LETTERS!

What a wonderful article on Ma and Pa Karas. Thank You! I lived in Escanaba until age 16 and knew them well. From our home at 1401 lake shore drive, I passed and very often stopped, at the Igloo on my way to the Barr School and the Junior High. In the warm store I would eat candy and listen to Pa practicing or giving lessons. We moved to California in 1943, but those memories are still vivid. Incidentally, my grandfather, architect Gothard Arntzen, designed the Karas band shell. Cordially,
**DAVID THORSEN, Emeritus Professor of Music, California State University, Fullerton**

I so enjoyed your article on the Karas family. (I read it on the on-line site) It certainly tied a lot of Esky history together. It's sort of amazing how one little old couple could make such an impact on a community. Thanks for writing the article.
**JAN CURTIS, Children's Librarian, deAngeli Library, Lapeer, MI**

Dear Patt (If I may be so informal), Once again my cousin Walt Peterson has called my attention to one of your articles. This time it was the one on Ma and Pa Karas! That did it, now I must get your book! I have fond memories of Pa Karas as I was a trumpet student of his back in the 40's, (1942-1946), played in the Jr. High orchestra, and the Sr. High band, graduated in 1947. Because of my lessons from Pa Karas I was appointed to position of "camp bugler" at Boy Scout Camp Red Buck for several years ('44,'45, and '46, I think). This meant "free room and board" and all of the fun of scout camp! I think that I knew some of the things you had in your article but that sure was a beautiful story, and filled with interesting details of these two dear people! Thank you and keep up your good work.

**ROBERT LINDEN, Ballston Spa, NY**

Patt: Another wonderful story. I had tears when "Ma" was invited to the pep assembly. As a former cheerleader for the little school of Nahma High, way back in '52,'53 and '54, what an honor and such excitement that must have been for "Ma." I can just picture that. You brought back memories and continue to do so each time I read your stories. Again, thank you for another wonderful story. I look forward to them each Friday down here in Florida.

**DARLA ERICKSON, FL**

What a wonderful article on Ma and Pa Karas! Thanks again for some wonderful and great memories of that wonderful and special little town (Escanaba) with the funny name.

**BETTY AND JIM HEIDEN, Glenn Mills, PA**

I just wanted to write and thank you for your story in the Daily Press about Ma and Pa Karas. It was an interesting story since I'm originally from Cornell and played the trumpet in the Escanaba City Band for a couple of years during high school ('81-'82). They sound like quite a couple, and it was fitting for the band shell to be named for Mr. Karas. Thanks,

**RANDY LAUSCHER, Fayetteville, GA**

## SCHOOL CLASSMATES:
## THE 49ERS CELEBRATE LIFE
## Friday, December 28, 2007

The 49ers are a unique group! Guys from the Esky graduating class of 1949 get together for a luncheon every couple of months at the Stonehouse.  It began when four of the guys golfed together: Herb Nicholson, Ron Sedenquist, Ray Oseen and Gary Abrahamson. They would have an occasional luncheon and soon began inviting other classmates. One week Matt Smith Sr joined them at Ray Oseen's request and the group just kept on growing. Eventually they included St. Joe '49ers.  That was almost 15 years ago.

At one time the group had over 30 classmates in attendance. The years have taken its toll and the '49ers have lost some of their classmates.  Some are deceased; some are disabled; while others have serious health problems.

Truly heart-warming is how the guys look out for one another. Larry Stein used to pick up Ray Slosson, who was on dialysis and lost a leg, until his death. When Matt Smith's health deteriorated, John Beaumier escorted him to the luncheon.  When Paul Laviolette developed Alzheimer's his brother-in-law and buddy, Rusty Markham made sure he got there. Rusty, disabled himself, helps John Gustafson, another brother-in-law to attend the luncheons.

Some of the guys come from other areas just to partake of the bonding with their classmates.  Phil Spade comes from Gwinn. Gilbert Kangas comes from Ironwood driving here and back in the same day—it is that important to him!  Ken Murray comes from Green Bay.  In the summer many classmates visiting the area from California, Texas, Arizona and other states join the group.

A few of the guys defy age: Gil Kangas couldn't make the December meeting because he took a new job as a ski instructor—incredible at age 76, but then he played baseball until age 60.  Dick Barron has had a couple of by-pass surgeries, but that hasn't impaired him from his after retirement job; cutting lawns and landscaping for a bevy of customers in the summer.  Kenny VanEffen, Bill Elliott and Herb Nicholson are in that age-defying group.

The group is a melting pot of teachers, doctors, lawyers, a sheriff, a pilot, small business people and many who worked for private industry. Does it matter when they sit down and break bread what anyone did for a living in their former life? No—of course not! They are the '49ers; bonding classmates all bringing their unique selves to the table.

What do they talk about? They discuss other classmates, the Packers, health issues, politics, sports and grandchildren. They reminisce about school activities, teachers, coaches and athletic events. They tease, joke and laugh a lot. They have talked about

*Members of the 49ers are, from left, Walter Casey, Dean Shipman, John Prokus (guest), Phil Spade, Ken Murray, Gordon Hermes, Norbert Murphy, Larry Curran (guest), Clarence Benoit, John Robitaille, Gary Abrahamson. 49ers also in attendance: Larry Stein, Ken VanEfen, Ed Millette, Dick Barron, Clinton Monson, Herb Nicholson, Ron Sedenquist, John Gustafson, Harry Markham. 49ers absent from luncheon: Ray Oseen, Bill Elliott, John Beaumier, Harold (Spike) O'Connell, Gilbert Kangas, Bob Martin and John Baker and Jack Slapp. Deceased members include: Matt Smith, Paul Laviolette, Ed (Tootsie) Gosselin, Ray Slosson, Bob Miller, Phillip (Tippy) LeGault.*

Miss Hilty, the 21-year-old teacher who was quite a looker. (Most teachers in the 40's were the old-maid type) They joke about Larry Stein and Dick Pryal's famous fist fights in the 40's. Occasionally, some bring photos to share from the past.

In the beginning the group met quarterly, now they meet every two months with a break in the winter when some of the guys head south. Dick Barron organizes the meetings; Gary Abrahamson helps with the phone call reminders.

The guys met December 12th for their Christmas luncheon. Yes, they are ageing; some have hip replacements; some have knee replacements; some walk a little slower; some are maybe a little stooped, some hear a little less but they ramble in the Stonehouse to laugh, joke, break bread and bond with their fellow classmates. Years have ticked by and may be taking a toll on their bodies but their spirit is soaring—alive and well! Every class should be so lucky.

## MELISSA AND JOHN BESSE:
### Capturing the American Dream

The Delta county area has spawned a host of talented individuals. Among them are skaters, singers, writers, musicians and painters. Some have attained notoriety on the national stage. We are extremely proud of them.

Others have purposely chosen to adopt Escanaba and the surrounding area as their home. They have given generously to the community in terms of community spirit, talent and generosity. John and Melissa Besse are an exemplary example.

We, as a community, are extremely grateful for their generosity that will continue to enrich our lives and those of our decendents for generations to come.

I said to Melissa, "I really would like to do a personal article from your point of view about you and John, about your roots, about how you met and your family."

Playfully, I added, "I don't imagine you were always 'rich and famous.'" Taking it in her stride she chuckled and answered, "Oh no! When we first married we were as poor as church mice!"

Ahhh! Now we have found some common ground! .

I met Melissa and John many years ago at a political fund raiser in a private home. Melissa's elegance, grace and typical Southern charm stood out. Not surprising—Melissa was born and raised in Raleigh, North Carolina.

"As an only child, there is no other way I can say it: I was spoiled." said Melissa. "I was blessed in as much as so many family members cared about me."

Her grandmother, whom she was named after, was years ahead of her time. She wasn't typical by any stretch of the imagination. Grandma Melissa, born in the 1800's, was her own woman—as an entrepreneur she owned a very successful drug store in a large hotel in Raleigh.

"When she was younger she was voted the most beautiful woman in Richmond," said Melissa. "She was very progressive; a real go-getter." She certainly wasn't the typical grandma in that era.

"How did you meet John?" I asked. "John was dating my friend," Melissa explained. John had already graduated from the University of Minnesota and was attending graduate school at North Carolina State University.

"I remember that I could barely understand John with his accent." said Melissa. His accent!? I was puzzled at first, knowing John was from Wisconsin. How funny—being from the Midwest we consider Southerners with the accent.

It reminded me when President Carter was in the White House. He remarked how great it was to have someone in the White House without an accent.

Melissa's aunt had baked a beautiful coconut cake for a cake walk fund-raiser at the college she was attending. The person who won the cake inadvertently also took her aunt's beautiful cake plate home. "John offered his help in a concerted effort to retrieve the plate—and he located it!" said Melissa.

After that, John called Melissa occasionally to talk. Melissa said, "He was always trying to set me up on a date with one of his friends. Finally, I told him, "I don't need anyone arranging a date

*John's Dad, Mother, Aunt and Grandmother Besse. The baby is John.*

for me. I am perfectly capable of attracting my own dates."

"Oh," said John, and after a moments pause, "Well, would you like to go out with me?" Melissa said she agreed and their first date was wonderful—they went dancing. She never dated anyone else after her first date with John. They were smitten.

They married when John received his master's degree and moved to Alabama. John's first job out of college was with the Tennessee Valley Authority as a forester.

The Besses' have three children and five grandchildren.

John, born and raised in Butternut, Wisconsin began his lifelong career at the age of 12. He worked in his dad's sawmill: Measuring logs, scaling logs, and building what is called a coal door on boxcars. John, in his youth, could have never dreamed where his ultimate career would take him.

The Besses' moved to the Escanaba area in 1963. In 1966, John, founder of Besse Forest Products Group (BFPG) began his operation with Northern Michigan Spliced Veneers and twelve

*John & Melissa Besse*

employees. In 1983 their son, Greg, joined Besse Forest Products.

40 years later, BFPG, is one of the largest privately owned producers of hardwood veneer, lumber, and specialty plywood in North America. Today the business consists of 16 manufacturing facilities operating in the United States and Canada.

Melissa talks affectionately about the relationship of son, Greg and his father: "They compliment one another. John has his strong points, and so does Greg. John is amazed at Greg's superior organizational skills."

They each bring to the table special strengths. John's values and enterprising spirit are matched by Greg's dedication to continue building on his father's foundation and business philosophy as he leads the Company into the 21$^{st}$ century.

Melissa is pleased that John and Greg have such a great working relationship: "Most importantly it is built on their mutual respect." says Melissa.

Melissa and John's love story has spanned more than 55 years.

The Besses' success is the quintessential American Dream story possible with dedication, determination and hard work. It doesn't end there though.

The Besses' philosophy to "give back" and their generosity paralleling the Bonifas' (Escanaba's lumber baron at the turn of the 20th century) will benefit Delta County residents for years to come—not to mention their significant gifts to other communities as well.

## ONE OF THE THREE BEST BOYS IN THE WORLD
### October 15, 2012

John Besse was born in 1926. The small town of Butternut, Wisconsin (population 600) is where John grew up. "I had such a happy childhood," said John. "My grandmother who lived with us always called me, "one of the three best boys in the world." The other 'two best boys' were my brothers, Robert and Arthur. My sister Helen completed our family and as the youngest of four I was the first to be born in a hospital.'"

"Grandma Besse was an integral member of our family household and still today, I smile when I reminisce about those happy times," says John. Black-eyed pick-a-pie was one of his grandma's favorite pet names for him. John wonders where that ever originated. Perhaps, the saying is one from Germany where she was born—or one made – up especially for John.

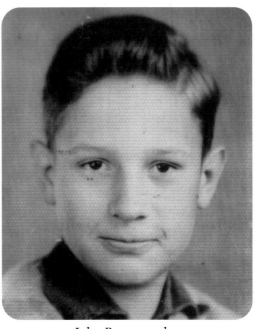

*John Besse aged 10.*

John relates, "We were poor, but then I didn't know it because nearly everyone in Butternut was in the same circumstance. My father was the postmaster during a Republican administration; however, he lost his job in 1932 when Democrat President Roosevelt was elected." John's dad was out of work until 1937 when he acquired a job as accountant at the local veneer mill. The Besse family was one of the few families fortunate enough to have an indoor toilet...and an outdoor toilet.

The Besse's had a garden like most everybody. His mom made sour kraut from the

*Relaxing at Guantanamo Bay while serving in the navy circa 1945.*

cabbage in a 10 gallon crock, and canned 200 quarts of dill pickles and tomatoes. She also canned partridge and venison (a secret...sometimes the venison was out of season). In those days, the first half of the 1900's, people were resilient and lived by the fruits of their labor.

Interestingly, John's grandfather, father and brother, Robert, all held the position of postmaster of Butternut. And at age 21 John's father was the youngest person to ever hold the position of President of Butternut.

John's siblings were all gifted musically; an endowment that escaped John. Alas! By his own admittance John couldn't carry a tune. However, John would rise to heights in life that most can only dream of, as the founder of Besse Forest Products. His success was not without stumbles. He filed chapter 11 bankruptcy at one point; eventually repaying all of his creditors. Five years later he would lose 100 percent of his suppliers, but his dogged determination would be an inspiration to all those that know John. When his luck turned around and he began making money, he sent his mom, whom he adored, six thousand dollars. His religious mom was overwhelmed about her gift and exclaimed, "Six- thousand dollars! Now I am a rich b---h!"

John speaks lovingly about his oldest brother, Arthur and his father who were band directors in the Butternut Band. Robert played the organ in church and recorded a song with Rodger Williams. Helen played the piano and organ. In the 1920's during the silent movie era, John's mother sang with his dad at the local theatre. That job ended with the advent of the first "talkie" featuring Al Jolson in 1927.

In the early 1900's Tuberculosis was prevalent. Two families close to John lost three of their children and four other family members contracted the deathly illness and survived. John's grandfather had TB when he married his grandmother. They traveled by train to Texas for his health. A train ticket in those days was about fifteen dollars. The trip was in vain and his grandfather died in Texas before John's dad was even born. His grandmother never remarried. Eventually she owned a hotel called The Butternut House, did the cooking and raised her only child, John's dad. John's mom and dad lived with Grandma at

The Butternut house for a few years. When she sold her hotel she moved in with her son and his wife and children. "I was so blessed," says John. "I had two mothers-both sweet and loving." Grandma was a beloved member of the household, doting on her "three best boys in the world", until death claimed her at age 87. Despite his happy childhood John remembers running away when he was 3 or 4 years old. He didn't get far; he hid in a neighbor's pig pen and got covered with pig lice. When he was 10 or 12 he talked glowingly about building a crude shack that would eventually soar three stories high. He raised chickens, ducks, pigeons, rabbits and guinea hens. The chicken coop was next to the shack. Every spring they bought about 100 chicks that were delivered to the post office from Sears & Roebuck or Montgomery Wards. Imagine the hundreds of chicks chirping away in the post office. John's job was to raise the chicks and kill them in the fall by chopping off their heads. Not a fun job! The chickens were dipped in boiling water to make it easy to pluck their feathers.

John's childhood friend John Jehn, is now 87, and still affectionately called by his nickname Booper. John fondly recalls the Model T Ford Booper bought around 1940 for five dollars. It had a fabricated top and the body sported yellow polka-dots painted all over it. They made quite a statement cruising down Butternut's main-drag in the yellow polka-dotted jalopy.

*John Jehn (Booper) and John Besse.*

*John and buddy*

*The U.S.S. Huntington*

John is quick to point out he didn't excel in academics in high school. Yet, he was Class President for 4 years. There were 24 in his graduating class and I suspect his winning personality with the girls garnered him that position. But that personality didn't get him into the University of Minnesota. His first attempt to be accepted failed. Luckily, a lady that worked in the high school office was a family friend and altered John's transcript so he was eventually accepted. And what a turn-around! John graduated com laude from the University of Minnesota and went on to get his master's degree at the University of North Carolina in Forestry.

John discovered early-on that he had a way with trees, converting them into plywood and eventually a multi-million dollar business. His love of wood started as a teen-ager and is still evident today. He eyes up trees and loves to relate information about them. Yes, John has an on-going love affair with trees.

In 1944, at the height of World War 11, John tried to enlist in the Air Force. That's when he found out he was color-blind and flunked the exam. Later he tried to enlist in the Navy and again flunked the color-blind exam. Luckily, the recruiter was an ardent fly fisherman and friend of John's brother. He allowed John to take home the charts and memorize them. Voila! He passed with flying colors and was now a seaman in the Navy.

Upon completing basic training at Great lakes Naval Station in Illinois he was stationed at Navy Pier in Chicago. John spent many evenings at a huge popular roller rink that boasted five men playing multiple organs. He was a good skater and since there was a shortage of young civilian guys, he and his

navy buddies made quite a hit with the young ladies. Like most young guys they played hard at night. He loved the USO where they had free hot dogs and admittedly partied like there was no tomorrow. The next day he would find a quiet corner in the office and tried to catch some shut-eye while standing up. And how did the young recruits clean their clothes? They used a huge tub and a

*High School graduation 1944.*

toilet plunger. The pressing was done between the mattresses.

While John was stationed at Navy Pier he was asked by his Commanding Officer to escort a young lady to her prom; apparently at the request of her parents and due to the shortage of young men during the war. He recalled picking her up in North Chicago, escorting her to the prom never to see her again. He didn't remember how he got there or what she looked like. No wonder! That was 67 years ago.

Rest and recuperation was enjoyed at Guantanamo Bay; the same place today where terrorists involved in the 9-11 attack are housed in prison. Hopefully, those prisoners still incarcerated there will have plenty of "rest time."

John may not be able to carry a tune but he surely knew how to run a successful business as founder of Besse Forest Products. His gentle character and modest personality comes through when asked for his success secrets. "Guess I was in the right place at the right time and ran my business by the seat of my pants," says John in his self-depreciating style. You gotta love him!

His generosity and philanthropy is unprecedented in Delta County. "I feel honored and blessed to be able give back to the community where I have raised my family and lived for over 50 years," explains John. His gifts now total 17 million dollars and counting!

*John and siblings. Clockwise: baby John, Robert, Arthur and Helen.*

# DON'T THROW THE BABY OUT WITH THE BATH WATER!
## Friday, January 4, 2008

Have you ever wondered where some of those sayings and expressions we have all heard over the years originated from? Or how some of our customs evident today were handed down—like a bride carrying a bouquet of flowers? A reader shared some of the following facts of life in the 1500s. Many are hearsay, many are not truisms and some are downright ridiculous. Folklore or legends, they are downright funny.

A great way to start the New Year—lighthearted with laughter! We will get into the WEIGHTY stuff next week. Meanwhile, go ahead and laugh. It is good for your health!

Bread was divided according to status. Workers got the burnt bottom of the loaf, the family got the middle, and the guests got the top—or the UPPER CRUST.

The floor was dirt. Only the wealthy had something other than dirt. Hence the saying, DIRT POOR.

The wealthy had slate floors that would get slippery in the winter when wet, so they spread thresh (straw) on the floor to help keep their footing. As the winter wore on, they added more thresh until, when you opened the door, it would all start slipping outside. A piece of wood was placed in the entrance way, Hence the term—THRESH HOLD.

Next time you complain while washing your hands that the water temperature isn't just how you like it consider this:

Most people got married in June because they took their yearly bath in May and still smelled pretty good by June. However, they were starting to smell so brides carried a bouquet to hide the body odor. Hence the custom today of carrying a bouquet when getting married.

Baths consisted of a big tub filled with hot water. The man of the house had the privilege of the nice clean water, then all of the other sons and men, then the women and finally the children and last of all the babies. By then the water was so dirty you could actually lose someone in it. Hence the saying, "DON'T THROW THE BABY OUT WITH THE BATH WATER."

Houses had thatched roofs—thick straw piled high, with no wood underneath.  It was the only place for animals to get warm, so all the cats and other small animals (mice and bugs) lived in the roof.  When it rained it became slippery and sometimes the animals would slip and fall off the roof.  Hence the saying, "IT'S RAINING CATS AND DOGS."

There was nothing to stop things from falling into the house.  This posed a real problem in the bedroom where bugs and other droppings could mess up your nice clean bed.  So a bed with big posts and a sheet hung over the top afforded some protection.  That is how CANOPY BEDS came into existence.

In those old days, they cooked in the kitchen with a big kettle that always hung over the fire.  Every day they lit the fire and added things to the pot.  They ate mostly vegetables and didn't get much meat.

They ate the stew for dinner and kept the leftovers in the pot to get cold overnight—then started it over the next day.  Sometimes stew had food in it that had been there for quite a while.  Hence the rhyme, PEAS PORRIDGE HOT, PEAS PORRIDGE COLD, PEAS PORRIDGE IN THE POT NINE DAYS OLD.

Those with money had plates made of pewter.  Food with high acid content caused some of the lead to leach onto the food and caused lead poisoning deaths.  This happened most often with tomatoes, so for the next 400 years or so, tomatoes were considered poisonous.

Meat was scarce and sometimes when they could obtain pork, it made them feel quite special.  When visitors came over, they would hang up their bacon to show it off.  It was a sign of wealth that a man could "BRING HOME THE BACON."  They would cut off a little to share with guests and all sit around and "CHEW THE FAT."

Lead cups were used to drink whiskey or ale.  The combination would sometimes knock the imbibers out for a couple of days.  Someone walking along the road would take them for dead and prepare them for burial.  They were laid out on the table for a couple of days and the family would gather around and eat and drink and wait to see if they would wake up.  Hence the custom of

"HOLDING A WAKE."

England is old and small and the local folks started running out of places to bury people. So they would dig up coffins and take the bones to a bone-house—then reuse the grave. When reopening these coffins, 1 out of 25 coffins were found to have scratch marks on the inside.

They realized they had been burying people alive. So they would tie a string on the wrist of the corpse, lead it through the coffin and up through the ground and tie it to a bell. Someone would have to sit in the graveyard all night (THE GRAVEYARD SHIFT) to listen for the bell; thus someone could be SAVED BY THE BELL or was considered a DEAD RINGER.

WISHING YOU A HAPPY AND HEALTHY NEW YEAR!

## THE BOSTON SWEET SHOP: PURE NOSTALGIA!
## Friday, January 11, 2008

The Boston Sweet shop was on the corner of Ludington and North Tenth Street where the Morrison Shop is presently located. The Boston was an institution for all of those that frequented the establishment in the 20's, 30's, 40's and 50's. It was truly a behavioral pattern of importance in the life of our community.

When you are young and living in the moment, you can't know of the wonderful fond memories being formed that will live on with you. The Boston qualifies: the meeting place of youth, the aroma of candy being made, the silver hammer breaking up the taffy, home-made ice cream, those wonderful olive and nut sandwiches, the tin roof sundaes and banana splits—not to mention the memorable Greek families, decked out in their pristine white bib-aprons, that created the institution.

Their fancy sundaes boasted the Esky High Boston Nut, the Lover's Delight and scrumptious Hot Fudge for 25 cents—my favorite. I wonder how many marriage proposals took place over a delicious sundae or their famous olive and nut sandwich?

Even as a young person I remember the place being clean as a

whistle.  I remember the marble table tops and dark wood booths where customers sat in the back complete with the decorative tin ceiling so popular in the early 1900's.

The Boston is also reminiscent of my courting days.  Another vivid memory: a sea of kids streaming down Ludington Street after basketball games at the Junior High.  The Boston would fill up and lock their doors while a long line waited outside to enter as patrons left.  On Saturday we stopped at the Boston on our way to the movies to purchase five cents worth of taffy.  It lasted all through the movie.

### 50c    EXTRA FANCY SUNDAES    50c

| | | |
|---|---|---|
| Dreamland | Cloverland | Hollywood |
| Three Graces | Showboat | Collegian |

### 35c    FANCY SUNDAES    35c

| | | |
|---|---|---|
| Banana Split | Banana Skyscraper | Banana Royal |
| Nut Salad | Fruit and Nut Salad | Pecanette |
| Rosemarie | Black and White | Angel Parfait |

### 30c    FANCY SUNDAES    30c

| | | |
|---|---|---|
| Esky High | Lover's Delight | Cherry Melba |
| Boston Nut | Buffalo Nut | Fruit Salad |
| Chocolate Temptation | Fresh Strawberry | |

### 25c    NUT AND FRUIT SUNDAES    25c

| | | |
|---|---|---|
| Hot Fudge | Chocolate Nut | Snow Ball |
| Marshmallow Nut | Hot Caramel | Cherry Fruit |
| Pineapple Fruit | Strawberry Fruit | Tin Roof |

### 20c    SUNDAES    20c

| | | |
|---|---|---|
| Chocolate | Cherry | Pineapple |
| Strawberry | Marshmallow | Maple |

### ICE CREAM SODAS
### AND
### 20c    FLOATS    20c

| | | |
|---|---|---|
| Strawberry | Pineapple | Lemon |
| Chocolate | | Lime |
| Maple | Orange | Grape |
| Root Beer | Vanilla | Cherry |

I also remember John Prokos, a classmate, working there. His parents, George and Koula Prokos along with relatives Sam and Helen Rouman, owned the popular establishment.

Recently I called John to spend an afternoon at our home so I might learn more about the Prokos and Rouman families—about how these two families emigrated from Greece and eventually settled in Escanaba. I was mesmerized with the history.

In 1910 John's dad, George Prokos, arrived in Chicago. Sam Rouman, who hailed from the same village in Greece, immigrated to America a couple of years later. Initially George worked in a

### FANCY DRINKS

| | | |
|---|---|---|
| Limeade ....... 20c | Fruit Orangeade, 25c | Egg Orangeade . 25c |
| Fruit Punch ... 25c | Fruit Lemonade, 25c | Egg Lemonade . 25c |
| Orangeade ..... 20c | Malted Milk ... 25c | Egg Malted Milk,35c |
| Lemonade ...... 20c | Jumbo Malted . 40c | Milk Shake ..... 25c |
| | Malted Milk Float 35c | |

### 10c    PHOSPHATES    10c

| | | | |
|---|---|---|---|
| Coca Cola | Root Beer | Lime | Orange |
| Cherry | Strawberry | Nesbit's Orange | Chocolate |
| Vanilla | | | Lemon |

Orange Juice ............ 20c    Tomato Juice ............ 10c

### SANDWICHES

| | |
|---|---|
| Olive Nut ...... 35c | Lettuce-Tomato . 30c |
| Ham .......... 30c | Cheese .........25c |
| Ham Salad .... 30c | Egg-Cheese .... 35c |
| Ham-Egg ...... 35c | Hamburger .... 30c |
| Ham-Tomato .. 40c | Cheeseburger ... 40c |
| Ham-Lettuce ... 40c | Bacon ......... 30c |
| Ham Let-Tomato 45c | Bacon-Egg .... 35c |
| Denver ........ 35c | Bacon-Tomato .. 40c |
| Tuna Fish ..... 30c | Bacon-Lettuce .. 40c |
| Egg .......... 25c | Bacon-Let.-Tom. 45c |
| Egg Salad ..... 30c | Cheese-Let-Toma 40c |
| Bacon-Peanut B. 35c | Peanut Butter .. 20c |
| Fried Ham .... 35c | Grilled Cheese .. 30c |

Campbell's Soups ................ 20c

### HOT DRINKS

| | |
|---|---|
| Hot Chocolate ........... 15c | Coffee, Tea, or Milk ..... 10c |
| Hot Lemonade .......... 20c | Hot Malted ............ 30c |

cigar store. Both moved to different cities in Minnesota to work in Greek establishments.

Meanwhile, Sam's relative, Leo Rouman owned Rouman's Candy Kitchen in Gladstone. A bit of trivia: Leo Rouman was Esky Coach Jim Rouman's father. Leo was instrumental in getting Sam and George together as partners to open a similar business in Escanaba. In 1920 they established their business in the Feldstein building on Ludington Street.

Leo Rouman helped them to

*George and Koula Prokos.*

*The Prokos's*

get started by teaching them the art of candy making and taffy pulling. John describes the taffy pulling: "Sam would hook the taffy and pull it a distance of about 25 feet, hook it and double back. Then it was laid on a marble table top 6 inches thick and left to harden overnight. Sam did most of the taffy pulling because he was bigger and stronger than my dad. In the morning it was broken up into chunks with a hammer."

In 1921 the business moved to

the corner in the building owned by the Papadakis Brothers—it was in that building their business was destined to become a famous Escanaba haunt and an integral and memorable part of Escanaba history.

Both George and Sam worked 16 hour days and were dedicated to their growing business.

In 1929 George went back to Greece specifically to marry.

*George Prokos*

"A family member informed him of a girl that was his for the taking," explained John with a chuckle. "My mother was only 16. It was customary for marriages to be arranged to someone you had never met. In Greece, school was only attended until third grade." When George and his new bride boarded the ship for America she was already pregnant for Charles, their first son, born in 1930. Four more sons would follow: Jim, John, Nick and Con.

John's mother had never seen snow and exited the ship without ever owning a coat.

In 1931 Sam went back to Greece; his purpose was to also bring back a wife through an arranged marriage. Their union would foster three children: George, Ted and Catherine (Tina).

Both of the wives did waitress work while struggling with broken English.

All of the children would grow up working with their parents. They washed dishes, waited tables and cleaned. In the summer the kids worked as many hours as their parents. John recalls, "We worked all day cleaning strawberries for 25 cents. In the summer we scrubbed and cleaned everything after 11PM when the store closed. In the winter we cleaned before school in the morning."

The children spoke mostly Greek at home. Charlie, Jim and John were kept back in Kindergarten until they acclimated to the English language. Every one of the Rouman and Prokos children became college graduates.

John's dad passed away in 1954. In 1955 the business was sold to Harry Gafner, proprietor of the bowling alley located upstairs next to the Delft Theatre. Time changes everything. The new owner didn't make candy; nor did he make his own ice cream. The atmosphere changed now that the Greek families donned in their signature white bib aprons were gone; business just wasn't the same. Consequently, Harry Gafner went out of business a year later ending the reign of the famous Boston Sweet Shop.

The building was leveled and the corner eventually housed Robert's shoes owned by Robert and Clara Mosenfelder.

In 1952 while John was in service and stationed in Germany he took a side trip to the villages where his parents were reared. He met many of his relatives. His mother's father came down from the village in the hills to bring John back to his home. John says, "I was overwhelmed to meet him and he was so happy to meet one of his grandchildren. We proceeded up the steep hills to the village reachable only by donkey. It was a hairy experience and when I started to get off the donkey, my grandfather said, 'No! no! John you must stay on the donkey!'" John explained that donkeys are sure-footed and wouldn't slip.

John's grandfather on his Dad's side has passed, but he met his paternal grandmother. "She was blind," explained John, "and so happy to meet a grandson. She explored my facial features with her hands. It was so emotional: she cried. I was young and struck

*The Prokos's*

by the experience."

I wasn't about to let John get away without giving me instructions for the olive and nut filling. The recipe is simple: olives with pimento ground up finely; then grind up walnuts very fine and mix with Hellman's mayonnaise. Spread on white bread toasted or plain. John explains: "We made just enough for one person at a time in a cup. Nothing was made in advance. The ham salad was ground up and mixed with lettuce chopped really fine—then mixed with mayonnaise—again, made fresh in a cup for each order."

When I worked at Harnischfeger as a computer operator in the late sixties I can remember Warren Fisher bring olive and nut sandwiches to work made by his wife Anne. Many of the women begged Warren to exchange half a sandwich with them—they loved the olive and nut concoction.

The Boston Sweet Shop will always dredge up the fondest of memories for those of us from that special era when life was so sweet and simple. Happiness could be a five cent bag of taffy!

(Readers: Please send your personal recollections of the Boston Sweet Shop for a follow-up article either to my P. O. Box 344, Escanaba, or my e-mail address.)

## THE GLASS CEILING STILL EXISTS!
**Friday, January 16, 2008**

Our founding fathers rejected the British dynasty and framed the Constitution based on a government "of the people, by the people, and for the people." The last thing they wanted was a coronation.

The men that put together our government were unquestionably brilliant. How could they know in 1776 how powerful the media would become? How could they know where present technology would take us? News in that era was transmitted by stagecoach, horseback (courier) or boat.

Lincoln's masterful speech at Cooper Union launched him as

a presidential candidate. His speech put in the context of the times—an era of racism, politicized journalism and the days when public oratory was considered entertainment—would not even reach many until AFTER his election.

Granted, after the pony express it was the telegraph and newspapers that got the word out; but consider this: Many thousands of people emigrated from other countries; they barely spoke the language let alone read English newspapers.

Telephones were non-existent and messages could only reach Lincoln on the campaign trail by telegram. His message was a cry for equality and democracy—not too different from today's message.

Contrast those times with today: air travel, cars, telephones, cell phones, television, polls, polls and more polls—-even voting exit polls. Political television shows and pundits geared to analyzing every little nuance.

Should Iowa and New Hampshire have that much power in catapulting an individual toward the nomination? After all there are 48 other states—over 300,000,000 Americans that need to have at least as much voice. Nothing in the Constitution says Iowa and New Hampshire vote first.

My case and point: Shouldn't our archaic way of running the primary be overhauled? Consider the fact that Obama won in Iowa and consider the polls proclaiming him the winner before the New Hampshire primary. For all intended purposes he would now be our candidate—steamrolled by two primaries. That sounds like a coronation. Are we a country of sheep?

For all practical purposes the New Hampshire Democratic poll was wrong. Why? I think it was a simple question of the media piling on Hillary Clinton. The tables and dynamics turned 24-hours before the primary—when Clinton exhausted from campaigning and poised to possibly lose, had a moment when she spoke from the heart and yes, became teary eyed.

That moment coupled with the previous debate when she was asked why she was not likable. She replied, "That hurts my feelings."

Then with a warm smile exclaimed, "But I will go on." Those two moments exploited by the media to make her appear weak and questioning whether her teary eyes were real—backfired. Women came to her rescue! They said hold on! Enough is enough! Let's have a look at both candidates again!

I am an Independent and had not seriously considered Hillary—that is before now. My husband is a conservative die-hard Republican and has voiced often, and not surprisingly, that he didn't like Hillary. Yet, those two defining moments affected both of us.

As political junkies we spent the evening glued to our TV during the New Hampshire primaries. Hillary's surprising small lead early on had both of us empathetically cheering for her—now the underdog. The real shocker! My husband jumped up and cheered when she was proclaimed the winner. Can you imagine!

If not for those two defining moments and media coverage Hillary would have lost the New Hampshire primary—and perhaps her bid for the nomination.

Now, the pundits are questioning the disparity in the polls because of the upset by Senator Clinton. They are raising the question of whether the race card entered in. Ridiculous! Barack Obama won handily in Iowa by a state of predominately white voters. The media (political pundits) could be the real culprit: the divisive element in our country. Gender, NOT RACE, appeared to have played a large roll in the New Hampshire upset with Hillary's win. Women saw what I did and REACTED!

Just maybe the New Hampshire voters thought deeply about the vote. Why? Maybe they agreed with her on the issues or because they thought she is the person to deal with our NO. 1 issue—the economy. Yes, according to national polls the economy outweighs the war.

It was a vote for Hillary—not AGAINST Obama. I believe the race card is lurking close to the surface—and will enter in this election; especially if Hillary takes the lead.

Now, the media questions if Hillary will "cry" when it comes to war issues or other serious issues. She can't win! First, they portrayed her without feeling and ruthless—an iron maiden; now they question her emotions as a member of the opposite sex.

Our country has come a long way from the early 1900's when a woman was not even allowed to vote. At one time women couldn't even own property. There has been and still is an invisible glass ceiling where women are concerned. My hope is that Hillary will break-through that ceiling. Two weeks ago I couldn't have written this article and put-forth this viewpoint.

A few years ago I thought it might be doubtful that I would live to see a woman Commander-in-Chief. Now I know that is possible. We have a qualified and accomplished candidate in Senator Hillary Clinton and it is time we don't get carried away by media swaying.

This is rounding out to be a historic election. Follow your heart, your intuition, and your basic instincts; but, by all means vote your conscience. Be heard in this election!

## GROWING UP IN THE U.P.
## Friday, January 25, 2008

Growing up in the Upper Peninsula has to be the best place in the world—not only by my standards, but also, according to the many readers that have contacted me through e-mail and phone calls. The same theme ran through their messages: how fortunate we were to have been raised in the Escanaba area.

A response from Mert Arntzen, Appleton, WI, (EHS 1953) on the Boston Sweet Shop article:

"Wonderful article. Aren't we lucky that we lived in the perfect era? Today's kids can't believe or understand how good we had it. I think that even back then we knew we had something special. We got to appreciate it more as we got older. I can't remember any specific happenings that occurred at the Boston. I just recalled that you walked in with a grin and came out with a smile. There never seemed to be a problem or a conflict. Just a lot of laughter. Thanks."

From Tom Fisher, West Bloomfield, MI:

"I am a graduate of the Class of 1952 (Eskymos) and have fond memories of the Boston Sweet Shop, even after 50 plus years. I grew up with Ted Rouman and Nick Prokos and spent half of my school years in the restaurant.

My mother owned Mitzi's Hat Shop, two doors away. My Junior High School lunches were spent at the Boston munching away on ham salad sandwiches and drinking tomato juice. Mr. Prokos called me "Tomato Juice Tommy." I grew into the olive and nut sandwiches later. I believe the sandwiches were 25 cents and the drink a dime.

I asked Mrs. Rouman once why she didn't write down orders for the boys to prepare and she said she couldn't write. No matter how many customers ordered, she always got it right. The Boston was "our hangout"; we were there most every night and never got into trouble.

When the shop was sold, it was a great loss. I would come home from college and our hangout was gone. There were other places, but none could match the mystique of the Boston Sweet Shop. I also took trumpet lessons from Pa Karas in the Igloo and have fond memories of both Ma and Pa Karas."

From Terry Burak, Bullhead City, Arizona

"Greetings from sunny Arizona. My wife Kathy and I look forward to your weekly column regarding Escanaba in our formative years. Although we spend most of the year in Arizona we do return to Escanaba during the summer.

Your column on the Boston Sweet Shop was enjoyable. I must have been only 13 when the store was closed and demolished...and replaced by a shoe store.

My recollection of the Boston was that my Dad would bowl at the Arcade on Thursday nights and if we were on our best behavior we would get to stop for ice cream. I think that our best behavior was to avoid being reprimanded by the manager and not to bother Dad for additional money to buy more candy at the Arcade.

The Boston was a magical place with the sights and smells of the front part of the store and to sit and eat ice cream in the dark booths with the marble tables was really special....We could also have Ely's potato chips and I can still recall the special taste of that treat. Thanks again for reviving some special moments from the past.

I ran into another Yooper at the golf course today. Asked where he was from and he said a small town in the Upper

Peninsula. When I asked what town he said Escanaba. When I asked what street he lived on he said he actually was from Rapid River but didn't think anyone in Bullhead City, AZ would know where Rapid River, MI was located. Turns out it was Jack from Jack's Restaurant in Rapid River. Small World!"

\*\*\*\*\*\*\*\*\*\*\*\*\*\*\*\*\*\*\*\*\*\*\*\*\*\*\*\*\*\*\*\*\*\*\*\*\*\*\*\*\*\*\*\*\*\*\*\*\*\*\*\*\*\*\*\*\*\*\*\*\*\*\*\*

How fortunate we were to grow up in a small town rather than an urban area! Granted times were different than today. We walked to school, to the beach, to the movies, to Club 314, to the band concerts, to the Boston Sweet Shop, to Sayklly's. We played with home-made scooters, we roller skated, flew kites, played marbles and jacks, played hopscotch and jump rope, and became entrepreneurs with Kool-aid stands—even though we drank most of it ourselves. There was no television—we made our own fun.

I remember the pure innocence of our youth. Our parents didn't worry or even thought about a predator lurking to kidnap or harm their children. Unheard of! Today our grandchildren are warned of the dangers in society and of the bad people out there. Some parents are concerned enough to not let their children play outside without supervision. What a contrast to the times and the way we were raised.

The notes from readers underscore how lucky we were to live in such a great era and in an equally great community. One of the favorite past-time of seniors, me included, is looking back and reminiscing about the way it was. Isn't it amazing how the passage of time jogs our memories even better?

Isn't it great that former residents from all over the country can pull up the Daily Press on the internet? They can keep informed of local happenings, check the obituaries, and reminisce. They look for familiar names from the past—and read my column! I feel fortunate to be the recipient of their many notes, stories and memories through e-mail.

# BIG HAIR-Y DEAL FOR MEN!
## Friday, February 1, 2008

To say hair styles for men evolve with the times is quite an understatement. The popularity of facial hair (beards and mustaches) can also define an era. Inherited hair-pattern genes also come into play.

Right now bald men are HOT! Completely shaved heads combined with revealing piercing eyes and riveting personalities are catching the eye of the ladies. No, hair doesn't make the man— and most women prefer that a man embrace his hair loss rather than hide behind a horrible comb-over or cheap rug. For younger women—think Bruce Willis, Vin Diesel, or Chris Daughtry. Hollywood does seem to set the styles.

Women aren't as judgmental as men; more often they don't judge a book by its cover. Hot is the man who is confident regardless of the amount of hair he has or doesn't have. In the end it is the chemistry that is important. Women are naturally attracted to men that radiate happiness and humor—with or without hair. Oops! Sometimes it could be fat wallets, flashy cars, or some level of fame.

Bald by choice is in—especially with closely-trimmed facial hair, such as a goatee; or a "soul patch" (a small patch of hair just below the lower lip and above the chin) think Howie Mandel on "Deal or "No Deal." Or a chin strap (not kidding—think of sideburns that just keep going under the chin and back up).

Facial hair helps the bald-by-choice dudes from looking like an embryo, a cue ball, or like they're undergoing chemo.

There was a time when only a few brave souls, like Yule Brenner, Kojak and Vladamir Lenin, shaved their heads (and when you think about it, Lenin was way ahead of his time with the shaved head and goatee thing). Not true today.

A school friend, the former Rosemary Erickson, now living in Arizona recently wrote me about an experience in the doctor's office. Apparently the subject of a bald head arose. One man exclaimed he was not bald, but rather the top of his head was a solar panel for the sex-machine. Priceless!

I recall hearing that a mother's genes account for whether her sons will experience male-pattern baldness or keep a full head of hair—not true, at least in my case.

My first son, Gary has a full head of hair at age 57; my youngest son, 49 year-old Jeff, who experienced gradual hair loss through the years, is one of those men considered hot with a shaved head, great eyes and teeth. He also exudes confidence, charm and brain power; attributes much more important than hair. Just keep in mind this is his mother talking.

Not one male in my husband's family has kept their hair, while the males on my Mother's side all had full heads of thick white hair. So how do you account for my two sons: one with a full head of hair; the other with a hair loss pattern?

Crew cuts (butches) were the rage when I was growing up. Anyone with longer hair was considered poor and unable to afford a haircut. Not cool. So how did our generation deal with the Hippie era and long hair? They didn't! Today you still see remnants of both: Some never gave up their crew cuts; and you will see an occasional older Hippie with a graying pony tail.

You just have to look as far as the presidential campaign trail to see 'big hair.' It is joked about and is part of the candidate's persona. For example: John Edwards paid over $1000 for a hair cut. Recently Letterman asked Edwards on his show if he could mess up his hair. John replied, "Go ahead!" He reached over and they both had a hair-messing fest.

Edwards and John Kerry tagged themselves as the 'dream team.' "We have better ideas, better vision and better hair," quipped Kerry: A statement that seemed lightweight and elitist. Guess Bush's hair beat them out teamed with bald and tubby Dick Cheney.

Mitt Romney said a surrogate on an opposing campaign mentioned they would like to punch him in the face: Romney retorted, "That's OK—but just don't mess up the hair!"

Rudy Giuliani ("the reality is"— guy) has a balding head but his dimples help rescue him. When he smiles you tend to notice deep dimples, not his hair. McCain (the "my friends"—guy) winks and has the ultimate comb-over. Huckabee has a bald spot in the back but his huge brown expressive eyes, and oh yes, the fact that he is a gifted orator outweighs his hair.

Then there is Barack Obama with his intentionally short-cropped hair. He is another gifted orator with a resonating message of change and hope. Hillary, if you become president then we will talk about your hair!

Hair did help shape images of former presidents. Both Kennedy and Clinton were partly defined by their hair. Reagan had an exceptional amount of hair for his age. And no, he didn't dye it. He used a little dab of Brylcreem which gave it the appearance of being darker.

Abraham Lincoln's decision to grow a beard was the direct result of a letter received from an 11-year-old girl named Grace Bedell: "You would look a great deal better (with whiskers) for your face is so thin. All the ladies like whiskers and they would tease their husbands to vote for you too." Lincoln's face was thought of as downright ugly. The beard worked. His face was softened and gave him a more distinguished look.

Of the next twelve presidents only William McKinley and Andrew Johnson were clean-shaven. Whiskers were even added to Uncle Sam's clean-shaven face in 1855.

Then came the advent of the disposable razor invented in 1895 and mass-produced in 1901. The transition from facial hair to clean shaven had begun. It is interesting to note that during World War 1, the military ordered 3.5 million razors and 36 million blades to keep our soldiers clean-shaven.

Equally interesting is the fact that with the election of Woodrow Wilson in 1912 no president has sported a beard or mustache.

Hair isn't always an asset. Great hair ala John F. Kennedy may help a candidate win the White House—or it could help contribute to his undoing ala John Kerry.

LADIES consider this: If your honey is hairless he is right in style and guess what? Personality and other attributes will win out every time over hair—that is, unless he is hairless and devoid of any other attributes—big bummer!

# A FAMILY MEMBER FIGHTS LYME DISEASE
**Friday, February 8, 2008**

Lyme Disease!  Sure I have heard about it.  I knew it was caused by a tick bite with otherwise limited knowledge —that is until it struck a family member.  My daughter-in-law, Peggy is fighting the insidious disease in its late stages.

Jeff and Peggy live in Virginia.  According to research, that area is one of the most prevalent areas for tick infestation.  Peggy loved to be outside gardening.  They lived on the edge of a wooded area that housed foxes and wildlife.  Beautiful country.

Peggy is 48 years old and works for the government.  She has a Masters Degree in English and is an accomplished speech writer for the Department of Energy on Capital Hill.  Over three years ago Peggy began to complain of vague symptoms.  A rash of doctors were puzzled with her numerous and vague symptoms.

Peggy's family of origin (mother, father, brother and sisters) became disenchanted with her ongoing health complaints.  They began to suspect Peggy was becoming a hypochondriac—that her symptoms were all created in the mind—there was no illness.

Lyme disease mimics many illnesses and is extremely difficult to diagnose.  Patients complain of 'strange' or 'weird' symptoms.  They visit many doctors and often it results in the patient being told it is psychological with referrals to psychiatrists for treatment—exactly what happened to Peggy.  Standard tests will miss over 90% of cases.

For people that live in the area where Lyme disease most often occurs (along the Atlantic coast, Midwest and parts of Oregon and California) the circular red skin rash is usually a sure sign of Lyme disease, especially when it appears in the summer months.  The disease is named after the town of Old Lyme, Connecticut where researchers recognized its nature in 1975.

There are three stages of Lyme disease.

Stage 1: Fatigue, lack of energy, fever and chills, muscle and joint pain, swollen lymph nodes.  (As many as 25% have only flu-like symptoms, no rash, or have no symptoms at all)

Stage 2: If not detected or treated in stage one, the infection may spread to the skin, joints, nervous system, and heart within weeks to months. Additional skin rashes; pain, weakness or numbness in arms or legs; paralysis of facial nerves; recurring headaches or fainting; poor memory or reduced ability to concentrate; or in rare cases serious heart problems.

Stage 3: If Lyme disease is not promptly treated, damage to the joints, nerves, and brain may develop months or years after you become infected. Swelling or inflammation in the joints (especially in the knees); numbness and tingling in hands, feet and back; severe fatigue; neurological changes; problems with memory, mood, and sleep or speaking; chronic Lyme arthritis which causes recurring episodes of swelling, redness and fluid build up in one or more joints.

Peggy is in Stage 3. Last summer after three years without a diagnosis, her knee began to swell to a point of using crutches and requiring an operation. Finally, Lyme disease was suspected and diagnosed. She received months of intravenous antibiotic treatment. A nurse came to the home daily to monitor her treatment as the disease raged on. However, Lyme disease can persist or relapse despite antibiotic therapy.

Peggy ran out of sick benefits. People in the government near retirement with accumulated benefits donated their sick days to her—a policy allowed by the government.

Her daughter (my granddaughter), Mary Pat, age 17 and a senior in high school was saddened and felt helpless by the downward spiral of her mother's health. Mary Pat, a student in a gifted program, garnered information on the internet. Last summer she ran across a grant offered by the Lyme Disease Foundation to help create awareness of this insidious disease. She applied for and received a 1000 dollar grant to plan an awareness fund raiser.

In January the fruition of her efforts culminated. Mary Pat organized a catered fundraising event in the D.C. area. Monies raised were the $12 per head contribution and revenue from several raffles. She solicited gift certificates from a host of restaurants and other businesses. She did the advertising, solicited raffle and door prizes, created the program and acted as MC. Her program included a physician (specialist in Lyme disease), and her mother speaking of her plight and experience since contracting Lyme disease.

She planned every aspect of the evening. It was a huge success attracting over 250 people. Her dad (my son) sat in the audience beaming with pride and misty eyes: proud of Mary Pat's accomplishment and Peggy's courageous fight and willingness to help create awareness. Also in the audience were Mary Pat's teachers and the principal of her high school. (Incidentally, Mary Pat, a gifted writer, wrote the prologue in my new book, *Through the Years.)*

Peggy continues to fight a battle with third stage Lyme disease. In December, a cyst was discovered on her lung and she underwent surgery. It was diagnosed as Melanoma. She will continue to have MRI's every three months. The standard antibiotic treatments are found ineffective against the cystic forms usually present in chronic Lyme disease. (The spirochete bacteria has the ability to transform to cystic forms) Meanwhile Peggy's Lyme disease rages on.

The pathos of Lyme disease appears to be centered on long-term persistence of the organism in tissues. It has been reported that the pathogen suppresses the immune system; perhaps preventing the elimination of the pathogen.

Because Lyme disease doesn't always respond to treatment in the latter stages; Peggy's Lyme disease specialist doctor has recommended Peggy start an experimental treatment. A treatment that is very expensive and not covered by any insurance and with no assurances it will work. Peggy's prognosis appears dismal. Her faith and courage sustain her.

The best way to prevent Lyme disease is protection from ticks. Cover up as much skin as you can when going into wooded or grassy area. Use a bug spray that has the chemical DEET to repel insects. You can spray it right on your skin. Check yourself and your pets for ticks after being outside. Ticks can fall off your pet and attach to you. (Peggy had two cats and a dog that romped in the woods) See a doctor if you have a tick attached to you that you can't remove.

It is important to clear brush during spring and summer months. Woods, deer or a bird feeder on residential property were associated with incidence of Lyme disease.

It's a good idea to be pro-active and vigilant regarding your health—that includes being informed. If you recognize some of the persistent vague symptoms described above—insist that your doctor prescribe tests specific for Lyme disease. Standard tests miss the diagnosis 90% of the time.

Meanwhile, if you believe prayers help (there is a consensus even in the medical community that they do) please consider offering some for Peggy. A million thanks!

**THE ESKY FIGHT SONG**
**AND ORANGE AND BLACK TRIVIA**
**Friday, February 15, 2008**

Go Escanaba! 'Fight, fight for Esky High! We want a touch down! We want this game!' Escanaba alumni and fans: Have you ever wondered about the origin of the Esky Fight Song? Or did you know orange and black were not always the team uniform colors? Or that the team was not always called the Eskymos?

I have a walking encyclopedia of Escanaba trivia living in my home—my husband, Gary. Guys in his class will often say, "Ask Gary, he knows who lived where in the '30s or '40s; who their parents were or what they did for a living." He never ceases to amaze me with trivia from years gone by—even if last week might be fuzzy. At any rate, he is my source for this trivia column supplemented with information from Jack Beck's book on Escanaba football.

In 1901 the colors orange and black were selected as official colors of Escanaba High School.

During Jim Rouman's reign as coach of both basketball and football in the forties he changed the colors of both teams. The basketball uniforms at one time were red, white and blue with stars on them. It was during World War II, and patriotism may have had an influence in his choice of colors. In the late forties, Rouman purchased used football uniforms from the Detroit Lions football team—the colors were blue and silver. No kidding—

sounds weird now, doesn't it? They alternated them with the orange and black.

At one time the high school was located in the old Franklin School. When the new school was built in 1908 on a hilly terrace located on eighth avenue South (now demolished) the team name became the Hill Toppers. Somewhere in the late twenties the team name was changed to the Eskymos. In 1929 Ma and Pa Karas started their little store and appropriately named it the Igloo.

The Escanaba Fight Song was written by John Lemmer, former superintendent of schools and principal of Escanaba High School. Lemmer wrote the words and Earl J. Clark composed the music. The song was copyrighted in 1925.

Gary attended the Escanaba-Kingsford football game in the early sixties. Mitt Romney's dad, Michigan Governor George Romney was on one of his "whistle-stops" while campaigning for re-election. He stopped at the athletic field. According to Jack Beck, "he spoke to the fans, talked with some of the people, kicked the football a little and then was off campaigning."

When Gary played basketball in the late '40s; the games were played at the Junior High School gymnasium. That was before the new school was built. The students were assigned to two balconies; one for junior high students; one for senior high students. They were always filled to capacity. Adults sat in bleachers on the main floor.

At every home game a musical group called the "Pep" band consisting of 10 or 12 students provided the music. They played the National Anthem, the Escanaba Fight song, and inspirational music of the time. The music was not only upbeat, but created excitement and inspiration for both the fans and the players. There was an all-around positive aura in the gym fueled by music and energy.

Fast forward to today: Gary likes to take in one game a season just for nostalgia and hear the Fight Song once again. After attending a recent game he lamented about the absence of a live musical group. Instead canned music over the loud speaker consisted of "rap" music: The "Fight Song" which has been a tradition since day one at all football and basketball games in the past was conspicuously absent. Gone was the excitement, the inspiration and energy that created the special aura—and no "Fight Song!"

At a recent game Gary observed the difference in fans: He estimated less than a 100 kids in the student section. However, there were 20 so-called cheerleaders. Contrast that with my generation. There were at least 300 kids in *each* balcony and maybe four cheerleaders.

When I was a majorette in high school we provided a half-time show with many crowd pleasers. I remember one basketball game in particular when Phyllis (Sissy) Villemure and I donned clown costumes; we did acrobats, cart wheels and fancy twirling to music. We spent hours practicing and looked forward to entertaining the fans.

Speaking of majorettes: My inspiration to become a majorette was Gayle LaChapelle Houle. Other majorettes in my era were Agnes Ogren Johnson, Sissy Villemure, Carol Christensen, Virginia Sodermark Johnson, Ruth Bullock DuFresne and Jackie Palmateer Smith. We strut our stuff at the half-time show during the football games.—the next best thing to being a movie star—or so we thought.

Back to football: The present coach seems to have a dress code for the players before the game. It seemed to consist of white shirts and a tie. Former Escanaba High School basketball coach, Harold Johnson, in a recent conversation with Gary talked about how he enforced the dress code during his tenure. They wore slacks and a black blazer with orange Eskymo embroidered over the breast pocket.

For out-of-town games the team paraded single file around the perimeter of the basketball floor prior to the game. They were classy and other schools were impressed at how the Escanaba team was dressed and the way they conducted themselves.

Just a suggestion: We have a unique team embroidery shop in Escanaba. I can just picture the team in orange and black polos. Perhaps there is a benefactor or organization out there willing to provide sharp classy polos for a team of 10. Wouldn't a "Pep" band be great too? It might be the catalyst to get more students supporting the team. "Yea orange! Yea black! Yea Escanaba, fight right back!"

# DEFINING MOMENTS IN CAMPAIGN HISTORY
## Friday, February 22, 2008

Do "dirty tricks" matter? You need only to look at the history of campaigns to know the answer: It could be a resounding yes—but then again, they can backfire.

A most recent one is John Kerry's bid for the White House in 2004. He put his Vietnam record out there front and center which caused his opponents to revisit a less than favorable period of American history. Attack ads followed claiming that Kerry had lied about how he earned his war medals.

The claims were bogus, but that didn't matter—they were out there. The campaign manager's decision was to NOT spend money on a rebuttal. Eventually they were forced to launch counter-ads when the story ballooned; too little too late. The damage was done.

In 1948 Harry Truman, incumbent was running against Thomas Dewey, a Republican from Owasso, MI. who was heavily favored to win. The 1948 race became the greatest underdog upset story in the history of American politics. I remember the front page photo of Truman holding the infamous early edition of the Chicago Tribune: Dewey Defeats Truman. But Dewey didn't even come close!

How did Truman win against such odds? He took the message to the people. Truman with his wife Bess, "the boss" and daughter Margaret, traveled 22,000 miles on a train "whistle stop" tour to 30 states delivering 280 speeches tailored to specific audiences.

Dewey's strategy was to play it safe aboard his Victory Special: Just talk in generalities. The defining moment was on Oct. 12, 1948 when Dewey's train pulled into Beaucoup, Ill. A thousand people ran toward the train to greet the governor; suddenly the train lurched backward.

"That's the first lunatic I've had for an engineer." Dewey said. "He probably should be shot at sunrise," he muttered into a microphone, "but we'll let him off this time since nobody was hurt."

The engineer insulted by Dewey was a 30 year veteran of the railroad. Word of Dewey's outburst spread while Truman took

full advantage. Supporters wrote on dusty boxcars, "Lunatics for Truman." Still many believed Truman's chances were still bleak.

On Election Day, the head of the Secret Service assumed his next job detail was Dewey and ditched Truman. Truman won handily with 303 electorate votes to Dewey's 189.

Pollsters and reporters THEN realized they had been sleeping at the switch. It has been said that, "Truman persevered like the Little Engine That Could," while Dewey sputtered and stalled.

My research took me back to the 1824 presidential election when no candidate won enough electoral votes to claim victory. It proved to be a history lesson for me when I found out congress stepped in to decide the winner.

Can you believe during this period the United States was dominated by one party called the Democratic-Republicans? As a result the four candidates who vied for the presidency were members of the same party: Andrew Jackson, John Quincy Adams, William Crawford and Henry Clay.

None of them earned the majority of electoral votes needed to win. The U.S. Constitution calls for the House of Representatives to elect the president and the Senate to pick the vice president. The House voted for Adams; the Senate chose John C. Calhoun for vice president.

After the election, Jackson and Adams became political rivals. Their bitter rivalry sparked two new parties. Jackson and a coalition of working men formed the Democratic Party; Adams represented pro-business interests mostly from the North and became the Republican Party.

The 1824 one-party system was now history. By 1828 there were two political parties.

It is truly amazing how an insignificant moment blown up by the press can bring down a candidate.

A snowy February day in 1972 helped to ruin Edmund Muskie's presidential bid. Muskie himself, called it "a watershed incident." Just before the New Hampshire primary, William Loeb, publisher of the Manchester Union Leader ran two scathing pieces. An editorial accused Muskie of using an ethnic slur against French-Americans.

Loeb published as evidence a letter from a Florida man that later would be determined a hoax planted by the Nixon White House. In a follow-up editorial Loeb accused Muskie's wife of unladylike behavior: drinking and telling jokes.

During that February press conference held outside during a snow storm, Muskie called Loeb a "gutless coward" with his voice breaking. The press accused him of crying; aides said it was melting snow on his face. None-the-less his fate was sealed. Call it the power of the press.

I'm sure most can remember the Florida fiasco in 2000: The legacy of hanging chads when eventually the high court decided Bush vs. Gore. Then in 1968 death and chaos reigned. Lyndon B. Johnson called it quits saying, "I shall not seek, and will not accept, the nomination of my party for another term as your president." Both Martin Luther King and Robert Kennedy were shot.

There is no question we are in the midst of a historic primary; a woman and an African-American running for the highest seat in the land—if not the world. One is likely to win.

If Hillary Clinton wins both Texas and Ohio it could become a race thrown into the hands of super delegates at the Democratic Convention. Before that Michigan and Florida and their disenfranchised voters will more than likely need to be addressed.

A scenario that could play out: The super delegates could give Hillary the win. Surely the Blacks will not accept that. It could fracture the party forever and cause Blacks and young Obama supporters to boycott the presidential election.

Quite a sad commentary if that were to happen.

Barack Obama can be praised for the energy he has brought to a presidential election. Democrats and young people are turning out in record numbers to be heard in this election primary. Let's hope a nominee is chosen before the convention.

One thing is for certain: The historic significance of this election will be mulled over, dissected and talked about for decades to come. Will it be a woman or an African-American? We may not know until August.

❧❦❧

## SENIORS: WE ARE IN THE WINTER OF OUR LIFE!
**Friday, February 29, 2008**

When I was young nothing could have prepared me for the WINTER of my life. No—nothing! I remember the SPRING of my life and that invincible feeling that comes from youth. I remember aging relatives but never ever fathomed myself in that way. I wondered how my grandmother, so beautiful in her wedding picture with her 22 inch waist, could have ended up looking old, graying and well—heavier.

I remember the bent frames of the elderly. And again, I just couldn't imagine them ever being young and vibrant. How could that much change come about over the years? Frankly, I didn't ponder the thought too much. Getting old seemed like centuries away. For me in the SPRING of my life everything was new, interesting, fun and fresh. Never would I allow myself to change *that* much. Ahh—how wonderful youth and naivety are!

The years continued. Like the song, "Life is Just a Bowl of Cherries" so it was for me. I was edging into the SUMMER of my life: Married life with three children; how could it get any better? The joyful holidays; the involvement in my children's activities; the fun times with friends; better economic circumstances; it just seemed that we had it all.

Milestones came and went: The decades flew by; I became 40, then 50, then 60. The babies had grown up. Life *was* changing. Some bad things happened like my son's brain-injury. We lost our parents and some of our siblings. Yet, we were resilient. Good things happened too. Our family grew with grandchildren and great-grandchildren. We basked in their accomplishments and great family moments. Where have the years gone? Suddenly the FALL of my life was upon me.

My interests turned to a healthy lifestyle and exercising: I became obsessed with running. Perhaps in some way I thought I was hanging on to youth and boundless energy was the path to take. The benefits were many. I felt great and kept the pounds at bay. I developed many interests now that the kids were raised: Going back to school and graduating from college; dabbling in politics; traveling; writing a couple of books; and entering in pageant competitions. FALL was without a doubt the most self-satisfying productive season in my life.

The WINTER I never thought would happen to me—well it's here! I must confess it beats the alternative. But here it is! WINTER! My friends look older; they are getting gray; they have lost their vitality and move slower. I see an older person now. And I have joined the ranks! Now we are those elderly folks we thought couldn't happen to us.

I guess you could look at it this way: We are fortunate to have survived; there is no guarantee you will experience all the seasons of your life.

Dr. Carl and Marilyn (Molin) Olson, former residents who now live in Florida, sent me a poem that says it all—laced with a little humor:

"Another year has passed and we're all a little older. Last summer felt hotter and winter seemed much colder. I racked my brain for happy thoughts, to put down on my pad, but lots of things that come to mind just makes me kind of sad.

There was a time not long ago when life was quite a blast. Now I fully understand about 'Living in the Past'. We used to go to friends homes, baseball games and lunches.

Now we go to therapy, to hospitals and after-funeral brunches. We used to have hangovers from parties that were gay. Now we suffer body aches and sleep the night away.

We used to go out dining and couldn't get our fill. Now we ask for doggie bags, come home and take a pill. We used to travel often to places near and far. Now we get backaches from riding in the car.

We used to go out shopping for new clothing in the Mall. But, now we never bother —all the sizes are too small. That my friend is how life is and now my tale is told. So enjoy each day and live it up—before you're too darn old!"

A recent experience: My daughter, Vicki, called and wanted to know how I dealt with "hot flashes" and how long will they last? My daughter having "hot flashes?" Yes, now I know WINTER has arrived for me. I didn't have the heart to tell her they may never end!

I sent her the above poem to which she replied, "You are so right Mom. We need to enjoy life before we are too darn old. After reading the poem; Dave and I made arrangements to go to Paris for our 35th Anniversary in March. We will be having dinner at the Eiffel Tower and thinking about you and Dad. Bon Voyage!"

I felt just a tinge of envy. Wouldn't it be great to experience SUMMER again? I guess we can—in the recesses of our minds! It's called reminiscing.

## A FOND FLASH BACK TO YEARS GONE BY
### Friday, March 7, 2008

People, places and events are what constitute the headlines. However, I can't think of anything to jog your memory more than hearing songs from a certain era. 1937, 1940, 1951 and 1958 will take you back to some of those historic happenings and facts; but the music of those years are what really captures your heart.

I was only four years old in 1937 but heard enough through the years to know the story about former King Edward the V111, and his abduction from the throne to marry Bessie Wallis Simpson, an American divorcee. He was then granted the title of Duke of Windsor.

1937 was also the year nylon, SPAM, Kit Kat candy bar and Kraft Macaroni and Cheese Dinner made their debut. Cobb salad was introduced. Shopping carts were introduced the same year.

The tragedy and shock of the Hindenburg, the famed dirigible crashed and burned in 1937. Thirty-six people lost their lives. It was also the year Amelia Earhart attempted the first around-the-world-at-the-equator flight. Her plane is lost between New Guinea and Howland Island.

Gone With the Wind by Margaret Mitchell is published.

1940 was the debut of Dairy Queen and York Peppermint Patty. I remember attending the Walt Disney movie, Pinocchio. He was swallowed up by a whale. At age seven I was so gullible and impressionable—I actually remember believing this could happen.

And how about the Gene Autry songs, You Are My Sunshine and Back in the Saddle Again? And later I remember his hit song, Don't Fence Me In.

Radio was huge in 1940—there was no TV, of course. During the first season of Captain Midnight; the show featured giveaway premiums. My husband remembers sending for a de-coder for secret messages. A million kids gained membership in the show's Flight Patrol.

Crime dramas were popular. Remember the Shadow and it's famous opening, "Who knows what evil lurks in the heart of men? Only the Shadow knows!"

Flurries of hit records for Glenn Miller's band were born. Pennsylvania 6-5000, Fools Rush In, In the Mood and The Woodpecker Song. In the mood, one of our favorite dance songs in years to come will always hold special memories.

I went to Washington School. In the second grade my teacher was Miss Hughes. I remember the winter time recesses in the basement. We did tumbles and handstands on the mats. The girls wore snow pants under their dresses.

The annual wage was $1,315. A Plymouth two-door sedan was $739. Gasoline was 18 cents a gallon and a first-class stamp was 3 cents.

The epic, Gone with the Wind, won eight Oscars. I remember all of the Bob Hope, Bing Crosby, and Dorothy Lamour "Road series" movies. They began with, Road to Singapore in 1940.

1951 is a year that is really vivid to me; especially the songs and the artists. That's when music was music; songs you could hum to. Too Young by Nat "King" Cole, A Guy is a Guy by Doris Day, The Four Aces and Tell Me Why, Tony Bennett with Because of You, Mocking Bird Hill by Patti Page, Johnnie Ray's chart topper Cry and Rosemary Clooney's smash hit, Come On-A My House. I remember seeing Clooney at the Chicago Theater—-what a thrill!

And then there were the comedic actors like Dean Martin and Jerry Lewis who appeared on the Colgate Comedy Hour, Abbott and Costello with their slap-stick routines. And who could forget Bob Hope?

CBS executives first turned down Lucille Ball's request that husband Desi Arnaz play her husband on her new show. She pointed out that no one would believe an upscale New York woman would marry a Cuban bandleader. Well, in real life, she had. Desi's accent proved to be one of the shows signatures and I Love Lucy climbed to one of the top three programs. You can still see reruns today.

1951 is also the year of color TV broadcasting, automobile power steering and direct telephone dialing. It is the year President Harry Truman removed General Douglas MacArthur as Commander of the United Nations forces in Korea for disagreeing with his policies.

1958 saw a huge jump in the annual income: $4,707. The first class stamp increased to 4 cents and gas was now 30 cents a gallon. New in 58 was the Pizza Hut chain, American Express charge card and the Hula Hoop.

Two popular books to hit the stands were Anatomy of Murder and Doctor Zhivago. (One of my all-time favorite movies)

1958 was a banner year of NEW happenings for me. In January we moved into our first NEW house—the cost was $12,000 with a monthly payment of $89. In August we ordered a NEW car. In those days it was necessary to order cars from the factory. You couldn't go to a dealer and drive home a new car. In August our car was delivered. Then in October we had a NEW baby—my third and last.

Elvis Presley entered the Army that year. Connie Francis had her big record, Who's Sorry Now?  Other hit songs include All I Have to Do Is Dream by the Everly brothers, Chantilly Lace by The Big Bopper, It's Only Make Believe by Conway Twitty and Smoke Gets in Your eyes by The Platters.

Other popular artists of the year include Frank Sinatra, Johnny Mathis, Peggy Lee and The Crickets with Buddy Holly.  In the same year debuts are made by Frankie Avalon, Bobby Darin of Beyond the Sea fame, the Shirelles and Neil Sedaka.

Sorry, but I can't even name one artist today.  Out of touch? Yes, I am almost happy to say.   But I am thankful for Music of Your Life on WDBC.  They play all of the familiar oldies that bring back memories and you can even hum or sing along.

An enjoyable part of life for seniors (me included) is spent reminiscing—either in our thoughts or in speaking with others. We seem to reach back into a time capsule whenever we get together with our peers.  Many of the memories shared above were found in that great magazine for seniors: Reminisce.

## Florida Insights
## Friday, April 11, 2008

A month's vacation in Florida was both gratifying and yet, made me realize how much I appreciated and missed Escanaba— because there is no place like home!

The change was difficult for my son, who has a brain injury, and benefits from a very structured existence: his own bed; his own place at the dinner table; familiar personal surroundings and being in Escanaba.  His aide Nick does daily routine exercises with him and also challenges him with games: chess, pool and air-hockey.  He missed Nick who has been with us for 8 years.

We enjoyed a visit from our son, Jeff and his two girls (18 and 6) during Spring break.  I knew age was rearing its ugly head when I couldn't or didn't want to do what I considered fun a few years ago—like going to the beach and lying in the sun or accompanying the kids to Sun-Splash Park, the Shell factory or Tin City in Naples.

My energy is waning. Guess you can't go back and capture what you thought of as fun years ago. I did manage go to the Edison Mall to see the Easter Bunny with the kids and dined at a favorite spot—the Outback.

I also observed many changes in Fort Myers. For example, Florida is one of the hardest hit states regarding the real estate meltdown. I watched prices of condos and homes double over a few years—not so anymore. The banks sponsored and advertised free daily bus tours to view homes that have been repossessed; one bus for moderate homes and another for high end properties.

One new entity with 113 new homes for sale in Cape Coral declared bankruptcy. A company bought them out and sold the majority of them for little more than half price: $150,000 villas sold for $86,000. $300,000 homes sold for under $175,000. They sold them all in less that a week. Guess if the price is right you can find buyers.

The 'for sale' signs and open houses were unprecedented in the community of 1300 where we rented; a real buyers market.

During our visit a giant Burmese Python weighing 400 pounds and 20 feet in length was discovered along US 41. Uggh! Apparently people buy them as pets and when they get too large release them in the wild. It is against the law and a bad idea—they can kill humans.

That evening on the local news they talked about an extended fight between a boa constrictor and an alligator. The boa won and burst while trying to swallow the gator. On another day a giant turtle sauntered slowly across the road oblivious of cars. It must have been four feet wide. It is not unusual to see an alligator sunning itself on the banks of small lakes or lumbering across a golf course. Florida wildlife is like a throw-back to pre-historic times.

We prided ourselves on not having a cold all winter then all three of us contracted colds with lingering bronchitis. When I entered a satellite medical clinic I was requested to put on a face mask at the door if I had a cold or cough. Not a bad idea! The antibiotics were free at Publix Super Market. Nice surprise.

I spent a lot of time at the library. I missed my computer. They had about 30 computers. A reservation was required and they were occupied all of the time. March was women's history month. I read four books about remarkable women.

The first day we were in Florida I met my former dance instructor, Betsy, at the grocery store. We reminisced about our tap dance group, the Sabal Springs Toe Tappers and how much we enjoyed performing around town.

Another day I had my hair cut in the Mall. The gal was from Green Bay, had lived in Ishpeming when her father was stationed at Sawyer and had attended the fair in Escanaba many times. She talked non-stop about Bret Farve and the Packers—even had her bathroom decorated in Packer colors with huge photos of Farve in every room.

Her mother took a close-up photo of Bret at his last game with a wide lens camera. She said it was beautiful with snow coming down on Bret. Her mom sent her the enlarged framed photo for her birthday. Anyway it was plain to see she enjoyed talking to someone about Bret.

Usually if you mention that you are from Michigan to anyone they think Detroit. Then I explain that is another world.

The Fort Myers area is full of Midwesterners. They are more laid-back than Eastern folks from the New York and New Jersey area. The Eastern people are easy to spot. They lack patience, sensitivities and can be abrupt, outspoken and aggressive in many cases. There are exceptions of course.

It is surprising how many Germans have winter homes in the area.

One thing we did enjoy is the great weather and eating at special places with outdoor seating at Bell Tower Shoppes. Yet in the back of my mind I was ready to come home after a week—-snow and all. I wanted the familiarity of my own home, my own bed and my own town where everything is convenient and comfortable. And oh, how I missed my friend the computer! Guess it takes a trip to make you appreciate what you have.

## Roe V. Wade: The Untold Story of the Controversial Landmark Case
### Friday, April 18, 2008

Most are familiar with the landmark case of Roe V. Wade: the case that traveled through district courts, appeal courts, state courts of Texas and finally through the Federal Court System; the case that would legalize abortion.

What many don't know are the specific details of the case or anything about the plaintiff, Jane Roe (Norma Mc Corvey). Henry Ward was the Dallas attorney who fought the landmark lawsuit.

The lawsuit would prove too late for Norma McCorvey. She bore her child and gave it up for adoption. Initially she sought a back-alley abortion—then through fate she hooked up with two ambitious newly graduated lawyers, Sarah Reddington and Linda Coffee, who were no doubt, bent on gaining some notoriety. And they did! They initiated and won the controversial law suit regarding abortion.

What was Roe (Norma McCorvey) all about: The woman that would affect generations of lives to come and spur a passionate movement still alive and well today to overturn the Supreme Court Decision?

Norma grew up in a chaotic household. She gave birth to three children: a daughter from a marriage that her mother adopted; another child born out of wedlock was placed for adoption; her third child, born out of wed lock, precipitated the lawsuit that would have unimaginable consequences for decades to come.

Norma certainly wasn't anyone's idea of a role model. She was a working-poor woman in her late 20's from Louisiana unable to face the psychological pain of carrying her unplanned pregnancy to term—only to give up the baby for adoption.

In her young years she experienced a marriage of abuse, rejection, a stint in prison, sordid jobs in gay bars; drugs and attempted suicide. Her chosen lifestyle of relationships was with both men and women. She became a self-proclaimed lesbian.

She told herself as she searched for a back-alley abortion, "You're in trouble, bad trouble. You're four months pregnant, broke and alone. You're a bad mother. You've lost touch with both of your children. I was lower than low—between a rock and a hard place. If I knew anything at all, I knew I could never survive having another child. I couldn't take care of it and I couldn't give it up either."

Through fate she met with the attorneys in a bar over a beer, eventually signed the papers and hoped that she could escape her pregnancy with their help. But trials and appeals bogged down in the legal system are slow to reach fruition.

When her pregnancy was too far along for any law to help her, despondent and dejected she retreated to the part of Dallas where all the hippies hung out. Everyone wore bellbottoms and tie-dyed T-shirts. She smoked dope and drank enough wine not to think about being pregnant—with total disregard for the child she was carrying.

While Norma was battling her own demons Roe v. Wade was moving forward—but not soon enough to benefit Norma. The lawyers "used" her to file the lawsuit and never kept in contact with her throughout the process.

She would deliver the child, give it up for adoption, and thought no more about the lawsuit. Until one day buried in page six or seven of the newspaper she read a small article that Roe v Wade had been decided—abortion was now legal. No hoopla and of course no mention of Norma—nor was she even contacted.

Most judges on the Supreme Court agreed with Sarah Reddington's argument and voted by a wide margin to legalize abortion. Voting for Roe were Judges Blackmun, Brennan, Burger, Douglas, Marshall, Powell and Stewart. Voting for Wade were justices Rehnquist and White.

The judges ruled just as Sarah had written: that abortion laws violated the 14th Amendment, the one that guarantees life, liberty and property. Anti-abortion laws did this, agreed the judges, by violating a woman's right to privately control her own body.

They ruled that the opposite argument: that a fetus was a separate human being entitled to legal protection was not backed up by anything in the constitution.

The Supreme Court's landmark decision on January 22, 1973 gave women the right to have an abortion.

Norma did not reveal that she was Jane Roe for many years.

When she did people broke windows in her home and left baby clothes scattered on the front lawn. She was reviled. She wrote a book, *Roe V Wade* detailing her experiences.

The following information was taken from the Catholic Review August 27, 1998.

In 1995 Norma began the process to join the Catholic Church by being baptized. In 1998 she received the sacraments of Holy Communion and confirmation and was fully accepted into the Catholic Church during a private Mass August 17 at St. Thomas Aquinas Church in Dallas. Leading up to her full entrance into the Catholic faith Ms. McCorvey made her first confession to Father Robinson.

"Father said he was going to use my book as a confession, so I was brief," relates Norma. "Even though I knew my sins had been washed away from my Baptism, I felt a sense of relief afterward."

For Communion she knelt at the railing in front of the altar to receive the bread and wine from Father Robinson. In a special closing address to the congregation Father Pavone said that, "by her receiving the body and blood of Christ, Ms. McCorvey is reconciled with the babies who were aborted during the time she worked in the movement to keep abortion legal."

The priest told her that every time she receives Communion Christ is "giving back to you all the babies that were lost through what you did." He added, "He has restored the friendship between you and the babies who didn't have a chance to play on the playgrounds."

Powerful stuff! I can only surmise that McCorvey's act of contrition twenty-five years after her input in the landmark lawsuit that legalized abortion must have weighed heavily on her conscience.

# Names We Are Stuck With!
## Friday, April 25, 2008

My mother named me Patricia Dorothy. Dorothy after my aunt and I guess Patricia because I am half Irish. My maiden name was Kidd—a good Irish name. I only remember being called Patricia by my teachers when I was in school. As a kid I was "Patsy" and how I hated that name!

My brother was 13 months younger than me. Apparently I couldn't say Francis so I called him brother and that stuck. We were Patsy and Brother. My sister, Pauline came along three years later. I never knew anyone else with that name.

My friend Joan was a grade ahead of me in school. She was always talking about Gary Abrahamson (before I knew him) and I thought what a strange name. Then I ended up marrying him and went from a one-syllable last name to one with four syllables—big change. We laugh about now whenever we get together.

I suppose most of us like our names. We can't imagine being called by another name. But then many of us have nick-names like Bill for William, Jack for John, Hal for Harold, Joe for Joseph and on and on.

Some nicknames for girls aren't shortened versions but entirely different like Betty for Elizabeth or Sally for Sarah or Peggy for Margaret.

Names are popular during different eras. Some of the family names we discovered in our genealogy quest were Ebenezer, Abner, Ferdinand, Adelaide, Angelique and Pierre. Many French names were from my mother's side. My grandfather's name was Horace. I can't imagine calling a little baby Horace.

I remember Bob, Jim, Bill, Joe, Tom, Dick and Ed being the most common names of boys in school. Common names for girls were Betty, Jane, Ruth, Jean, Ann, Mary, Janet and Joan. Short and simple.

Now the names have changed so much that I am amazed when an obituary mentions the names of grandchildren. Popular boys' names are Jacob, Joshua, Matthew, Ethan, Daniel, Christopher, Jaden and Anthony. Many of the boys' names are biblical. Common girls' names now are Emily, Emma, Hannah, Olivia,

Ashley, Madison, Taylor, and Samantha.

My husband's name was not real common during our school years. I only knew of two boys named Gary. He says his mother was reading a magazine about movie star Gary Cooper when she was expecting him and decided on that name.

His brothers' name was Elliott Glenn, but probably no one knew that since he was always called Glenn. Elliott was his mother's family name and the connection to first cousin Thomas Edison. Edison's mother was Nancy Elliott.

Everyone in his family and our children were called "Abe" in school. Even the teachers called my husband Abe. Some of his classmates that had nicknames were Warren Gustafson (Moose), Harold O'Connell (Spike); Don Carlson was called Baldy (his dad clipped his hair short) and Ed Gosselin was called Tootsie.

Some were called by their dad's names. Dave Johnson was "Big Al." Harold Pearson was called "Fred"—Gary still calls him that even though he has graduated to "Hal" in other circles.

Some of the names our teachers were unknowingly tagged with were: Bulldog Drummond, Black Ed, Puck, Hank and Big Al.

I wonder if there was some thought when naming George W. Bush—different than George H. That way no one would call him Junior. It just doesn't seem like a good idea for a president to be called Junior. It sounds so demeaning. I named my son after my husband—bad idea. There have been so many mix-ups over the years not to mention the confusion.

Less often girls are given their mothers names. Yet if they are named after their mother no one ever calls a girl Junior even though the word is not gender-specific.

Some presidents are identified by three initials: FDR, RFK and JFK. Teddy Roosevelt was tagged TR. Eisenhower was Ike.

Some people have three names. It makes them sound important. I just read a book by Joyce Carol Oates—a few others with three names were Louisa May Alcott, Henry Wadsworth Longfellow, George Bernard Shaw, Martin Luther King Jr. and Alexander Graham Bell. Impressive, right?

Southern people especially like the sound of two names like Billy Joe, John Henry, Cindy Lou, or Ellie May (ala the Beverly Hillbillies). My twin cousins from Indiana were called Ruth Ann and Dorothy Mae—always the two names together.

My granddaughter is named Mary Pat, after both grandmothers. Nobody calls her just Mary but some family members and friends call her MP.

How about the Olympic ski gold-medalist Picabo Street? Her name is like in the childhood game Peek-a-boo. Her parents, typical '50s hippies, were going to let their kids name themselves when they got older.

My husband always checked the phone books when we traveled to other cities. Numerous times he found another Gary Abrahamson—even called one up in Denver. One time we found a husband and wife with our same names. On the internet we found 26 Gary Abrahamsons'.

Have you ever noticed people look like their names? You couldn't imagine calling them anything else.

For years when we went to a restaurant my husband gave his name as Mr. Gary. He hated to hear them mangle his last name or laugh at the length.

Guess we are victims of our parents when it comes to our given names. Like it or not they give us a name and we're stuck with it. There is one way out—a nickname, but again we don't give ourselves nicknames.

A name is a brand we are given at birth. If you are unhappy with your name keep in mind that some folks like our names so much they steal them. It's called "identity theft." A growing problem in today's society.

## HOBEY BAKER: AN AMERICAN LEGEND
## Friday, May 2, 2008

Sports have got to be the greatest pastime ever—for those that participate and of course for the spectators. When I was in school there just weren't the opportunities for girls. I played volley ball in gym and that was the extent of my participation.

There were no organized sports for girls to participate in and it would take years for that to happen. I doubt I would have been interested in say, being competitive at track related sports. The mindset of the time would have been: How unfeminine!

Most girls in my era were only interested in sports as a spectator primarily because of school spirit and the interest in boys, you know, the big jocks on campus. How that has changed! Years later I did become an avid runner. I competed after age 50 and placed first two years in a row.

By then I owned a health spa and running was a craze. Health and fitness became "catch" words. Terry Ahola, recently inducted into the UP Sports Hall of Fame, reminded me that he trained at my former business, Hawaiian Sun Fitness Center.

When Gary and I attended the recent UPSHF induction we were moved to tears when one young lady, Shana (DeCremer) Ojala, a star basketball player gave her acceptance talk. Humbled and choked up with emotion she held up her award for her twin boys to see as an inspiration. Yes, she was a difficult act to follow.

When Joe (Jocko) Ricci received his coveted award for being a stand-out football, hockey and baseball player he brought the house down. Amidst the whistles, hoots and cheers, he kidded that all of his Italian Mafia family showed up. It brought me back to a time in the Sault when my boys played hockey.

We traveled to many International tournaments in Canada when our boys competed. Eventually I became such a fan of the game I wanted to see the "big boys" like the Red Wings play. When we moved back to Escanaba there was virtually no hockey program or at best primitive: Outdoor hockey at the water tower rink—certainly not well organized in 1966.

Our son, Gary, was so despondent with our move and the local hockey program that we agreed to let him go back to the Sault to room and board with a hockey family. He was the league high scorer that year—quite a feat in a hockey town that churned out world class hockey players. Many of them are in the UPSHF.

The Hobey Baker Memorial Award for hockey is equivalent to the Heisman Trophy Award for football. Recently U of M captain Kevin Porter won the Hobey Baker award. Brendan Morrison (1997) was the only other wolverine player to garner the award.

Which begs the question: Who was Hobey Baker?

Baker was the stuff of legends. Not only was he the first

*Hobey Baker*

American elected to the Hockey Hall of Fame but he is the only athlete enshrined there and in the College Football Hall of Fame. He was an Ivy-Leaguer from the East. By the time he arrived at Princeton as a freshman the national spotlight had already focused on him.

His contemporary in college, F. Scott Fitzgerald would pattern several of his memorable characters after Baker. Fitzgerald said, "Hobey Baker is an ideal worthy of everything in my admiration, yet consummated, and expressed in a human being who stood ten feet from me."

You could compare his athleticism to George Gipp from the UP in their uncanny ability to excel at every sport they undertook. Both died in their twenties as heroes; but that is where the comparison ends.

Hobey was from a wealthy family with good breeding. His athletic ability, reputation of a gentleman athlete gave him star power before the Great War (WW1). Hobey's sense of duty made him a celebrated flyer in France with the elite Lafayette Flying Corps when the life expectancy of a pilot was just two weeks.

Hobey was on his last mission (a test mission) a month after the war ended when his plane crashed in December, 1918. He died enroute to the hospital with the gash in his head partially hidden by his long blonde hair. He was twenty-six years old. The report of his death was sensational—reported in every major newspaper in Europe and the United States.

Hobey, the Prince of Princeton, had become the most famous amateur athlete in the country during his Princeton Tiger (orange and black) career.

I found it interesting that football was a work in progress during that era. The rules changed. The results were more broken bones and crushed heads. The game was primitive, vicious and lethal.

Variations of mass plays were created such as Harvard's infamous flying wedge and Princeton's deadly V wedge. A smaller player would literally springboard himself into orbit on the back of the center. Even biting occurred. Crowds were horrified at the carnage of the unprotected players. Death and injuries were rampant.

Cries came for the abolishment of the game, after a particularly bloody Harvard –Yale game. The two schools cancelled "The Game" for two years. Football had become more brutal than prize-fighting or cock-fighting.

In the fall of 1905, with calls for abolishment of the game, President Theodore Roosevelt summoned the Big Three—

Harvard, Princeton and Yale to discuss the state of the game. He advocated for changes in the rules which eventually occurred. Can you even imagine life without football—or the Packers?

The year (1910) Hobey Baker enrolled at Princeton, also marked the end of the vicious mass plays and collisions of muscle and bone. In addition, the game was divided into fifteen-minute quarters instead of twenty-minute quarters. The new rules moved the game closer to the sport that we know today.

Hobey Bakers's first love was hockey. His abilities on the ice are even more extroadinary when framed in the context of the time. Skates were long, flat and thick making it difficult to turn quickly or change directions on the ice.

But Hobey could stop at will without turning his skates sideways. He was a wizard when handling the puck. He curved and glided through fields of skaters effortlessly with unmatched speed and never having to look down at the puck.

His hockey stats speak for themselves. In three seasons on the Princeton varsity team, he scored 120 goals and over 100 assists. He averaged about three goals and three assists a game, a feat never equaled in college or professional hockey. He was an All-American three times and led the Tigers to two National Championships on the ice.

He is the only amateur in both the Canadian and American Hockey Hall of Fame. Each year since 1981, the best college hockey player in America is awarded the Hobey Baker Memorial award. Hobey, the gentleman athlete whose feats were almost mythical would be a spectator's delight today.

## Today's Dollar and Senior Frustrations
## Friday, May 9, 2008

I doubt that our generation of seniors ever gets really comfortable with a multitude of things (progress?) as decades pass. I probably will sound like Andy Rooney on 60 Minutes—bewildered and maybe a bit negative about changes and what is happening in the world today.

I hate to think like "older is better" but here are a couple of examples: Recently we purchased a new refrigerator after 6 repairs on the old one in 10 years. We had the one before that for 20 years and no repairs. They just don't make things as good as years ago. Then the salesperson informed us that the warranty is good for only a year. Would we like additional insurance at a whopping price?

In our day (the olden days) you had confidence when you bought a major appliance. Not so anymore. We were informed they make refrigerators with a smaller compressor now and they don't last as long. Really?

We recently purchased a new car. I don't relish the haggling that ensues over the trade-in and price. You have to do your homework on the internet and be prepared for their doublespeak. And in the back of your mind you think, "Jeez, I could have bought 3 or 4 houses in the '50s for the price of a car today."

The salesperson runs back and forth to the sales manager like a rat after cheese. He brings us back a new price and when it looks like we are going to look elsewhere—only then does he sharpen his pencil.

Can you believe that the paint was listed on the invoice as an extra? Yep, 495 dollars for white-chocolate tri-coat! A week later my husband scratched the bumper. It was a minor half- inch scratch—incurred while hoisting the wheelchair in the back. He went in to the dealer thinking they would "touch it up" at no cost. He explained, "That paint has four coats and to cover this scratch would be several hundred dollars." Needless to say the scratch stays.

The wheel covers were options too. 895 dollars! My husband kidded the salesperson, "you can buy that car a lot cheaper but it doesn't include the paint or wheels. How about the engine? Is that an extra too?" An option is not really an option. All of the cars had trailer hitches listed as an option at 495 dollars.

The one thing I wanted was the navigation system. I didn't realize I would have to go back to college for an engineering degree to operate it. My head spun as the salesperson gave us instructions. Then he said, "oh well, don't feel badly—it took me a couple of years to master this." If we have to wait years to master it—we don't have years left!

My husband agued against a navigation system: He put forth the argument that we know our way to the store, the doctors office, hospital and funeral home; that I didn't need that to go to the casino—the car knows how to get there on its own.

Then the salesperson proudly announced the car was equipped with a Sirius satellite system. What's that? Buying a car made us feel like out-of-touch relics. He added that a "blue tooth" cell phone can be hooked up to the navigation system. Bluetooth?? I did find out it is a short range wireless technology that connects electronic devices. High tech leaves us frustrated, bewildered and anchored in the past.

Our trade-in car was six-years old. Only when we were about to trade it in did we find out we had heated seats—never used them; didn't even know we had them.

Our next purchase will be a mattress: an important commodity since we spend one-third of our lives lying prone on it. We began the process and became utterly confused lying on every mattress in the store. You no longer have to turn a mattress since they are one-sided. There are pillow tops, hard, firm, plush, extra firm, tempur-pedic (the mattress of astronauts) developed in Sweden, hypo-allergenic and companies galore. And the list goes on.

More confused that ever we haven't made a choice yet other than it will be a king mattress like we have now. I wondered how an ample-sized couple in the '40s and '50s ever slept in a standard size bed; the only choice years ago.

Now another grumble—taxes for instance. We paid taxes on our last car and then paid taxes again when we traded it in. You end up paying 12% taxes on a trade in the state of MI. What about property taxes? Our property (home) is being devalued, yet our property taxes continue to increase.

How about the price to maintain a home? Our utility bill is over 300 dollars a month—the heating bill is extra. Couple in taxes and insurance and even if you own your own home (no mortgage) it's an uphill battle to make the bills. Most seniors are on fixed incomes and as the prices increase many have to make choices between groceries, medications and housing. Like us they may have to pay to have maintenance help if they want to stay in their home.

Then if you are forced to sell for financial or health reasons you have already lost a bundle due to the devaluing housing market. The domino effect enters in: Even if you find a buyer they can't buy because they can't sell their house.

Seniors that depend on social security can barely survive now. You get an increase, of say 30 dollars a month, on one hand then the government takes half back for increased insurance rates. Look at the increasing prices of groceries and gas. Filling a tank can cost almost 70 dollars. And the end is nowhere in sight.

Some seniors depend on interest income from CD's. Their penalty for saving for old age is that the rates are so low now they barely keep up with the cost of living.

The airlines claim they are going broke with the price of jet fuel. So now if you want a window seat or aisle seat some airlines are charging 5 dollars extra. Or if you have more than one bag the cost is 25 dollars extra. Remember when an airplane trip offered a first class meal? Well, now you can buy a half-frozen sandwich for 6 dollars.

Yes, I took a page right out of Andy Rooney's 60 Minutes negative spoof. Guess we can grin and bear it or just laugh outright and go with the flow. Are there any other choices?

## CRISIS IN THE NIGHT
**Friday, May 23, 2008**

On any given day something can happen that could turn your life into a tailspin. It could be an accident, the loss of a job, the death of a loved one or any number of happenings. Last week it was our turn. We endured a crisis.

About 3 AM one morning I heard a terrible crash. My son Gary, who lives with us, had fallen out of bed.

We called 911. An ambulance sped him to the hospital. An examination revealed he had a fractured hip. By 6 AM he was on his way to Marquette in an ambulance for hip replacement surgery that same day. Lacking any sleep we followed closely behind.

Hip surgery is very common but Gary experienced complications. Our week was like being on an emotional roller coaster—up and down—tears of sadness and tears of joy. One moment we were in the depths of despair; the next moment floating on cloud nine.

Toward the end of the week Gary's situation became less critical and we experienced some welcomed funny moments: One afternoon Gary asked me, "where his Dad?" I explained he was in the lounge across the hall. "Is Dad a drinker now?" he asked.

We were especially impressed with one resident doctor from Pakistan. Her name is Farah. She came to the U.S. for her education and met her husband (also a Muslim) at Columbia University. She is working on her citizenship now that rules will allow her to retain her Pakistan and British citizenship.

She visits her family in Pakistan but expressed that she will never return there to practice medicine. The conditions in a third world country are deplorable. There is no health care plan in place. The people are poor and die because they have no money to get a needed operation, medical attention or drugs.

She explained that many doctors even pay for tests etc. because they can't bear to see their fellow man in need of medical attention. If you live in Pakistan and have resources (money) you are expected to help others. Some live with dirt floors and many children don't even have shoes.

The day before Gary left the hospital we met Chubbers, the well-known dog from North Escanaba. He was in the lounge with his owner, Bud Irving. Gary reached down from his wheelchair and petted Chubbers. He brought a smile to Gary's face.

Chubbers wears a vest identifying him with Pet Partners Nationwide. That recognition allows him to visit any hospital or healthcare facility nationwide. Chubbers seems to have a sixth sense that he is cheering up folks in the hospitals. Bud says the vets at the Jacobetti Center wait for his visits.

Bud also says, "When Chubbers and I go over the crosswalk at Marquette General I always know when a good-looking nurse is coming toward us. Chubbers waves his tail vigorously. If they are homely his tail doesn't wag."

Chubber's will be in the Memorial Day parade in Rapid River. He'll be wagging his tail (his way of smiling) as he sits proudly on Duane Berro's golf cart. Look for him!

Bud also drives patients to Marquette for tests and therapy. One gentleman has Alzheimers. As they drove to Marquette he said to Chubbers, who was sitting up in the front seat, "how are you today Chubbers?" Bud answered saying he was just fine. The man, in all seriousness declared, "D—- it! I wasn't talking to you. I was talking to Chubbers!"

Gary stabilized and was taken by ambulance to Christian Park village. He will spend weeks, perhaps months, in rehabilitation. That costly, deadly moment when he rolled over and fell out of bed has changed all of our lives for now.

The first day he was at Christian Park we attended a scheduled activity with him. A country and western band provided music for the residents. It was heart-warming to see some of them clapping their hands and snapping their fingers to the music. One elderly lady (about age 90) even grabbed my husband's arm and said, "Wanna a dance?"

The room was filled with a sea of wheelchairs. The volunteers that donate their time and loving ways to help the residents are living proof of the great community that we live in. Not to mention the special caregivers—and it does take special people to care for the elderly nursing home residents. They are the unsung heroes.

Justin, a therapist at Christian Park Village also takes his dog, Hazel, to work with him. The patients all love him. He rolls over so they can pet him. It is common knowledge that animals do impact the lives of people. Guess that is where the age-old adage "A dog is man's best friend," comes from.

We have been exposed to a different world, the nursing home world, one we knew precious little about. At some time in our lives we probably will all face a crisis of sorts. It is amazing how you get through them with sheer determination—and by taking one day at a time. Some losses leave a hole in your heart that never quite heals, but life is precious and we must go on.

## MEMORIES FROM LONG AGO
### Friday, May 30, 2008

So often when I meet people in the community they want to talk about their memories of long ago. The oldsters (like me) love to reminisce. Sometimes they bring to mind memories that I hadn't thought of in years.

For example, I go to Christian Park Village to help feed my son everyday. A gentleman who was seated at the same table as Gary told me he reads my column. George Labre is 87 and a wonderful conversationalist. He remembered my mom Edna and step-dad, Tootles Flath.

He talked about Tootles (Earl) playing baseball. He was a great ballplayer and catcher for the Escanaba Bears. He came from a long line of Flath ballplayers: his dad, Julius (Ching) Flath; brothers, Wally and Bill Flath and nephew, Allan Erickson. Allen played professional baseball for the San Francisco Giants in their farm system.

Wally played for a team while in the army. A major league

*House of Ludington, Escanaba. Recommended by gourmet duncan Hines and A.A.A.*

scout from the St. Louis Cardinals discovered him and invited him to a try-out camp in Georgia. When he got to the camp he was stricken with pneumonia and came home to Escanaba. He also played for the Escanaba Bears and managed them. Wally played ball until he was 50 years old. Bill also played for the Bears.

George talked about their hunting escapades and stories: hunting deer and violating. Yes, I do remember when they went out spotlighting and we were never without venison. My mother cooked it every which-way and even canned the steaks. We were poor by today's standards (like many in that era) but had many steak sandwiches—food was always plentiful.

George and I laughed heartily when we talked about Ritchie's pop shop. My family lived next door. When my age was in single digits, I remember roller skating. Remember the skates hooked on to your shoes and you had a key to tighten them? You hung it around your neck on a string. And ouch! The skinned knees!

After skating my brother and I sat on the receiving deck to the pop shop swinging our skinned knees. We looked like little beggars waiting for them to offer us a pop. Finally, they would have us come in the shop to pick a flavor. Our eyes would be big as saucers as we watched the machine fill the clanging bottles with pop. Strawberry, grape or orange. Which would it be? Big decision!

George reminisced about the pop shop. He chummed around with Ray Taylor's younger brothers. They passed by the pop shop on their way home from their hike to Second creek. If a truck was there unattended they would swipe a bottle of pop. Ah, it tasted so good!

Second Creek! Wow that brought back memories. First Creek or Butchers Creek was on the city side of Lincoln Road. But Second Creek was further out. Mom would fix us a baloney sandwich slathered with mustard, pack a Twinkie in a little sack and we would hike to Second Creek for a picnic.

The boys would try and dam the creek with boards and branches so we could swim. Can't believe that now. The water was dirty, shallow and mucky. We thought it was a big deal to swim there. Until one day a huge snake was swimming in the creek. I never went back.

There was a funeral home on the corner of Stephenson Avenue and First Avenue. My friend Joan and I stopped in the funeral home every few days to see if there was a different body laid out. How weird when I think of it now.

Funerals were quite different than today. I was five when my grandfather died. In 1938 he was laid-out in his bedroom off the parlor. All the furniture was removed and folding chairs were all along the walls. The service was held in the home.

I still remember how scary it was to see him laying in the casket and my mother having me climb up on the rail of the casket to see him. There were lamps at each end shining to the ceiling. I still remember the frightening experience today.

I received a letter from Walt Peterson, who grew up on a farm in Bark River. "Patt, thank you for the memories," he says. "Your articles have brought back many of them."

Quotes from his letter:

"Dad had a large milk and egg route in Escanaba in the 1930s and early 1040's. The Karas Igloo was a good customer. One name I heard frequently was Abrahamson. Somehow I associate it with the day old Danish sent home with Dad for our chickens. We were six kids and the Danish never saw the chickens.

The family grew up on eggs. We had hundreds of chickens and we ate all the eggs that were cracked or for some reason did not measure up.

At Christmas time in 1952 I came back from Korea. I flew to Chicago and took the 400 back to Bark River. I remember Chicago was gosh-awful cold. I had stowed my gear and was looking out the window when a very distinguished looking man and a girl came up to the car on the platform. They stopped right outside of the window and said their good-byes. Then the man looked into the train and said to the girl, 'Honey, stay away from that serviceman.' I read his lips...

The only vacant seat was next to me. I was 22 and Julie was in high school. I drove up to Ishpeming to see her on my leave. Their home smelled pleasantly of wood smoke from a wood heater. And I can verify that the refrigerator had a number of fresh fish rolled up in wax paper.

Tom Swift's fish fries. They did it right with fresh fish!

The Casino. Our farm was on the Delta-Menominee county line. From our place you could see the Eastern edge of the reservation. I remember Indians coming with their pails. We had a separator that put cream out one spout and skim milk out the other. Dad would let them put their pails under the skim milk spout. At that time there was no sale for skim milk and we gave it to the calves or pigs.

Our farm had some big hills on it and the farm was sold for a song. When a new road was being built to the reservation there was a need for gravel. The hills had good gravel and they were leveled. To stabilize the foundations for the expansion of the casino they needed lots of sand. That came from a different part of our old farm. Too late we realized we should have retained mineral rights when the farm was sold.

Thanks again for the memories. If you live to be 100 plus I hope you will always look like your picture in the paper."

Oops! Guess I need to update that photo. And thank you Walt for sharing your memories!

## BONIFAS PROJECT IN FULL SWING!
## Friday, June 6, 2008

A caring and loving community—that's who we are! That explains how all of the great projects are implemented and funded by wonderfully generous benefactors and the people in our community. One just needs to look at the Escanaba Athletic Field project as an example of a community coming together. And we, as a community, are going to make it happen once again with the Bonifas Project.

William (Big Bill) and Catherine (Kate) Bonifas have left their footprints in this community with gifts of untold magnitude; Gifts that have touched every person who has ever lived here.

Did you attend Escanaba or Holy Name High School? Have you attended mass at St. Josephs Church? Have you utilized the Bonifas Fine Arts Center or attended a play there? Have you

attended the Civic Center, the senior activities and meals or a council meeting there?

Has a loved one resided in Bishop Noa? Have you visited the state building to purchase a license? Have you attended Bay College? Or perhaps you or a family member has been the recipient of a Bonifas Scholarship. Have you been to the library and city hall? How about the courthouse and St. Francis hospital?

These are just a few of the projects or injections of monies

*Bishop Sample dedicates the renovations and celebrating
the life of William and Kate Bonifas.*

made possible by the generosity of Bill and Kate Bonifas. An examination of their will revealed the funding of the aforementioned projects or gifts plus many, many more too numerous to list.

So how can we as a caring community leave their resting place

(Mausoleum and grounds at Holy Cross Cemetery) in desperate need of repair, restoration and beautification? We can not and we will not!

For that reason a strong committee was formed: The Bonifas Mausoleum Restoration Committee. Jerry Shapy, former mayor and councilman and project manager for the athletic field has lent his talents and heart to this project. Also on board is his wife Kay, who says, "This is a project I really felt compelled to get involved with."

Other committee members are: Pat Baribeau (councilwoman), Jillian Jamison (Lifestyles Editor, Daily Press) George Rusch, (former mayor and councilman), and Master Gardeners, Ann Savage and Judy Schroeder (DDA Administrative Assistant) plus yours truly.

Major work is required to the inside of the Mausoleum. Granite blocks have tumbled unto the caskets. Windows and doors have been frosted to hide the unsightliness. We can only surmise that Bill and Kate had beveled glass doors and windows installed so that rays of sunlight could shine into their resting place. The plan is to restore the major structure to its original form.

*Ann Savage, George Rusch, Patt Abrahamson,*
*Jerry Shapy, Kay Shapy and Pat Baribeau.*

Possibly a brick apron, benches, large flower urns, landscaping stones and small plants will be part of the plan—maybe even an arbor. The Master Gardeners are in the process of drawing up the final plan. Also to be included will be some sort of stand or rock with a plaque listing the contributions Bill and Kate made to the community.

It will ultimately be a place of beauty and reverence where people can visit, sit on a bench, give thanks and offer prayers. It will be the community's way of giving back and giving thanks.

The completion is planned for late September when a celebration of their life will take place. Plans include extending an invitation to Bishop Sample, the Bonifas family descendents and the community at large to attend the commemoration ceremony.

In conjunction, another consideration that will be explored is the naming of a street or a place in honor of William and Catherine Bonifas. Many streets are named after pioneers of the community such as: Ludington, Stephenson. Ogden and Jenkins drive. Also some places: Ludington Park, Royce Park, and Aronson Island.

In lieu of the Bonifas generosity there is a distinct absence of the Bonifas name in the community other than the Bonifas Fine Arts Center. There has been very little recognition bestowed upon them in light of the fact that they have been the community's foremost and greatest benefactor.

In today's money the Bonifas will would be worth approximately 30 million dollars.

Seed money has been pledged to help get the project off the ground. The Bonifas restoration account has been set up through the Community Foundation.

Now we need to enlist the community to open up their hearts and contribute whatever they can to this worthy project. Checks may be made out to the Community Foundation for Delta County, 2500 7th Ave. So. Suite 103, Escanaba, MI. Be sure to include in the memo section: Bonifas Mausoleum Fund.

In the future look for more in-depth articles in the Daily Press regarding the lives and times of Bill and Kate Bonifas.

# FATHER'S DAY AT CHRISTIAN PARK VILLAGE
## Friday, June 13, 2008

Comfortable daily living routines can stay the same for months—even years, then something happens to change that. Your comfort zone is altered. My son has lived with us for almost twenty years. Everything was business as usual until he broke his hip when he fell out of bed.

Now our daily routine includes visiting Christian Park Village three or four times a day. Gary is getting rehabilitation therapies to help him regain his ability to walk.

We are experiencing a whole different world never having a loved one in a nursing home. The residents have become part of our life too, along with the caring staff and the many planned activities they provide.

The activity director, Linda Paulin and her husband Dave are honoring fathers on Sunday. Dave is an avid fisherman and will prepare walleye on the grill. This is the 9th year they will do a special fish fry at the Village for Father's Day. I offered to bake cookies for the occasion—ya, unlike Hillary, I bake cookies.

*Gary Abrahamson at walleye dinner at Christian Park Village.*

Gary has adjusted to his new routine and so have we. We have had some funny and some precious moments with some of the residents.

My husband was talking to a lady resident about the old days, where she lived and about her family members he knew. She was in a wheelchair and very lucid—really with it! Then as he was about to leave she asked. "Do you mind giving me a ride home?" He said sure but then asked the nurse who said she has been a resident for years.

Another lady with Alzheimer's wanders in the halls. She has something attached to her in case she tries to walk out the door. Many times we hear the alarm go off. The aides gently turn her around. She is docile and willingly comes back in.

One lady calls for her Mama, and has a rubber doll that she thinks is her child. Gary asked her if it was a boy or girl. "Well, can't you see, he is a boy!" Hugging and kissing him, she exclaimed, "You beautiful boy!"

Gary asked one gentleman how old he was. "Well", he said, "now you got me thinking." Gary then asked what year he was born. Since he seemed a bit confused, Gary said, "I was born in 1931. Were you born before that?" "Oh no," he said, "I am much younger than you!" I asked his wife his age the next day and she asked her husband to guess. He thought he might be 117. He will be 92.

Every day there is a different planned activity for the residents. Bingo, musical exercise, social hour with donuts on the week-end, happy hour on Friday, an occasional musical group, and many more innovative things.

You can sense the caring and empathy of the staff when they feed residents that require help. They gently encourage them to open their mouth and take a bite.

Don Goulais is a resident there and has a good mind. Gary reminded Don of when he was a young lawyer for the state. Gary was returning from Alma College for the week-end—hitch-hiking of course. Mackinac Bridge was non-existent in 1949. Don gave Gary a ride home from St. Ignace.

George Labre's wife brings their adorable young grandchildren to visit PaPa—the residents love the kids. Many other young kids visit relatives and you can just see the eyes of the residents light up.

Kathy Shine is the beautician. She takes pride in gussying up the ladies hair and gives them a sense of pride. He husband Bill's mother is a resident there and he is there every noon to feed her. It's like one big happy family.

When I think about years ago, there were no nursing homes. There was the Poor Farm across from the Buck Inn. The conditions were appalling. Many slept in one room. There was a lack of cleanliness. At that time there was no regulations overseeing conditions. Gary remembers seeing old men with canes sitting on a bench near the highway.

Pine Crest in Powers was a sanitarium for TB. Family members with dementia (I don't believe Alzheimer's was a word then) went to the Newberry State Hospital—what a shame! One of Gary's family members was admitted to the Traverse City State Hospital in the 1890's—that was before the opening of the Newberry facility.

In reading her admittance from court records she was going through menopause and it affected her emotionally. Zikes! We'd all be in an institution. Today many women experience similar symptoms but there are drugs to help them weather the storm.

Newberry State Hospital was closed during the Reagan Administration. In the 1800's people were caged and chained without the benefit of medications available today. Conditions were squalid and not regulated or monitored like today.

People at the nursing home aren't restrained. They can roam freely in their wheelchairs or walk in the halls. They can watch TV all night if they choose. They are treated humanely. Some have family members that take them out for Sunday dinner or even a beer. Some have no one left to visit them. Their family is caring staff members and the volunteers who come daily to feed those that require help.

Audrey Halgren, age 87, has been a volunteer for 7 years. Tiny 70 pound Audrey buzzes around the dining room delivering meals to the residents; lovingly buttering their bread, cutting their meat, touching them and calling them by name. I reminded Audrey about the fun we used to have at her bar, The Idle Hour, years ago.

And the times we dined with her and her husband at the Ludington.

Margaret Therrian, soon to be 90, has been a volunteer for 18 years. She bustles around like Audrey helping some folks that are much younger than her. There are many other "saints" that volunteer. I am sure it is gratifying to them and adds to their life.

When we visit Christian Park Village we hug and greet residents. They seem to purr with the attention. I hug Fred Sayklly's widow, Kathryn. She is receiving rehab for a stroke and making tremendous strides. She waits for those hugs and so do I.

Shirley Lundquist visits daily to feed her husband Rodger, a stroke victim, who has been there for five years. Shirley says, "Sometime I think he knows who I am; other times he thinks I am a staff person." He had tears in his eyes recently when he seen her arrive.

The nursing home world I described will more than likely touch most of us—either visiting a family member, or even residing there ourselves. Lucky for us the landscape has changed since the days of state hospitals.

Guess what? My son likes it there as much as he does being home. I think the activities and people are fascinating to him. He is making strides in his attempt to walk again.

Father's Day will be extra special. We are looking forward to Linda and Dave Paulin's fresh caught Walleye dinner in the parlor.

Life goes on and we must adapt to change.

## KATE BONIFAS HAD HUMBLE BEGINNINGS
**Friday, June 20, 2008**

When Kate Nolan arrived in America from Ireland she must have been in awe. People were starving in Ireland. In 1845 the potato crops had failed changing the destiny of Ireland forever. The potato crops had failed before, but it failed again in 1846 and 1847 and to some degree every year through 1851.

Potatoes were the main crop for tenant farmers and when the

crop failed they were not only unable to feed their families but they were also unable to pay their rent. People were both starving and homeless as landlords evicted them from their property.

During 1845-1900 the population of Ireland shrunk from 8 million to 4 million with an estimated 1 million dying in the famine and more than 3 million migrating to America, England, New Zealand and Australia.

My Irish great-grandfather, Charles Kidd, was one of them. At age 20 in 1879 he emigrated to the U.S. and Escanaba where he worked on the railroad all of his life. He fathered 18 children, including my grandfather, Frank.

Kate Nolan was a beautiful Irish girl who worked in a lumber camp in Garden. It has been said she was Bill Bonifas's greatest find. Bill was a lumberjack who arrived penniless from Luxembourg in his early twenties. America was thought of as the land of opportunity and the Upper Peninsula was one of its frontiers.

The strapping broad-shouldered, six-foot Bill married Katie Nolan, a waitress at a lumberjack boarding-house in August of 1894. Their story is one from rags to riches, but neither Bill nor Kate ever forgot their beginnings in Garden.

This story is about Kate and her life after Bill Died. Kate Bonifas lived in a beautiful three-floor mansion on Lake Shore Drive. Her husband, Bill, a millionaire eight times over when he died, had it built for her.

I wonder if Kate was ever comfortable with the fortune Bill had amassed. She came from such meager beginnings. That reminds me of my mother and folks who grew up in the Depression: For a great many folks from that era they were never comfortable spending or indulging themselves even though in later life they could afford to do so. So it was with Kate.

In fact, Kate was less than pleased to have to contend with Big Bill's money. Churches, neighbors, friends, and beggars hounded her for money. Eventually she sought help from the well-respected John Lemmer, then Superintendent of Schools.

He helped her ascertain how she would disseminate her vast fortune: a fortune that would include and enrich the school system, City of Escanaba, and the Catholic Church.

Kate was shy and lonely. She feared being alone and hid when a storm produced thunder and lightning. In 1944 she asked Cleotabelle (Cleo) Bonifas, a niece from Garden, to come and live with her. Cleo was a junior in high school and reminisced about those days while attending St. Joe School: 'I couldn't eat in the cafeteria. I went home for lunch. Aunt Kate probably thought she was saving money."

Cleo remembers little things like the fruit cake Kate kept hid in the basement. Cleo said, "I would sneak down there every now and then and pick off a cherry to eat—then rearrange the rest of the cherries so she wouldn't suspect."

"I remember she had a lady make her bloomers out of cotton Pillsbury flour sacks. "I also remember when Grandma LeMire joined us along with another lady for Thanksgiving dinner," says Cleo.

"Aunt Kate shopped at Lauerman's. She called the store to have two dresses delivered for me. They both fit perfectly but I was allowed to only pick one of them to keep."

"One day a salesman came to the door selling fur coats. I tried it on but Aunt Kate didn't buy it."

"I slept on the third floor where the maid's quarters were. She didn't have a live-in maid at that time. I remember Joe Hirn was her hired hand and chauffer. If I went roller skating he was sent along to watch over me. I was allowed to go to school dances."

"One day when I was dusting under the dining room table, the doorbell rang. When I answered it no one was there. I continued dusting and it rang again—again no one was at either door. Then Aunt Kate asked where I was when the doorbell rang. Under the table I answered. Then she told me I was sitting on the buzzer for the maid."

"I used to sit on the stairs and listen to Aunt Kate and John Lemmer talk. He visited often. I was in every room in the house except one which she kept locked. I believe that was her liquor room."

"I dried my hair in front of the furnace in the basement. I drove Aunt Kate to purchase flowers and took her to the cemetery. I went into the Mausoleum with Aunt Kate while she said prayers for Uncle Bill."

"John Lemmer was going to teach me to drive the big Cadillac but I told him I already knew how. I was a farm girl from Garden and drove tractors, set forks and stacked grain."

"When Uncle Bill was living he slept in a huge 'movie-star' bed at one end of the hall and Aunt Kate slept at the other end on the second floor. Aunt Kate's secretary slept in the room next to her."

"I remember they had a beautiful place in Florida. And their Grandfather Clocks were beautiful." I visited Aunt Kate when I got married. She gave me a statue of the Blessed Virgin for a wedding present."

"I attended her funeral. Aunt Kate was laid out in the front parlor room. The casket was covered with glass."

Thanks to Cleo Bonifas Hermes, now age 80, we were able to gain a small snapshot of Katherine Nolan Bonifas, the beautiful Irish lassie who went from rags in Ireland to a millionaire in Escanaba. She would live in a mansion on Lake Shore Drive—but would never feel comfortable with her wealth. Her real fame came through her will with the many benevolent projects that touched us all.

The Bonifas Mausoleum Restoration Committee is poised to begin the restoration, repair and beatification work at an estimated cost of 50,000 dollars. Karen Moore, Master Gardener, recently presented the committee with the site plans for approval.

The Bonifas contributions to our community are unprecedented. Now we need to enlist the community's help to fund the Mausoleum Restoration Project. We graciously accept any amount small or large. You can be part of this historical happening by mailing a check to the Community Foundation, 2500 7th Ave. S., Suite 103, Escanaba, MI 49829. Be sure to include in the memo section: Bonifas Mausoleum Fund. Please direct any questions to Kay Shapy, Treasurer, 786-4340.

## POLITICS: OBAMA, HILLARY AND RUSSERT
### Friday, June 27, 2008

Barack Obama is the presumptive Democratic nominee and there is a very good chance that he may even be our next President of the United States. Barack Hussein Obama! He calls himself an African –American; in essence, he really is an inter-racial American. The title of African-American leaves out his Caucasian roots.

I read his book *Audacity of Hope* more than a year ago; just recently I read his first book, *Dreams From My Father* which really gave me a feel for who the man, Barack (called Barry while growing up) is.

Barack was named after his father. His mother was only eighteen when she met his father at the University in Hawaii. Barack was just two-years old when his father left to attain his Doctorate at Harvard. He never returned to live with his wife and young Barack. Instead he returned to Kenya, his country, where he already had a wife and two children.

In Barack's own words from his autobiography: 'How and when the marriage occurred remains a bit murky, a bill of particulars I have never quite had the courage to explore.'

Although Obama claims his father was an atheist; he was raised Muslim and given a Muslim burial at Barack's family's request.

Barack would not meet his father until he was 10 years old. His father, recuperating from a motorcycle accident, spent two months living in the complex where his mother and grandparents lived in Hawaii. He father was stern; Barrack was not impressed and was even relieved when he left.

Through the years they passed a few letters between them—then a six year absence of any communication. One day Barack received a call from his half-sister: their father had been killed in an accident! Barack was nineteen and stunned.

He was troubled and would grieve over never knowing who his father really was. Eventually he would visit Kenya, meet his relatives and gain knowledge about his father's life, his country and the huge family he was a part of.

He learned that his grandfather was a Muslim, a strict disciplinarian with a mean disposition. Multiple wives are a way of life in Kenya. Barack's father also married another white woman he had met at Harvard. She bore him two sons and during the same period he frequently visited and stayed with his first wife, again fathering two more sons.

\*\*\*\*\*\*\*\*\*\*\*\*\*\*\*\*\*\*\*\*\*\*\*\*\*\*\*\*\*\*\*\*\*\*\*\*\*\*\*\*\*\*\*\*\*\*\*\*\*\*\*\*\*\*\*\*\*\*\*\*\*\*\*\*

The dream of millions of women (that a woman would possibly be Commander-in-chief) was dashed with Hillary's loss of the nomination to Barack Obama. Hillary had been vetted for years—inside and out. It has been said she wasn't given a fair shake by the media.

Barack's meteoric rise early on was fueled by the media. He was, in essence, the media's darling. I remember being frustrated while watching *Hardball* with Chris Matthews: Not because I was necessarily in Hillary's camp, but because he was so biased and unfair. I must have gauged it right because Matthews eventually had to begin one program with an apology for his biased treatment of Hillary—no doubt the 'powers that be' insisted on that apology after thousands of women bristled and called in complaining of his unfair treatment.

Did it stop? A resounding "no!" He may have tempered his bias somewhat but it still seeped through. If not by him, he stacked guests that were anti-Hillary. He wasn't alone though.

The story about Obama's relationship with his minister, Rev. Wright actually surfaced months before it broke in the mainstream media. Journalists were scared away by the racial aspect. But then as a result of the Wright stories, Obama's double-digit lead over Hillary vanished toward the end of the campaign. Too little too late! If the media had picked up on the stories earlier Obama very likely would have come out behind Hillary in the primaries.

In my opinion, disengaging himself from his church wasn't enough. What about sitting in that church for twenty years and listening to the Liberation Theology views presented by Rev. Wright? His disenchantment with the church was for political reasons. My question is: Do we really know enough about Obama or his real leanings?

The media has become way too powerful. Herd mentality of journalists covering the campaign in a slanted, partisan way really decides elections—disturbing to say the least.

As an Independent I haven't yet made a choice in the general election. My husband has. He is unhappy with both choices and plans to vote for himself as a write-in candidate in the general election. He is fed up with the politics of both parties and what's happening in the county today.

He rails on about declining morality; the war and the economy (gas and food prices) just to name a few. As a conservative and a patriot he is concerned about the direction our country is taking and worries about where it's headed.

My analytical son, a conservative at heart, works on Capitol Hill and has worked for several Republican congressmen before attaining his law degree. He revealed his take on the upcoming election. In the past he most always voted Republican and has worked on many political campaigns, including George H.W. Bush and Bob Dole.

He is unhappy with the Bush Administration and feels a change is needed. I believe this time he will vote Democratic. He sent me a double-speak cleverly worded e-mail recently:

"Mom, since you're only going to have two choices in the Fall (unless you vote for Dad) you must decide which among the two is the lesser of two evils. It may be better to have someone making the right decisions for America; even if for the wrong reason, rather than someone making the wrong decisions for the "right"reason...for four more years."

If you're ambivalent and inclined to not vote at all; how about a protest vote—for my husband, "honest Abe", as a write-in candidate? I say that tongue-in-cheek; but I think he is serious. He claims he's running on the Yooper ticket.

Vote "Write-In" for

# "Honest Abe"

### Gary Abrahamson
### For President of the United States

### Yooper Party

Keeping in the sphere of politics one last thought about the recent sudden loss of Tim Russert, moderator of NBC's *Meet the Press*. There was no one as tough with questions and yet, more fair. I just re-read his book, *Wisdom of our Fathers*. What a gem! He was the consummate father to Luke and son to Big Russ. And he was genuine!

He had that perpetual smile and extra special way about him. He has always been a favorite of mine. This year he gave a talk at the Library of Congress revealing how he got reluctant presidential candidates to go on his show. Russert told (the candidates) he would hold a "virtual" show and address his questions to an empty chair for each candidate. Soon each appeared on *Meet the Press*.

Yes, Tim Russert was special. He will be sorely missed. It's doubtful that anyone will be able to fill his shoes.

# SLEEP PROBLEMS ARE COMMON
## Friday, July 4, 2008

While I was in the OSF emergency room some months ago; about 9 p.m. a gentleman came in with his pillow. Apparently he was going to sleep at the hospital sleep center for an evaluation. I witnessed the same scenario at Marquette General. I chuckled to myself. Who would have ever heard of a sleep center years ago? My grandmother would have hee-hawed too. She was so basic. I can hear her saying, 'Nobody would have sleep problems if they worked hard." She came from the old school.

As I recall my early years; sleep never seemed elusive. So, naturally, I linked sleep problems with age. Imagine the surprise when my research found that age alone does not cause sleep problems. Disturbed sleep, waking up tired every day, and other symptoms of insomnia are not a normal part of aging.

Sleep is so important to your physical health and emotional well-being no matter what your age. The experts disagree about whether you need less sleep as you age. Many seniors complain about sleep problems such as: difficulty falling asleep; frequent waking during the night and lighter sleep; waking up early and not feeling rested; being tired in the daytime; and needing naps during the day.

As we age we may perceive unwelcome changes in our sleep patterns. The changes may be more in the quality of sleep rather the quantity of sleep. As we age a good night's sleep is important because it improves concentration and memory formation, allows your body to repair any cell damage that occurred during the day and refreshes your immune system needed to prevent disease.

So why do I have such a problem getting a good night's sleep? I found several reasons in my quest for sleep information. Pain can elude sleep. I occasionally have Sciatica pain or Restless Leg Syndrome. Taking a daytime nap late in the day will also affect your nighttime sleep.

Menopause (hot flashes) is another reason for disturbed sleep. Finally I have overcome that one.

My mother complained of lack of sleep. Her reason was probably drug related. Seniors tend to take more medications than younger people. Combinations of drugs, side-effects of drugs can impair sleep and even stimulate wakefulness. She also had Restless Leg Syndrome and Sciatica which can run in families.

Health conditions affect more elderly folks: nighttime heartburn, osteoporosis, asthma, arthritis, sleep apnea, diabetes, menopause, a frequent need to urinate and Alzheimer's.

Other reasons for sleepless nights could be a snoring partner or alcohol in the evening. Consuming alcohol before bedtime is another culprit. You may feel tired and fall asleep, but after a couple of hours the effects of alcohol has a tendency to disrupt sleep later in the night. A bad mattress or pillow could also be the culprit. My husband carries his own pillow whenever we travel.

Many times my mind is racing overtime with thoughts, a to-do-list and even thinking about some topic for this column. Some of my best ideas are formulated in bed. I hatch an idea or certain phrase; then get up at all hours to record it on the computer And although I know I should let go of thoughts running through my mind when it is time to sleep—it is difficult. I have even tried counting backwards from 100. Sometimes that works.

Psychological stress and significant life changes like the death of a loved one can rob you of sleep. Anxiety or sadness can also keep you awake—and there are many worrisome problems we sometimes take to bed with us.

I found an interesting list of sleep tips for the elderly:

Expose yourself to sunlight. Get at least two hours of bright sun each day. Sun increases your body's production of melatonin, which regulates your sleep-wake cycles.

Separate yourself from a snoring partner.

Monitor your medications. Drugs you take for medical reasons may be interfering with your sleep.

Go to bed and wake up at the same time every day, even on week-ends

Develop bedtime rituals. Create soothing bedtime rituals, such as taking a bath or playing calm music.

Take only a brief nap (15 to 30 minutes). Napping longer puts you into a deeper sleep and your will feel groggy for a while. If you take a nap too late in the day, you won't be able to fall asleep at night.

Keep in mind these tips were compiled for the elderly. Don't you just love this one? Combine sex and sleep. Sex and physical intimacy, such as hugging and massage, can provide relaxation and the physical release that lead to restful sleep.

Other tips that improve sleep: Limit caffeine late in the day. Some people are still affected by caffeine eight hours after ingesting it. Refrain from eating three hours before bedtime.

Of course exercise helps. If you are too sedentary, you may not feel sleepy.

My best sleep aid is reading a good book in bed. I devour books. Probably the best advice is: If you have tried some of these remedies and are still having a problem, discuss it with your doctor. There are aids available that may help you. A date with the sleep center may be in order to uncover your sleep deprivation problems.

Untreated sleep disorders can even be hazardous to your health. A British study released in September 2007 found that people who didn't get enough sleep are twice as likely to die of heart disease. Eight hours of sleep, the recommended amount, is as important to your well-being as a healthy diet and exercise. Sleep amounts to one third of your life.

Pleasant dreams! Dreams, now there's a topic for another day.

## 107 Years - It's A Great Life!
## Friday, July 11, 2008

"It was so much fun!" says 107 year-old Helene Merki, who presided as Grand Marshall of the Fourth of July parade in Gladstone. "I got to wave my hand and I want to tell ya, my hand got tired."

We felt privileged to attend Helene's 107th birthday party at Christian Park Village recently where she has resided for the past ten months. She rooms with a very dear friend, Dorothy Shram from Gladstone. Helene is amazing, witty, and delightful. She still has that twinkle in her eye as she speaks of her life experiences.

*Unretouched PROOF from The Scott Studio Chicago*

She was born is Chicago June 30<sup>th</sup> 1901, the daughter of Jane Ogden, concert pianist and Karl Hunter, concert violinist. "Mother had a studio in the fine arts building in Chicago," says Helene. "My parents were accomplished and well-known in their field."

Musical talent was in the genes. Helene taught piano, organ and voice for years before moving to Gladstone. Her only son lives in Escanaba. Helene's marriage was short lived when her husband died of leukemia after only 15 years. Her son was age 12.

That became the catalyst to move to Gladstone, a great small community to raise her young son. Bob Key, a teacher and choir director originally from Gladstone, was instrumental in her move. Helene's husband and family were all deceased. The year was 1956 and there was no reason to stay in Chicago. She was eager to venture in a new direction.

*Helene with Leo Evans (Escanaba Mayor)*

"I grew up with a good education," says Helene. "My family was all well-educated. Mother graduated from one of the first women's colleges in Pennsylvania, and Father from a music school in St. Paul. My grandfather helped start up oil in Pennsylvania. The family was always wealthy and we always had a maid."

"I brought my husband Gary along to meet you," I told Helene. "He is a history buff and wanted to hear about your early years." After some interesting conversation she said to Gary, "We should get together and talk about old times," then gesturing to me, she continued, "she's too young for you —she asks the questions—but we know all the answers!"

And did she know the answers!

She was in high school during WWI. She remembered her mother attending meetings and being very active in the Woman's Suffragist movement and the struggle for the enfranchisement of women. (Women were not allowed to vote until 1919)

She spoke of her mother's sinus problems. "The doctor prescribed smoking. It cured the sinus problem," says Helene, "but she became addicted to smoking which eventually killed her. You know, smoking then was considered the 'thing'."

Gary asked, "Did you ever go to a Speakeasy during Prohibition?" "Well, yes, everyone did!"

George Gobel attended their church in Chicago. Helene recalls, "George sang in the choir and Mother gave him voice lessons." George became a child singing star on the radio.

"George was born funny," says Helene. "I asked him after he became famous, George, you had such a beautiful voice, you should have pursued that. His response was, 'that's not where the money is.'" Small world—George got his start as a comedian at Helsings Vaudeville Lounge in Chicago—the same place where I worked in the '50s while my husband attended Loyola University. I met George when he returned to Helsings to visit long after he became famous.

Helene and her husband lived on the North side and on occasion patronized the Green Mill, a well-known Jazz club during the reign of Al Capone. It was a frequent haunt of his. Helene's husband, John, was also a great musician and sometimes they would go there after a band gig. They traveled the country for four years. John played with Art Castle, the Dorsey Brothers and other famous bands.

"When I was expecting a baby," recalled Helene, "my husband said traveling with a dance band was no life to raise a child." "He took a job as the manager of an ammunition factory in Dayton Ohio during WWll."

I was dying to know about the Roaring Twenties—my favorite era in history. And yes, Helene danced the Charleston during the Roaring Twenties! Her roommate, Dorothy Shram (age 87), chimed in about how she loved the Charleston—so I spontaneously danced a bit of the Charleston for them. "That's it!" said Dorothy. "You know how!"

"I wasn't a Flapper though. My mother wouldn't have approved." said Helene.

Helene has seen many changes and experienced many things, but when I asked her about computers, cell phones and other inventions, she said, "Most of those things I hardly know anything about."

She couldn't put a finger on her longevity other than, "good genes, a positive attitude all my life, never smoked and I was fortunate to have a good education." She played the organ at the Episcopal Church in Gladstone until she was 99 years old.

Helene has lived through the administrations of 18 Presidents of the US—from Teddy Roosevelt in 1901 to George W. Bush. She has lived through the advent of flight, the beginning of the automobile, the sinking of the Titanic, two world wars, silent movies, talkies and a man on the moon just to name a few.

When asked by the activity director at the Village, if she enjoyed bingo—her answer was, "Heavens no, that's for old people!"

That says it all. She is one incredible lady with a wealth of life experiences, a great mind, and a love to reminisce at the age of 107. My husband and I feel richer for meeting her!

## SOMETHING OLD—SOMETHING NEW—
## SOMETHING BORROWED—SOMETHING BLUE
## Friday, July 18, 2008

Attending my granddaughter's wedding this month was the catalyst to research wedding history and the changes in weddings just in my lifetime.

Weddings and traditions have evolved over time, yet some traditions have remained steadfast. It is interesting to know the origination of the words bride and groom. Bride comes from old

English for the name of "cook" while the word groom comes from "male child." Wow! A cook? Is that why men get married? Who would have thought?

Most brides keep the old Victorian Wedding Tradition: Something Old—Something New—Something Borrowed—Something Blue—and a Silver Sixpence in her shoe. The good-luck saying originated in the Victorian era.

Each item in the poem represents a good-luck token for the bride. As for the colorful item, blue has been connected to weddings for centuries. White was not always the chosen color for brides. In ancient Rome, brides wore blue to symbolize love, modesty and fidelity. Christianity had long dressed the Virgin Mary in Blue, so purity was associated with color.

White became the choice after Queen Victoria wore a white gown for her marriage to Prince Albert. Many brides today wear a blue garter for the something blue. Even the dress style has changed from high neck and conservative to strapless and more skin showing—and of course, the sought after suntan.

Many stories abound on the origin of the bridal veil. Some say the origin was due to circumstances of an arranged marriage. Men bargained with an eligible young ladies father. After the ceremony the veil was lifted to reveal the brides features. This was to keep the groom from backing out of the deal if he didn't like what he saw. So, then the "cook" wasn't that important after all!

Times have changed the meaning of wearing a bridal veil. Now wearing a bridal veil signifies a special event—a wedding! It signifies joy, highlights the brides' appearance and features and finally a veil is the final crowning touch. Over the last twenty years bridal traditions have changed even more. Veils were worn more frequently over the face (a blusher). Now, you don't have to wear it over your face if you don't want to. Star Jones, once on the popular TV show, *The View,* wore a 27 foot veil—the longest known in history. Her veil was two feet longer than Princess Diana's bridal veil.

One thing that caught my husband's attention at our granddaughter, Heather's wedding was the outrageous prices: $750 for the wedding cake as opposed to about $35 in 1950. The photographer was $1000 and took about 700 to 800 photos.

Compare that with maybe 25 photos and a price tag of less than $50 in our era.

Heather is 34 and has four children. That was different. The kids were all prominent in the wedding, including her five-year-old twin sons in little tuxedos. Her daughter was one of the bridesmaids.

Many years ago I gave my daughter a diamond necklace made with my original wedding ring. My daughter had the diamond necklace reset into a ring for Heather's wedding. And one day Heather's daughter will wear that ring.

The dinner was a sit-down affair at round tables with elegant linen. Bottles of wine decorated every table for over 250 guests. Their friends were many and no doubt dictated the music for the dance. We managed a few requests of what we call music, but much of it was loud—a pounding beat that my husband likened to African drums. No, it was not the dreamy and sentimental music from our era.

An added touch was a caricaturist at the reception. He was busy all evening with a line waiting to be drawn at the price of $10 a person. We had him draw Gary and I. What fun! It will be framed as a memento of the evening.

As people left the reception a limousine was available to escort the guests either home or to their hotels. It was held in West Bend, WI. Of course the great part of weddings is seeing relatives you haven't seen in years. My young brothers attended: Jim Flath from Reno and Dennis from Kenosha.

My son, Jeff's wedding in Washington D.C. was a bit more sophisticated. A string ensemble played in the church for the actual ceremony. It was held in St. Peters Cathedral in downtown D.C. with many congressional people in attendance since they both worked on Capitol Hill. A receiving line of the bridal party and parents was held on the church steps. Photos shoots were taken in front of the Capitol Building with the Dome as a centerpiece. The reception was held at the Fort Myers Officer's Club next to Arlington Cemetery. It was an elegant affair to remember.

My grandson chose a small family wedding in Las Vegas on the roof-top of a hotel. His proposal and engagement was in New

York's Times Square on New Years Eve.

Married during the Depression; my parents never had a wedding photo. They were lucky to afford their four dollar a month rent. They were too poor to buy groceries so they ate at their parent's house. I do have beautiful treasured wedding photos of ancestors in the 1800's. None wore white gowns though.

During World War11 many weddings were the bare essentials. Perspective brides traveled to a military base to marry their sweetheart. The wedding was simple, probably a civil ceremony, the groom in uniform and the bride in street clothes wearing a hat. Then the groom left for overseas after a brief honeymoon. Sadly, some never returned.

So much planning and hoopla goes into a wedding. Sometime the reception place is reserved a couple of years in advance. But alas, marriages have a higher failure rate now—over one in two ends in divorce. In Missouri, three in five end in divorce. Today, a divorce is easier to obtain, there is less stigma and 'for better or worse' doesn't enter in. Then again, many couples today openly live together skipping the marriage vows.

Weddings will never go out of style though and are very much in vogue. Young people still revel in a big church wedding with the whole expensive nine yards: beautiful gowns, tuxedos and fancy receptions. The Ludington Park gazebo can attest to that. It's a busy place all summer and quite heart-warming to ride by and see a wedding in progress with all the pageantry.

## A VISIT, A KIND WORD AND A LITTLE HUG!
### Friday, July 25, 2008

Last week-end was sad for my son, Gary, who is receiving rehabilitation at Christian Park Village. He was painfully aware that it was his class's 40th reunion. He wouldn't be there. He wouldn't see his old friends—but he would realize the horrific changes in his life; he would question why this has this happened to him?

*Dr. Al Gossan and wife Jan.*

My daughter, Vicki and husband Dave Cass came for the reunion. Dave is a class member. Class members questioned Vicki about Gary's circumstances and remarked that they thought about him. But alas, people have busy lives and really don't visit Gary unless they are family members. That happens with many people who are confined to a nursing home—not just Gary.

Perhaps visitors don't know what to say. They may question how do I act? Maybe they don't know the extent of the injuries and aren't sure if the person can communicate. Whatever the case; confined people become forgotten. If they are elderly perhaps there are not many friends around anymore. If they have Alzheimer's and don't make a lot of sense perhaps people are uncomfortable with that. They don't visit for a myriad of reasons.

So you can imagine how happy we were as parents when a caring class-member and his wife took time to visit Gary. Al Gossan, son of Dr. Al Gossan, and his wife Jan spent time with Gary.

Al Gossan is Pastor of a large congregation in Holland, MI. In April of this year a Booklet of Al's conversion testimony was published. He left a copy with Gary with the inscription: Gary,

God bless you!

I read it and appreciated even more Pastor Al's road to discovery. Young Al was like any other youth of the time: partying, playing drums in a rock band, in other words, interested in fun and games. His ultimate plan was to pursue his chosen career and follow in his father's footsteps to become an Optometrist.

Al was accepted into the school of Optometry at Indiana University. It was there that his path was altered and he would eventually become a man of divinity dedicated to doing God's work. In his words, "I solemnly committed myself to pursue my calling into the preaching ministry."

Pastor Al reflects on his life in his booklet: "It has been forty years since my conversion took place. Since then, I have become an ordained minister of the Gospel. I have been abundantly blessed with a national and international Bible teaching ministry, a faithful Christian wife, four beautiful daughters, nine grandchildren (so far) and countless, "spiritual children and grandchildren." The Lord continues to surprise me, over and over again, with people being saved, healed, and delivered from demons as I have shared God's word with others in the power of his Spirit. All Glory goes to God for the things He has done."

Pastor Al has a Doctorate of Literature degree, Religious Education AWCU. Most importantly he is a dedicated spiritual person and has touched many lives. That calling takes very special people.

Our son who has a short-term memory problem has kept Al's visit in his mind. We are grateful for his kindness toward Gary. His humanity shines through and touches many. The path he chose was certainly the right one.

Charlene Carlson, a Eucharistic Minister at St. Anne's Church, is another example of a great person doing spiritual work. She came to our home regularly administering Communion to Gary. Now she visits him at the nursing home to give him Communion.

I am amazed at her dedication. She recently spent a month in California with her sister who has cancer. Yet, she was concerned about Gary when she heard he fell out of bed and had surgery. She called from California to inquire how everything was going with Gary. Charlene is so special!

I have a special affinity for the many residents at the nursing home. I know their names, hug them, talk to them and have become concerned about them. The experience has given me compassion for the struggles that many people endure and their loved ones—their advocates.

This past week, Don Goulais a resident was taken to the hospital. I was concerned and called his wife Betty to check on him. Darlene Bichler, a newer resident, is someone I have known since childhood. I try to comfort her and orientate her as much as I can. I hug her and kiss her forehead. Dick Wiles was recently admitted. He is another school mate and Gary and I are concerned about him.

Shirley Lundquist is another friend from school. She has visited and fed her husband for five years—he is unable to talk. When she isn't there I talk to Rodger and get him to smile.

The nursing home has changed our outlook. Our world has grown. It isn't just our family that has been affected by a loved one who needs care and attention. It is a real eye-opener to have people we know (our age) in need of 24-hour care.

I have become more aware and more sensitive to the needs of others. A short visit, a kind word, a little hug—those are the things that really matter.

## A Community That Keeps on Giving!
## Friday, August 1, 2008

A football story seemed in order with all of the hoopla going on with Brett Farve and the Green Bay Packers of late. The opinions can spark some pretty heated dialogue—but that story is for another day.

The real story is about generosity and a community that steps up to the plate whenever a need arises.

On a local level: if you haven't been out to the Escanaba Athletic Field yet, you are in for a great surprise. Not only will your eyes pop out when you see the thousands of dollars in renovations, but to know that our community came through again to fund such a tremendous project is really gratifying. Believe this! Community donations contributed over $350,000 to the project— then add over $300,000 of donated labor! Nearly $700,000! That's absolutely incredible!

It has been said of the project—it could only have happened in Escanaba! Jerry Shapy was at the helm along with countless others who donated their time, talents and resources to the project. Kudos' to them all.

You will see many names on the granite brick walls and the stone slab walkways. Names on the walls that will stand the test of time and if yours is absent; it's not too late to contact Russ Bluse, Jerry Shapy, Gary Seehafer or Karen Moore to be included. Your name or a name in memory of someone can be added for 75 dollars. Anyone can proudly be a part of Escanaba's great sport history.

A special event is planned to kick off the football season in Escanaba. All of the living Gessner/Pfotenhauer Award winners have been invited to be honored at the season's first football game on August 29th against Gaylord. The recipients will be recognized at halftime. Kick off is 7:30 p.m.

The Eskymo Fan Club has also invited the Veteran's to the game and a meal before the game. They will be recognized before the game—this is the second year for special recognition of Veterans. Any questions? Contact Rusty Bluse, Fan Club President, Jack Beck, Gary Seehafer or Sue Roberts, 789-9291.

Following the Eskymos "winning" their first game; everyone is invited to the Elks Club for a Fan Club mixer. Pizza and refreshments will be served.

## Gessner Trophy Winners 1924 - 1991

| | |
|---|---|
| 1924 – Ovila Savard | 1931 – Gilbert Byrnes |
| 1925 – Herman Miethe | 1932 – George Call |
| 1926 – Edward Curran | 1933 – Harry Monson |
| 1927 – Gladwin Oberg | 1934 – Leo Alperovitz |
| 1928 – Hilding Olson | 1935 – Stanley Jensen |
| 1929 – Leon (Dick) Shram | 1936 – George Anderson |
| 1930 – Don Anderson | 1937 – Robert Embs |

1938 – William D. Peterson
1939 – Thor Nilsen
1940 – Robert Barron
1941 – Don Pfotenhauer
1942 – George Shomin
1943 – Robert Pfotenhauer
1944 – Boyd Peterson
1945 – No Award
1946 – Jack Finn
1947 – Wendell Buckland
1948 – Richard Lough
1949 – Gary Abrahamson
1950 – Alfred Nelson
1951 – Richard Shomin
1952 – Warren Johnston
1953 – Paul Davidson
1954 – Marshall Judson
1955 – James Beck
1956 – Lawrence Erickson
1957 – Ronald W. Johnson
1958 – Mike Mileski
1959 – John Lindquist
1960 – Barry Andrews
1961 – John Fisher
1962 – Mickey Moses
1963 – David Hunter
1964 – Walter Schultz
1965 – James Clairmont
1966 – Steve Ohman
1967 – James Boyle
1968 – Jerel Brazeau
1969 – John Moberg
1970 – Gene Timmer
1971 – Tom Kangas
1972 – Bill Johnson

1973 – Bob Kleiman
1974 – Wayne Schwalbach
1975 – Jack Hirn
1975 – Ann VanDyke
1976 – Jim Rogers
1976 – Sharon Schultz
1977 – John Sankovitch
1977 – Mary Dulek
1978 – Bob Boyle
1978 – Jeanne White
1979 – John Moore
1979 – Cindy Courneene
1980 – Tammy Sovey
1981 – John Tolfa
1981 – Chris Martin
1982 – Rick Frazer
1982 – Jean Tolfa
1983 – Dean Altobelli
1983 – Hope Laviolette
1984 – Paul DeHaan
1984 – Carolee Boudreau
1985 – Scott Peterson
1985 – Tammy Funke
1986 – Paul Sundquist
1986 – Jean Ammel
1987 – Kile Zuidema
1987 – Phyllis Hauser
1988 – Brian Barrett
1988 – Kim Picord
1989 – Jim Hirn
1989 – Cheryl Jacobsen
1990 – Nick Bink
1990 – Judy Skradski
1991 – Dick Englund
1991 – Lisa Kuckhahnssner

*****************************************************************

Speaking of community projects; the Bonifas Mausoleum Project is now underway. Trees and dead branches over-shadowing the mausoleum have been removed. Flowering trees have been ordered for fall planting. The first phase is in progress. The actual acid cleaning of the mausoleum's roof and exterior will began the first week in August. Marble has been ordered to replace the stones that have tumbled to the floor inside of the mausoleum.

The project has four phases for completion as contributions allow. The bronze door will be refurbished. A large granite area will hold two granite benches. An obelisk will grace the center highlighting the numerous contributions William and Catherine Bonifas so generously bestowed on our community.

More contributions are needed for this important project to reach fruition.

I received a welcomed phone call from Jane Gundry. She is sending a contribution for the Bonifas Mausoleum project and related to me why it was so important to her.

"I have so many reasons for wanting to contribute. First, I was the 1967 recipient of The Catherine Bonifas Scholarship," says Jane, daughter of Don and Mary Jane Wertz of Escanaba. "I attended Bay DeNoc College which was also funded in part by the Bonifas's. I worked at the State of Michigan office building. Another project funded by Catherine Bonifas's will. I have attended and enjoyed many events at the Bonifas Art Center built by the Bonifas's. The Bonifas's have touched my life in so many ways and continue to do so today. I discussed a contribution with my husband Craig and he agreed with me. I am happy for the opportunity to give back."

In the spirit of "giving back'—if you would like to contribute to the Bonifas Mausoleum fund for the repair, restoration, beautification and perpetual care of William and Catherine's final resting place, please make out your check to the Community Foundation. In the memo section specify: for the Bonifas Mausoleum Fund.

Send to Kay Shapy, Treasurer, 520 South 8th Street, Escanaba, MI 49829

See you at the Eskymo/Gaylord game on August 29th.

## THE BRAIN AND ALTERED STATES OF CONCIOUSNESS:
### Dreams and Hallucinations
### Friday, August 8, 2008

Some people claim they never dream. The reality is that all people dream—you just may not recall your dreams. So what are dreams and why do they occur?

Dreams are the images, feelings and thoughts experienced while asleep. The purposes of dreams are not fully understood, although they have been a topic of interest throughout recorded history.

For the last couple of weeks I kept a journal of my dreams as soon as I woke up in anticipation of this dream column. If you don't they disappear into oblivion as soon as you are wide awake. My dreams almost always seem troubled.

For example, I dreamt there were thick dust balls under the bed and I couldn't sweep them up. The cleaning girl was here the day before and I pondered if that was why I had that thought. Another dream had me washing clothes in a huge tub but the water level was too low.

In one dream I went to Publix grocery store in Florida and was shocked to find my husband was the Greeter—what's more he didn't even recognize me!

A nightmare last night had my twin great-grandson's falling into a pool. I jumped in to save them. I saw their blue jackets in the bottom and retrieved one. I couldn't understand why no one else sitting around the pool seemed concerned. I woke up with my heart pounding.

I do remember years ago I used to have flying dreams. If someone was chasing me I was able to fly up above everything and escape. Those dreams were reoccurring and scary. I hope thinking about them doesn't cause them to reoccur.

I tell my husband to bring a banana to the nursing home every morning when he goes to feed our son. My latest dream: I watched strangers eat all of the bananas and there were none left for my son.

Some research explains the most common emotion expressed

in dreams is anxiety. Negative emotions are more prevalent than positive feelings. That is some consolation that my dreams are somewhat normal.

My husband experiences the same type of anxiety in dreams. He was a route salesman for Fairmont Foods years ago when we lived in Sault Ste. Marie. His worst nightmare was reaching one of his good customers like the Red Owl and discovering he had ran out of products and the store had sold out. The dream was reoccurring and filled with anxiety.

We owned dry-cleaning establishments years ago. A reoccurring dream my husband had was that the dry-cleaning fluid escaped from the machine or that the machinery broke down and clothes were piled up sky high. More anxiety and frustration!

Research claims that sexual dreams are experienced mostly in young to mid-teens and account for less that 8 percent of dreams. Many common reported dreams include: situations relating to school, being chased, running slowly in place, sexual experiences, falling, arriving too late, a person now alive being dead, flying, embarrassing moments, failing an examination and not being able to focus vision.

Dreams can also be linked to actual sensations such as incorporating environmental happenings into dreams. Examples are hearing a phone ringing in a dream while it is ringing in reality or dreaming of urination while actually wetting the bed. Hopefully that is a dream of young people.

Dreams are more apt to be recalled if a person is awakened while dreaming. Women tend to have more recall than men. A dream journal can be used to help dream recall for psychotherapy or entertainment purposes.

Hallucinations are all together different. Some are caused from chemicals like LSD. Others could be caused by a mental illness like Schizophrenia.

My husband had his aortic valve replaced three years ago in Houston. It was touch and go—a matter of life or death. At first they couldn't wean him off the heart/lung machine. Finally, they did, but left his chest wall open with a sterile drape for three days. The consensus was that if they closed his chest; his heart would stop. The plan included keeping him asleep so there wouldn't be movement until they closed his chest. That meant a heavy drug regiment.

What a shock when he woke up! He said, I never visited him (I was there day and night) and left him in a 13 dollar-a-week flea bag. He continued, "Look at the rats and spiders climbing all over the floor and walls. We went to England last night and saw John Lennon's house. I was tired and you didn't bring me a sandwich."

Bewildered I asked the nurse if he had a stroke. She explained that being in ICU on morphine and not knowing if it is day or night can cause ICU psychosis. She was sure he would be OK.

He continued on, "will we sleep here tonight? The bed floats. Does *USA Today* say anything about me or this place? Are we on a boat? They are clever here. Joe is the boss. Can we leave? Let's get out of here!"

He railed on, "They wrapped me up in plastic like a picture and said they wouldn't take the bag off until we came up with the money and paperwork. Jeff (our son) was on the table with me and held my hand—then he looked down from the cubicle in the ceiling. Last night I begged them to kill me, but they wouldn't. I hassled with them to take this thing out of my mouth but they wanted $500 dollars. I didn't trust you; I thought you were in on it." And on and on!

Today Gary remembers every small detail of those horrid hallucinations unlike dreams. I didn't know if I should laugh or cry when all of this took place. He was in the Houston hospital for six weeks. The end result: he came home and underwent rehabilitation in Green Bay with a new lease on life.

Sweet Dreams? I don't think so!

## JEANETTE LECAPTAIN:
## AN ICON OF DANCE AND SKATE
## Friday, August 15, 2008

Jeanette LeCaptain and husband Lyle—her lifetime partner, best friend, lover and father of their three children—awoke on the morning of July 8th eagerly anticipating an overnight trip to a favorite chalet in Wisconsin.

It wasn't to be. Lyle said, "I don't know if I can go this morning. I feel short of breath." "Maybe you should sit down and rest a while," said Jeanette. Minutes later, "Call 911 for an ambulance. I need to go to the hospital!" said Lyle.

The ambulance sped off with Lyle. Jeanette followed shortly. Stunned when she arrived at the ER Lyle was near death. "Do you want us to use extreme measures...?" "Yes, yes do everything you can!" Jeanette replied.

Lyle, Jeanette's partner of 63 years died a short time later. The shock and loss was almost unbearable.

I recalled practicing my dances for competition in the Ms Senior MI pageant. Jeanette, the "Queen of Dance" and owner of LeCaptain's studio choreographed the numbers and worked with me personally. Lyle was there like a fixture everyday. I witnessed the love and respect between them. They were a team! Lyle always encouraged her to continue to work at what she loved.

I thought what will Jeanette do now that Lyle is gone? I soon found out.  Jeanette, age 83, is an incredible lady with 50 years of running her dance studio plus over 20 years of designing and sewing costumes; a flourishing business on a national basis.  Now Jeanette was making plans to start a new pre-school dance class for children 3 and 4 years old.

Jeanette is the published author of *Learning to Skip;* written especially for nursery schools, Special Ed Teachers and Dance Schools.  Her credentials are many.  She has authored numerous articles and organized Summer Workshops for Dance School Teachers at her Studio.

The Pre-School Dance Class will offer hand, eye activities and gross motor skills before dancing begins.  "Gross motor skills first develop with walking, running, jumping (two feet) and hopping on each foot individually," Jeanette explained with the enthusiasm of a teen-ager.

Kalisa LeVigne, an accomplished instructor will teach the youngsters.  The children will learn Hop skipping.  "The skipping movements are first learned in "parts" and began to flow together within a few tries," relates Jeanette. "The final goal is performing these same skills moving backwards.  At this level the small child can begin to do simple dances."

What a role model Jeanette is in so many ways.  Anyone who loses a loving mate after 63 years and jumps back into the work place with fresh ideas and an enthusiasm usually reserved for someone decades younger is truly a role model for seniors devastated by a similar loss.

Does that mean Jeanette doesn't experience profound sadness? Of course not!  During my interview with her, she became teary eyed when discussing Lyle—especially when I asked how long they had been together.  I hugged her; she composed herself and continued talking about her new venture that begins in September.

During the war (1940's) when Lyle LeCaptain was in service he met the love of his life in Texas.  Jeanette was a professional dancer and skater performing in an Ice Show in Dallas Texas.  How fortunate for Escanaba that she married Lyle and would literally take the city of Escanaba by storm—ice storm that is.  She became the director of the "Biggest Small Town Ice Revue in the

World" and parleyed what was once a handful of skaters to a cast of over 350 in a dazzling colorful extravaganza on ice.

Jeanette toured with "Holiday on Ice" and later performed in several upscale night clubs in Dallas and Philadelphia. She would witness many of the Escanaba performers she tutored go to the ranks of the Big Time professional shows. Mary Goodreau skated with the famed Shipsted and Johnson Ice Follies.

"Word of the small town Ice Show got around," says Jeanette. "Ice Capades called and wanted to come to Escanaba and check out the local skaters. The scout that covered the show offered jobs to over half of our precision line girls."

Other skaters were offered jobs and skated with the Ice Capades, the Ice Follies and the Sonja Hennie Show. They included Bob Schwalbach, Kathy Nelson, Martha Gruber, Howard Sullivan, Johnny Flannigan, Jeanne Groos, Jean Farrell, Jo-Ann Beck, Carolyn Johnson, Glenna Falmer and Shirley Girard. Jeanette's shows were closely watched by the "big time" and considered one of the "sand lots" of the business.

*Jeanette teaching tap dance at Club 314.*

"1951 was another big year," Jeanette continued. "Life Magazine contacted us wanting to cover our Ice Show. I believe the Editor of the Daily Press got them interested. The biggest draw was my 24 month-old toddler, daughter Jeanne, featured in our show." The article depicted Escanaba as a skating crazy town.

1955 was a really exciting year for Jeanette. Escanaba's professional quality Ice Shows and a host of skaters now performing in the Pros really put the little town in the U.P. on the map. Jeanette was offered a job choreographing the skating show that was in conjunction with the St. Paul Pops (equivalent of the Boston Pops).

Jeanette reminisces about the incomparable Bill Clark, who played the organ at CJ's Bar and the Sherman Hotel. He played for and was an integral part of the Ice Revues. "He prepared my music and helped prepare me to work with the huge orchestra in St. Paul. The Pops ran all summer long playing several times weekly."

A review from the St. Paul Press: "Jeanette LeCaptain, the new skating revue director, has trained a line of 24 precision skater-dancers into the finest unit I've seen locally."

Jeanette has touched the lives of hundreds (perhaps thousands) of youth through her dance studio and years of directing the "Biggest Small Town Ice Revue in the World." 60 years later, she is still actively involved. The young pre-school children of today will be benefactors of Jeanette's unique and tested teaching abilities available in September.

Jeanette will always miss the 'love of her life' Lyle. However, she is grateful she is able to do what she loves doing; teaching children, and designing and sewing costumes. Her days are busy and active. The "Queen of Dance" has recorded a lifetime of fond memories. She remains enthusiastic about life. Like the song excerpt; Fairy tales will come true if you are among the very young at heart—that's Jeanette.

# KNOW THE TEN WARNING SIGNS OF ALZHEIMERS
## Friday, August 22, 2008

Perhaps you have noticed slight changes in your memory and it worries you. Perhaps a family member or friend has Alzheimer's and you are worried that changes in your memory are the beginning symptoms of the dreaded disease. Some change in memory is normal as we grow older. It is important to know the warning signs.

The Alzheimer's Association has developed a checklist to help you recognize the difference between normal age-related memory changes and possible warning signs of Alzheimer's disease.

1. **MEMORY LOSS.** Forgetting recently learned information is one of the most common early signs of dementia. A person begins to forget more often and is unable to recall the information later.
   **WHAT'S NORMAL?** Forgetting names or appointments occasionally.

2. **DIFFICULTY PERFORMING FAMILIAR TASKS.** People with dementia often find it hard to plan or complete everyday tasks. Individuals may lose track of the steps involved in preparing a meal, placing a phone call or playing a game.
   **WHAT'S NORMAL?** Occasionally forgetting why you came into a room or what you planned to say.

3. **PROBLEMS WITH LANGUAGE.** People with Alzheimer's often forget simple words or substitute unusual words, making their speech or writing hard to understand. They may be unable to find the toothbrush, for example, and instead ask for "that thing for my mouth."
   **WHAT'S NORMAL?** Sometimes having trouble finding the right word.

4. **DISORIENTATION TO TIME AND PLACE.** People with Alzheimer's disease can become lost in their own

neighborhood, forget where they are and how they got there and not know how to get back home.

**WHAT'S NORMAL?** Forgetting the day of the week or where you were going.

5. **POOR OR DECREASED JUDGMENT.** Those with Alzheimer's may dress inappropriately, wearing several layers of clothes on a warm day or little clothing in the cold. They may show poor judgment, like giving away large sums of money to telemarketers.

**WHAT'S NORMAL?** Making a questionable or debatable decision from time to time.

6. **PROBLEMS WITH ABSTRACT THINKING.** Someone with Alzheimer's disease may have unusual difficulty with performing complex mental tasks, like forgetting what numbers are for and how they should be used.

**WHAT'S NORMAL?** Finding it challenging to balance a checkbook.

7. **MISPLACING THINGS.** A person with Alzheimer's disease may put things in unusual places: an iron in the freezer or a wristwatch in the sugar bowl.

**WHAT'S NORMAL?** Misplacing keys or a wallet temporarily.

8. **CHANGES IN MOOD OR BEHAVIOR.** Someone with Alzheimer's disease may show rapid mood swings—from calm to tears to anger—for no apparent reason.

**WHAT'S NORMAL?** Occasionally feeling sad or moody.

9. **CHANGES IN PERSONALITY.** The personalities of people with dementia can change dramatically. They may become extremely confused, suspicious, fearful or dependent on a family member.

**WHAT'S NORMAL?** People's personalities do change somewhat with age.

10. **LOSS OF INITIATIVE.** A person with Alzheimer's disease may become very passive, sitting in front of the TV for hours, sleeping more than usual or not wanting to do usual activities. **WHAT'S NORMAL?** Sometimes feeling weary of work or social obligations.

\*\*\*\*\*\*\*\*\*\*\*\*\*\*\*\*\*\*\*\*\*\*\*\*\*\*\*\*\*\*\*\*\*\*\*\*\*\*\*\*\*\*\*\*\*\*\*\*\*\*\*\*\*\*\*\*\*\*\*\*\*\*\*\*

New facts compiled in 2008:

Alzheimer's is a progressive disease—that only gets worse—no coming back from it or containing the disease.    People usually live on average 8 years and up to 20 years after onset.

As many as 5.2 million people in the U.S. are living with Alzheimer's.

10 million Baby Boomers will develop Alzheimer's in their lifetime.

The risk of developing Alzheimer's grows with old-age, doubling every 5 years beyond the age of 65 and growing to nearly 50 percent for those over 85.  It is more common in women due to the fact women live longer than men.

\*\*\*\*\*\*\*\*\*\*\*\*\*\*\*\*\*\*\*\*\*\*\*\*\*\*\*\*\*\*\*\*\*\*\*\*\*\*\*\*\*\*\*\*\*\*\*\*\*\*\*\*\*\*\*\*\*\*\*\*\*\*\*\*

My experience has been with my son's brain injury.  And that is totally different.  His injury arrested after the initial insult.  And he continues to improve—especially in the area of memory—even after 20 years.

My recent experience with the disease has been visiting the nursing home.  There are more women residents with Alzheimer's. The ladies I am familiar with are manageable.  In fact, they are so sweet, sometimes funny and very loveable.

If an individual becomes violent (a danger to staff or themselves) a nursing home is not equipped to care for them. Those individuals are cared for in a special facility like Pine Crest in Powers.

The State of Michigan regulates nursing homes.  A couple of things that I became aware of after my son became a resident for rehabilitation are: No side rails are allowed on beds. Residents are allowed to roam freely as long as they are safe regarding balance etc. Residents are not allowed to be restrained (tied in a wheelchair). The system is so much more humane than state facilities of the past.

Years ago people in state facilities were tied up, locked up, drugged up and forgotten about. Not so today. Of course, the heartache of watching a family member deteriorate mentally cannot be summed up in terms or words. Only those in the trenches can identify with the wretchedness of Alzheimer's and dementia and how it affects all of the family members.

I remember when former President Reagan announced that he had Alzheimer's and would be ending his public life. His wife, Nancy, shielded him from the public eye for the next ten years to protect his image and legacy. She wanted him to be remembered and endeared the way he was.

Granted they had the financial means to keep him at home. However, Nancy like thousands of others had to stand by and watch the "love of her life" drift into the shadows—a valley of death that only those that experience it could explain. Eventually, they could no longer even reminisce about their life together. For him the memories were wiped out, erased, gone, like they never happened. At the end he couldn't even recognize his "Nancy Pants"—his term of endearment for her.

Recently I viewed the movie, *The Notebook* for the third time. It portrays the life of a couple and what happens when one falls into the deep hole of Alzheimer's. I cried while viewing it for a third time just as I did the first time. It's available at the video store. Be for-warned! It's a tear jerker.

The Alzheimer's Association Memory Walk will take place tomorrow August 23rd at the Civic Center. Registration is from 11:00 to 12 noon. The walk begins at the Senior Center and is approximately 3 miles. It will end at the Senior Center with a picnic and Children's activities to follow. All donations from the walk stay in the U.P.

## UNDECIDED ON A PRESIDENTIAL CANDIDATE?
**Friday, August 29, 2008**

I heard a profound statement on Larry King Live: "If God wanted us to vote; he would have given us a candidate." Precious!

You would think after almost 2 years of debates, primaries, speeches, political ads (mostly negative) and exposure on untold talk shows that both parties would have got it right.

However, either party's base is not completely enthralled with their candidate. Take John McCain: Even his mother, Roberta, when asked how much support she thought he has among the base of the Republican Party said,

"I don't think he has any. I think holding their nose they are going to have to take him." OUCH! That comment is kind of strange coming from Mama—but very perceptive.

She was right. He still has a problem with the Evangelicals. Roberta McCain went on to say, "He worked like a dog to get Bush re-elected...He's backed Bush in everything except Rumsfeld. Have you heard other senators and congressmen backing Bush over eight years? Find me one—give me a name."

I wonder if Roberta knows Bush's popularity and record is not exactly a great premise to run on. In fact, his popularity numbers (presently 29 percent) are at an all-time low for any contemporary president.

Quite frankly, my choice in the primaries would have been Mitt Romney. What's wrong with having a president who is intelligent and can speak well? "My Friends" as McCain begins every other sentence; wouldn't that be a breath of fresh air? And Romney would have been a giant regarding one of our biggest problems; the economy. And let's not forget that he is a Michigan native.

American's do have a real concern and dilemma over John McCain's independence from President Bush's policies. They are also concerned about Obama's readiness to lead and his level of experience.

Now let's look at Obama, the media "Darling." Until now he has been given a pass. He has inspired young people to vote—that's true, but Obama does have a problem with Hillary's supporters and the lunch bucket brigade—blue collar workers.

As of now Obama and McCain are running neck and neck in the polls. Many are puzzled that he doesn't have a commanding lead. The prevalent question now; is he ready to lead? I wonder about his decision to ignore Hillary Clinton who had garnered 18 million votes in the primary. She wasn't vetted or even a consideration for VP. She didn't even receive a phone call from him on his selection.

Obama has angered the women behind Hillary; not a good way to heal wounds that run deep. A good percentage will not support Obama. Seems Osama's wife, Michelle, had a hand in his decision to stiff Hillary—she dislikes her intensely.

That is not unusual for a spouse. They feel the wounds of a hard fought campaign. They remember the nastiness, the stretching of the truth, the negative stuff. Michelle didn't like hearing those things about 'her man, her honey, and the father of her babies.' Likewise for Bill Clinton.

Pundits have said if Obama loses the election it would all boil down to not including Hillary on the ticket. They also agree that the next best choice was Joe Biden. Obama is decidedly thin in Foreign Policy. Biden is considered a heavyweight in that area.

The notion that a VP should do no harm remains to be seen. Joe Biden is colorful and candid. The talk shows love him. Often he shoots from the hip, says what he thinks and could create a gaffe that may be difficult to overcome at this late stage. The Obama camp may have to muzzle him. Overall, the polls say he is a good pick. Certainly he is ready and qualified to step in if called on to be president.

I will admit I became a Hillary supporter when Romney ended his bid. But I like Biden's background, his experience and his ability to overcome adversity. I wondered about the Freudian slip when Obama introduced him by mistake as "the next president of the United States." Republicans picked up on that!

I have mentioned before about my husband, Gary's conservative leanings and his disenchantment with either candidate which prompted his decision to vote for himself. It definitely is a protest vote. All tongue-in-cheek or so I thought— but wait—he has even had cards printed up! Claims he is running on the Yooper ticket.

I humor him somewhat. He is a senior citizen frustrated with the world and the declining morals where anything goes; so venting gives him something to do everyday. What's the harm? But now he has even worked up a campaign platform. Has he gone too far with this silliness? I wonder? Many of his peers agree with him on issues and where this country is headed. Many have said (I hope, in jest) that they will vote for him as a write-in candidate.

Take a look at his Yooper Presidential Platform: Humor is good for the soul!

1. Bring the Packers to the U.P. and rename them "Da Yoopers."
2. Change the national Thanksgiving meal from a turkey to a pasty.
3. Make the first day of "hunting season" a national holiday.
4. Appoint all cabinet members from the U.P.
5. Make toothpicks the symbol of the U.P.
6. Build more taverns and drink more beer to help the economy.
7. Lower retirement age to 50 giving seniors more time to drink beer.
8. Make the U.P. a separate state called Superior.
9. Have Polka dances in the White House weekly.
10. Start a war with France and England to divert attention from Iraq.

\*\*\*\*\*\*\*\*\*\*\*\*\*\*\*\*\*\*\*\*\*\*\*\*\*\*\*\*\*\*\*\*\*\*\*\*\*\*\*\*\*\*\*\*\*\*\*\*\*\*\*\*\*\*\*\*\*\*\*\*\*\*\*\*\*

If you are in a quandary about your choice for president and who you are going to vote for, you are not alone. The race is fluid and changes every time there is a poll; a real indication of indecision among American voters.

Next week look for an in-depth article about the two VP picks.

# DO NO HARM!
## Friday, September 5, 2008

The first consideration of a presidential nominee when choosing a vice president resembles the Hippocratic Oath: Do No Harm. In this day and age candidates for VP are heavily vetted to ferret out any personal skeletons that could be dug up by the opposition.

Of course any public speech (even 20 years ago) or any other uttering is fair game to use negatively in a heated contest. God forbid if the candidate has changed his course on issues over the years. He or she will be held accountable, nailed to the cross and labeled a flip-flopper.

There are many other reasons to consider for a VP pick. Geographic's enter in as well as certain key states—and what the candidate brings to the table to strengthen the ticket. Much thought goes into the pick including will he or she be ready to lead if an emergency should occur; how well will he or she handle the "attack dog" persona that is part of the job and of course all-important is the chemistry. Do they share the same values? Ideology?

And if Mama ain't happy—ain't nobody happy! So out the window goes the pick! It's no secret that today wives have a huge input in their husband's running mates.

The exception I remember is the Kennedy/Johnson ticket: There was no chemistry. Lyndon Johnson was thought of as brash, a clod devoid of class by the elitist Kennedy's, but they knew his rapid ascent in the US Congress, his tenure as a Senate Majority Leader from Texas made him an attractive addition to the ticket. So they held their noses, won the election and treated him badly.

JOE BIDEN, the 65 year old Senator from Delaware has the Democratic nod for VP. Born in Scranton, PA, Joe moved to Delaware at age 10 with his parents. Like Obama, Biden's life story is dramatic. Biden overcame his stutter as a kid by relentless drills. Tragedy struck Biden early in life. He was age 29 when he was elected to the Senate. Before he could assume office, his wife and young daughter were killed in a car crash as they shopped for a Christmas tree; his two young sons were badly injured.

He was persuaded to take office as planned in 1973 by his sister who helped him look after the boys during the day. He commuted home to be with his recovering boys every night. He married Jill Jacobs in 1977 and has continued to commute on Amtrak ever since. His son Beau says his dad "wanted to be home at my ballgames and be at the dinner table."

In 1988, Biden suffered a life-threatening aneurism. 1988 was also the year Biden was driven to run for president. He withdrew after he failed to credit a British politician for a passage used in a stump speech, thereby being accused of plagiarism.

Biden's mother lives with him. He said she kissed him as he left for Springfield to be introduced as Obama's running mate. "Joey, everybody in Scranton will be so proud," she told him.

Certainly his heavy credentials as chairman of the Foreign Relations Committee and his experience has got to be a huge plus for the ticket. David Axelrod, senior strategist for Obama said, "Mostly, I think what attracted Senator Obama was Biden's wisdom. And not the kind of wisdom you get in Washington. D.C., but the kind of wisdom you get when you overcome adversity, tragedy in your life as he has..."

The question Biden has brought up himself: Can he adapt to working for someone else—playing second fiddle? I doubt he will be a VP that is seen and not heard. Good choice overall. That is if the Clintonites unite behind the party.

SARAH PALIN, 44 year-old Governor of Alaska, and McCain's VP choice stunned and shocked everyone. "Who is she?" everybody is asking. McCain is really rolling the dice. USA Today reports, "McCain was ready to throw a long ball; a Hail Mary pass in an election in which more than 8 out of 10 Americans say they are dissatisfied with the country's direction." McCain has defied conventional wisdom. "Do No Harm" doesn't seem to apply.

Again, the choice begs the question, "Who is she?" Virtually unknown, she was born in Utah, and graduated from high school in Alaska. She went from PTA, to city council, to mayor of a town of 9000. For the past two years she has been the sitting Governor of Alaska.

She has five children; her 4 month old son has Downs

Syndrome. She knew early in her pregnancy that her baby would have Downs Syndrome. For her abortion was not an option.

Evaluating the pros and cons of the pick; although she will appease the party base (Evangelicals and Social Conservatives), her thin credentials are being questioned. Foreign policy and national security are as far from her realm of expertise as Alaska is to the mainland. McCain has had several bouts with cancer and one would have to consider his age. Would she be ready to step in as president of the U.S.?

In my younger years I chaired the Republican Party in Delta County and attended the state convention in Detroit as a delegate in 1988. Back then I ate, slept and devoured politics—a real junkie.

Perhaps the most exciting political event I was involved in was held in Iron Mountain; the Secret Service was in the U.P. weeks in advance staking out the location. I was privy to being one of 15 people in the state of Michigan invited to a brain-storming meeting with then Vice-President Bush. I remember being escorted into the meeting room by Secret Service. My husband and I were also invited to Bush's Inaugural Ball. Memorable occasions!

Over the years my interest in politics waned somewhat—until this year. I guess it was the historical nature of the candidates that lured me back; a multiracial man (black and white) and Hillary's historical bid winning 23 states.

My son, Jeff with conservative leanings, was one of 84,000 attending the historic nomination acceptance speech of Barack Obama at Invesco Stadium—and of course, attended one of the after-parties.

Jeff, soon to be age 50, had just turned five when we witnessed historical happenings on TV. President Kennedy was shot and killed. We, like so many Americans, were riveted to our TV on Sunday morning as history continued to unfold. We actually viewed the shooting of his assailant, Lee Harvey Oswald, as he was being transported in a jail hallway. It was so bizarre; you weren't sure if that was really happening. Those images have been played over and over through the years.

One thing for sure; we are witnessing firsts in presidential election history.   Will it be a multi-racial man as president or a white woman as vice-president? Time will tell when the American people make their choice in November.

## A SLICE OF LIFE
## Friday, September 12, 2008

Summer's end is nearing.  And what a summer this has been for my family:  Trauma, near death, pneumonia, heart attack and sandwiched in between a delightful family wedding.  Guess that's a slice of life.

It all began in May when my son fell out of bed and fractured his hip.  We spent days in Marquette when he had surgery and nearly died when he went into shock from a blood transfusion.  He was transferred to a local nursing home for a three-month course of rehabilitation.  That meant being there three times a day to feed him because he has a delayed swallow.

We were exposed to a life we knew existed—but not up close and personal.  We met many elderly residents at the nursing home that we came to love.  We experienced funny moments, endearing moments and yes, sad moments too.  Several residents we came to know expired during the three months.  We felt sadness almost as if they were family members; their deaths affected the staff that cared for them too.

We also enjoyed some fun times at the nursing home.  For the past eight years they have planned a special fish fry for all of the male residents and their families on Father's Day.  Our son was so happy; he sang Beatle songs as he sat outside in his wheelchair and watched them grill fresh perch and walleye.  Alas, four of the men that enjoyed that special day have died.

Three weeks ago we took our son home.  His home coming has been riddled with anxiety.  He doesn't walk as well—at least not yet—maybe never.  We are barely able to transfer him from bed to wheelchair.  He has been with us for twenty years needing 24-hour care.  Nothing stays the same and we knew that caring for him as we advanced in age may not be possible. The jury is still out—yet, the stress and sadness we feel over the possibility of having to place him in a nursing home is overwhelming. Many a tear has been shed as we wrestle with a decision.

Two weeks ago was a happy time. My husband was honored along with 40 plus Gessner and Gessner/Ptotenhauer recipients during the half-time of the Eskymo/Gaylord game. He was the 25th recipient in 1949. Wendell Buckland was the oldest recipient (1947). Both Wendell and Gary were interviewed by Kevin Scannell who is creating a documentary about Escanaba football. Gary loves to talk so I am sure Kevin got his monies worth. Plus Gary has a phenomenal memory for the past if not yesterday.

Looking back on the evening I should have realized Gary was having serious problems. We parked about a block and a half from the field. He stopped every few steps—"to rest," he said. I was frustrated with the time it took to walk that short distance.

We reached the field and Gary met several of his classmates: Kenny VanEffen, Bill Elliott, Herb Nicholson and Ron Sedenquist. They joked about Gary's outrageous protest bid for president and the card he had printed up stating he was a write-in candidate for the Yooper Party. He laughed himself silly all of the way up to the stands. Anyone who knows him is aware of his outrageous and sometimes strange sense of humor. He loves to laugh.

We sat in the visitors section so he could be close to the field at half-time. He seemed concerned about having to walk a great distance on the field at half-time. Jack Beck sat behind us; he mentioned to Gary that perhaps the older guys should follow the younger ones on the field. Gary laughed but wholeheartedly agreed.

Just before the game ended Gary asked me to get the car and pick him up at the entrance. Even as he entered the car he seemed breathless. When we got home I suggested he should get checked out at the ER

"I'm just tired," he said. "I'll be fine after a good night's sleep." We retired. Early the next morning I discovered he wasn't in bed. He was sitting in a chair and reluctantly said, "Maybe I should go to the ER. I'm really short of breath." I checked his oxygen level and it was low—in the 80's.

I drove him to the ER. Within two hours he was being rushed to Marquette General. He was in congestive heart failure, had pneumonia, had a heart attack, and was bleeding internally. He lost half his blood.

Wow! In just twelve hours: from a fun evening at the football game to being rushed in an ambulance to Marquette with your life hanging in the balance. To complicate matters I had to leave my son alone while I waited in the ER for my husband's status. Is it any wonder my blood pressure went haywire?

The good news: Gary rallied! Again! I tease him that he is the "cool cat with nine lives." He has been to the brink of death so many times and his strong will to live has always prevailed.

Gary's home now and the lesson learned from his latest serious episode: Don't wait to go to the ER or to see a doctor. Don't just attribute a decline to "getting older." Be vigilant about changes, take charge of your health and for goodness sake, listen to your wife!

Seriously though, seniors carry a heavy load mentally—especially in the 7th and 8th decade. The last thing you think about when you are young and healthy is death, dying or losing your freedom through being bedridden or in a wheel chair. Young folks are in the main-stream: raising a family and earning a living. That's normal—as it should be.

The reality of demise is glaring for seniors. They witness the decline in the health of their peers and attend more funerals. How can they not be affected? They may not talk about their fears: the possibility of losing their freedom through disability, dementia or even their fear of the unknown; of dying. But the thought is there—lurking. Taking one day at a time, having a sense of humor and a strong faith helps.

## The Rich Football Tradition
## of Escanaba and Menominee
## Friday, September 19, 2008

Escanaba has shaped many a youth with their football program and rich tradition that spans more than a hundred years. The Escanaba Eskymos and Menominee Maroons is the oldest inter-county series in the 15 county Upper Peninsula. The rivalry dates back to 1897.

Both schools churned out programs and teams that ranked among the best not only in the U.P. but in the state.

When I was in high school the 'big game' was Menominee. I especially remember 1948. It was a week to behold: Constructing the floats for the snake dance and parade highlighted the week as the crescendo built toward 'the game'.

At the time there was no mall. No TV. There were no fast food restaurants and no Wal-mart. Friday night in downtown Escanaba was the only game in town: it was payday; stores were

*Yours truly, lower left. Note: Tommy's EAT sign.*

open; fish fries at local bars like the People's, Sandberg's, and the Michigan were jammed. Downtown was bustling.

Homecoming parade started at the foot of Ludington and turned down 14th street as it made it way to the old high school like the Pied Piper. Cardboard boxes were collected all week and piled high in anticipation of the huge bon-fire that lit the skies and was seen from all over town. The coach and a couple of the players gave talks. The pep rally fired up everyone with cheers for the 'big game' on Saturday. A stuffed Maroon player on a stick was burned in effigy—all in fun of course.

Back then Escanaba didn't have a lighted field. Saturday afternoon games were wholesome: crispness filled the air as leaves dressed in their fall colors of red, yellow and orange swirled in the wind. After the game cars raced up and down Ludington Street (the main drag as it was called) tooting their horns—win or lose! The town knew when the game was over.

The school dance was held at the old high school. Music was provided by fellow classmates. I remember a few: Jack Frost, Betty Lemirand, Betty Houle, Dave Zerbel, Harold Cloutier and Susie Lindstrom on the piano. The cost was 10 cents.

However, the 1948 game was played in Menominee. It was also the year that the "Hinker Bell" was introduced and became the glory crown that traveled with the winning team. The bronze bell was a symbol of Escanaba and Menominee heritage.

According to Larry Ebsch, former editor of the Menominee Herald-Leader, "The bell came from a locomotive that powered a logging train transporting raw products from the lush forests of Menominee and Delta Counties. The 110-pound bell was given by John Hinker, a Menominee coal dealer. He donated it to the school as a prize in the Menominee-Escanaba football series. The year and game score were inscribed on the bell."

Ebsch continued, "Cheerleaders of the previous victorious team would push or pull the carriage to the 50 yard line before kick-off and ring the bell. It added to the spirit of rivalry."

The locomotive was built in Philadelphia 1906 and the bell was cast in a railroad foundry. The Menominee-Escanaba series (1897) is nine years older than the bell.

Apparently the bell disappeared sometime in the sixties while in possession of Escanaba. Some say about the time the new school opened. Efforts to track it down have proved futile. Does anyone have any idea where that historic trophy bell is hiding?

And what has happened to the team players of that historic game in '48 when the undefeated Eskymos lost to the Maroons in the forth quarter 13-12? One lousy point separated them from an undefeated season. The guys still talk about it—play by play.

According to Ebsch (Maroon's class of '49), "The undefeated Eskymos of Coach George Ruwitch were guided by such stalwarts as Herb Nicholson, Howard Perron, Warren "Moose" Gustafson, Gary Abrahamson and Don Carlson." All are still living.

The four members that comprised the legendary Menominee '48 backfield either played college football or in the semi-pro Wisconsin State Football League. They were Phil Johnson, Emil Pontow, Billy Wells and Ray Johnson. All have passed away. Dick Deschaine, a former Packer, is still living.

Ebsch says, "The Wells story is enduring. It stretches from his prep days at Menominee, to the glory years of Michigan State in the early 1950s, to a sterling seven-year professional career. He was a radio sportscaster, dated Debbie Reynolds, had small bits in the movies, dabbled in movie production and had his own popular band, Billy and his Bachelors." He was the MVP in the 1954 Rose Bowl Game.

Billy was handsome, modest, and even a bit bashful then—he made the girls swoon. Wells came from a wealthy background; but his classmates knew only the modest Billy. He liked to Jitterbug at teen dances and at the Silver Dome in Marinette. Incidentally he was a great dancer. He did the "Charleston" on national TV.

Mike Shatusky was in touch last week. He played on the 1947 Menominee team and for the University of Michigan. Mike was a great athlete and is a U.P. Hall of Famer. Several years ago he had a stroke and since has founded the Strokes Fore Strokes golf outing in the Ann Arbor area. Stroke victims play in the tournament to raise money for research. 'Michigan Mike' as he is now called has been an inspiration to all that know him.

One last important thought in regard to the Hinker Bell: Wouldn't it be great if some sports benefactor or the Escanaba Fan

Club presented the school with a meaningful traveling award to continue the age old and longest rivalry in the U.P.? Perhaps some symbol of Escanaba and Menominee Heritage. Then it would seem logical to reinstate the rich historical tradition of having Homecoming before the Menominee game.

Larry Ebsch stated in his column, ByeLines, "If the Hinker Bell can't be found, another one should be introduced. The rich tradition of the Menominee-Escanaba rivalry merits it."

Upon investigating on the internet I found that a steam locomotive bell in bronze is available for sale at $1995. It could be named the Fan Club Bell or the name of any private sports donor. Now there's a worthwhile project!

## FOOD FOR THOUGHT
## Friday, September 26, 2008

Food! Our bodies require it. It sustains us. Holy Wah—it is so much more than that! We talk about food everyday. We shop for food at the grocery store. We prepare the food. We plan special occasions around food. We dine in restaurants.

The book stores are filled with diet books, health books, and cook books. In fact it is a multi-million dollar industry. Perhaps everyone at one time has been on some sort of diet to lose weight or to gain—better nutrition?

The first Atkins diet book was published in 1972 and millions of copies have been sold. His diet allowed a lot of fats but few carbohydrates. The Pritikin diet advises the opposite; eating a lot of carbohydrates.

There has never been a study on what long-term effect diet books have on overweight people. Not much I suspect. I have bought a few diet books myself including the South Beach Diet. Most are filled with recipes to cut calories. Even if people do lose weight the long-term success of keeping it off is less that 2%. It takes a lifestyle change for permanent weight loss.

Birthdays, anniversaries, holidays, picnics and family

gatherings all center on planning a menu. We anticipate eating. Food makes us happy.

Families have special recipes. Nationalities usually will dictate the recipes. I think of my grandma's French meat pies and orange cake recipes that have been handed down through the years.

The French are frustrating, but then so can family members be difficult. Whatever you think about the French they are incomparably better with food than the people of any other country. They enjoy it and savor every morsel. They love the long sticks of crusty French bread; I agree it beats Wonder Bread!

Andy Rooney of 60 minutes fame says, "Commercial bread in the United states is terrible. How it ever came about that the French eat such great bread everyday and Americans eat such bad bread is a mystery."

People just seem to love Italian food: Pastas, pizzas, great sauces. I don't think I am the only one that really misses the old Crispignas. I love going to Olive Garden in Green Bay or Carrabba's in Florida. I have never been fond of Asian food but I know that's a favorite of many.

I always laugh when I see the homes on the TV show House Hunters. The ultimate kitchen features a gas stove with at least six burners. Then it will show a huge island with the new owners lovingly cutting up veggies together. I wonder how much use that kitchen will get on an everyday basis.

The rich and famous eat out often at exotic restaurants. Those not so rich and famous settle for fast food. Check out the local restaurants on Friday and Saturday evenings. Makes you wonder: Does anybody eat at home?

I used to love tomatoes. Now over the past twenty years they have deteriorated because of genetic alterations made to their seed by scientist in the business of horticulture. Tomatoes are harder and not so red and juicy as they used to be. It makes them easier to ship and the loss due to rotting in transit is reduced.

I love real butter. It makes everything taste good. I remember in the forties when my mother bought margarine (butter was rationed during the war) and it looked like a pound of lard. Yuck! It was my job to mix the capsule of food coloring in the lardy looking margarine trying to get it yellow looking and more appealing, but it still tasted like h—-.

Too much sugar or too much salt is bad for us, but we all recognize a direct relationship how good something tastes and how bad it is for us. The better it tastes, the worse it is for us.

Food and drink is like butter is to bread. I never ever drank milk—oh, maybe as a kid I drank chocolate milk because it didn't taste like milk. Guys seem to like milk more than girls. Nowadays everyone carries their water bottle with them—including me. We take a ride to Green Bay and I need my special spring water free of chlorine.

I never drank hard liquor. I drink wine only on special occasions. Once in a very great while I enjoy a beer, usually only with food though, like pizza.

For a soft drink I like Sprite in the little glass bottles. My husband loves coke in the bottle similar to what was available in the '40s. My son drinks cranberry juice by the gallons.

Andy Rooney says, "One of the strangest success stories in American business is Coca-cola. It's strange because no one who drinks it knows what's in it. It won the legal right to be called by its nickname "coke" years ago when it was sued by Pepsi-Cola. The best idea the Coca-cola Company ever had was that small, original, green-tinted pinched waist bottle."

Coke is available now in the grocery stores for about 3.99 for a six-pack of the old-fashioned 8 oz. glass bottles. Why does coke taste so much better in smaller glass bottles? Guess we will have to defer that question to the Binks. Maybe they will even divulge the secret of what is in it!

**READERS TAKE OVER THE COLUMN**
**Friday, October 3, 2008**

The 50's and 60's are reminiscent of the popular Perry Como Show on TV. Remember the clever ditty that played before the request segment: We get letters—lots and lots of letters! Dear Perry...

With today's technology that ditty would no doubt reflect e-mails. A huge portion of letter writing, even card sending today is generated through e-mails. It is instant, does not require a stamp and a reply can happen in minutes or hours.

Comments received about my column are mostly by e-mail. I do receive an occasional letter—those are mostly from folks that are my age and don't do e-mail. Let me share a few gems with you.

Letter from Jane Rice Lippold, Escanaba: "Hello Patt, Surprise! I'm cleaning up and sorting pictures and found this one of you in 10th grade...I enjoy your articles each Friday, then cut them out and mail them to Audrey Beach Carlson in Arvada, CO. She passes them on to Pat Palmateer Menard in Wisconsin Rapids, and she sends them on to her younger sister Jean in California. So you see, you really get around!"

An e-mail from Mr. Makumi, Nairobi, Kenya: "Dear madam, Let's cut the crap, shall we? Your article on the WC-or toilet as it is commonly called—was a pleasure to read. Rarely does one encounter articles that capture varied aspects of fact as yours did.

But I feel you should have taken it a step further and reminded your readers of places where the flush toilet still remains as hard to find as chicken's teeth. There are places in urban centres where hundreds of people have to co-exist—but without benefit of a toilet. It's shocking but true.

Lastly, I wonder if you could e-mail me your past (or future) articles. I won't lie. I was delighted. You brightened my day—and for a long time. Thank You."

Nairobi, Kenya, wow! I'd say the Daily Press really does gets around!

An e-mail from Dale and Jo Skogman, Gladstone: "Hi Patt, "Your column in Friday's paper regarding purchasing a car, mattress, etc. really hit home with us. Having just bought a car and mattress your column caused us to laugh till the tears rolled. Bravo!"

An e-mail from Paula Schroeder Jorgensen, Appleton, WI: "Dear Patt, Another fan letter...As so many people tell you, I am another of those that thoroughly enjoy your columns. And your book. I have sent it to Minnesota, South Carolina and Wisconsin.

The lady at Canterbury book store laughs when I come in to buy another of your books to obviously give away.

I was born and raised in Esky...left Esky in 1958 but am "home" very frequently as I have wonderful family in the area. I was particularly touched by your column about the Bonifas cemetery plots and the condition of such...

I read and reread your book and also Erol Beck's books of which I have also purchased and given away. They are all so very rich in memories and I am thankful that you and Erol have shared your talents with us and cared enough about these "memories" to bring them forth for all to share.

Do you remember the floats and huge bonfires we used to have for Homecoming? I worked at Harry's Soda lounge across from Anderson Funeral Home and after the games, both football and basketball, it would get so busy in there that I literally couldn't move to serve refreshments.

And a tune on the jukebox was 5 cents so we could always dance. And nobody frowned if a couple of girls danced together. And we had 'live' music to dance to at the Starlight across the street. White "Bucks" and saddle shoes were flying till we couldn't jitterbug one more note. Such good times! And trouble was almost nonexistent among kids. Oh how the memories flow..."

E-mail from Barbara Main, Oklahoma City, Oklahoma: "Hi Patt, I really enjoyed your article "Caregivers need care, too." Maybe it strikes me closer because I am a 24/7 caregiver for our handicapped daughter.

You may remember us. Greg was the director of CUPPAD when we lived in Esky from 1970-1986. Our Elizabeth was born in 1981. She has Down Syndrome and medical issues.

Your nightmares with Gary's caregivers over the years makes me remember that sometimes you just have to change your plans, and do it yourself, in order not to put them at risk. I am sure being an advocate has helped you. I know that helping others has helped me.

Finding respite care here in Oklahoma is a nightmare. There is a waiting list of about 5-7 years to get into a program and no agency that I can find will do respite for handicapped 'kids'. The day programs for kids who have graduated from high school will only take kids that can feed and toilet themselves. That eliminates a whole group of the population… Hope this is a great day for you and yours."

(Barbara's note and the difficulties they are going through to find any kind of respite care brought tears to my eyes. Sadly they are not alone.)

E-mail from Ken Schubring, Dunwoody, GA, University of MI BBA '48, MBA '49

Appreciated your "Rivalries" article, not only your take on the OSU/U of M competition, but also the historic info about the States of Ohio and Michigan. As a Michigan alum with yellow and blue running through my 85 year old blood, I think the OSU/U of M rivalry is certainly one of the best among major schools in the nation.

Even though most folks focus on OSU/Michigan, I can take you back to a day and age when the OSU game was almost an afterthought insofar as Michigan's schedule was concerned.

There was a time when the big one was with the Golden Gophers of the University of Minnesota. Of course, the hoopla that accompanied this annual scrap was nourished by the competition for the legendary Little Brown Jug…and this continues as we speak. But I agree that the big game nowadays for the U of M nation is the OSU game."

\*\*\*\*\*\*\*\*\*\*\*\*\*\*\*\*\*\*\*\*\*\*\*\*\*\*\*\*\*\*\*\*\*\*\*\*\*\*\*\*\*\*\*\*\*\*\*\*\*\*\*\*\*\*\*\*\*\*\*\*\*\*\*\*

So you see, the Daily Press and I really get around—even to other continents. Keep the letters coming! They make my day. Every now and then I share your wonderful gems in the column.

## 911 CALLS
## Friday, October 10, 2008

The 911 emergency phone number is a great service. I have had a couple of occasions that I thought warranted a 911 call.

What I recently found out is: a rule of thumb to call 911 should be to stop a crime, save a life or put out a fire.

I called 911 in Florida several years ago. My son was choking and turning blue. My husband and I were frantic while trying to perform the Heimlich on him. Thank goodness we were able to rectify the situation. The EMT's arrived at our home about 6 minutes later.

On many occasions I have had to call 911 locally. Two times my son had fell and couldn't get up—nor could we lift him. The police arrived pronto to help us. What a great service. It wasn't life threatening though; so I should have checked the phone book and called the police station. Several times I called for an ambulance; of course that was warranted

Today I had a bizarre occasion to call 911. I received a call from Monitronics International. Thinking it was an advertisement I was ready to hang up. Then he said the security alarm alert went off in my son, Jeffery's home in Alexandria, Va. Did we want him to send the police squad car to the house?

"Wait a minute! I am in Michigan. Of course send someone. He may be in some type of mortal danger or a robbery taking place at this very minute!" I answered excitedly.

Less than 5 minutes later the security company called back and said the police refused to investigate because my son hadn't registered for a permit.

"That's it! No one is going to check on him?" I said.

That's correct." he answered, "Our hands are tied."

"Give me the number to the Fairfax, VA police department," I said.

I called and explained the situation to the Fairfax Police Department. An officer said he couldn't do anything about it until I called my local police department in Michigan and have them teletype the information to Fairfax.

I couldn't believe it! "Policy," he uttered nonchalantly.

I called our local 911 and explained the situation to a dispatcher. Why are you calling us if this is in Virginia? After a lot of questions and answers he took the home address of our son in Virginia and the Fairfax police department phone number.

"You'll contact them immediately, right?" I asked.

"We'll contact them." He answered.

"Exasperated, I asked again, "immediately right?"

I asked him four times before he reluctantly acknowledged he would contact them right away.

Five minutes later I called the Fairfax Police Department back. This time a woman officer answered, "No, they hadn't heard from Escanaba yet, but I will dispatch a police car out there. No mention of 'policy' this time.

She proceeded to tell me they should send a car in an hour or so depending on priority. "PRIORITY? " My son may be in danger!" I screamed exasperated.

While I was talking to her a call came in from my son. "Everything is fine here. Kelly (his daughter) went outside on the upper level and I hadn't disengaged the security alarm." Guess all is well that ends well. Of course we were relieved but shuttered to think of the outcome had it been a real emergency.

Many 911 calls are downright hilarious—Ok, ridiculous... Take the woman that locked herself in her car with her keys inside. "I'm having a panic attack. I can't get out of my car."

Or the lady that called to say, "There is a spider in our house that bites. I'll open the door but I need someone to come in to look at the spider and make sure we're OK."

Dispatcher "How big is the spider?"

Caller, "Just a little one."

How about the lady that wants her burger done right?

Dispatcher: Sheriff's department, how can I help you?

Woman: Yeah, I'm over here...I'm over here at Burger King right here in San Clemente.

Dispatcher: Uh-huh.

Woman: Um, no, not San Clemente; I live in San Clemente. I am in Laguna Niguel, I think, that's where I'm at.

Dispatcher: Un-huh.

Woman: I'm at a drive-in window. I ordered my food three times. They're mopping the floor inside, and I understand they're busy...they're not busy, okay, I've been the only car here. I asked them four different times to make me a Western Barbeque Burger. Okay, they keep giving me a hamburger with lettuce, tomato and cheese, and I said I'm not leaving.

Dispatcher: Okay, what exactly is it you want us to do for you?

Woman:  Send an officer down here.  I want them to make me...

Dispatcher:  Ma'am, We're not gonna go down there and enforce your Western Bacon Cheeseburger.

Woman:  Well...that is...you're supposed to be protecting me.

Dispatcher:  Well, what are we protecting you from, a wrong cheeseburger?

Some calls are serious dispatcher errors:  Kids today are taught to call 911 in case of an emergency.  A young Detroit boy did just that when his mom could not be aroused.  The dispatcher told him to hang up and dismissed his call as a joke; just playing with the phone.  He called an hour later and was dismissed the same way.  Ten hours later he was found crying next to his dead mother.

You also hear of the ridiculous questions a dispatcher may ask that can cause a delay in response in real emergencies. How about when they say, "You need to calm down."

Stupid 911 calls tie up the system.  Remember the rule of thumb to call 911.  Is the call to stop a crime, save a life or put out a fire?

❧❦❧

## BIG TIME CHANGES OVER THE YEARS
## Friday, October 17, 2008

Generational changes occur in society over time; they may seem small and incremental to young people, but the changes become whopping to the folks that live to their 8th and 9th decade.

Take business for example: I remember the way people came to the house to conduct business.  Gump Olson was my mother's insurance man.  He sat down over coffee and chit-chatted with my mom like it was his only stop for the day.  Never in a hurry they talked about everything but the kitchen sink.

The delivery man from John's Market brought the groceries to the house and arranged them on the kitchen table all the while having a heart to heart talk with my mom.  Groceries were charged to your account. In bad times during work lay-offs my mother always appreciated how Johnny Chylek "carried us".

The iceman brought ice to the house for the icebox. More conversation ensued! Everyone was folksy. Coal and heating oil was delivered to the home. Everything was charged.

Doctors came to the home with their little black bag. They even made house calls on Sunday or in the middle of the night if an illness deemed it necessary.

Magazines like Colliers, Life and Good Housekeeping was also personally delivered to the house. Dry cleaners delivered to the home.

The Jewell-Tea man came regularly to our house. More folksy conversation as he sat at the kitchen table and unveiled his gems: coffee, tea, Jell-O, dry goods and household items.

I couldn't help but contrast school differences when we were young. The recent image on the Daily Press front page of students having their back-packs examined for bombs or explosives was so—out there. What is this world coming to? To even think that kids would want to bomb their schools and fellow students.

I think back to the '40s and attempted to dream up a scenario of being searched at school—for what, chewing gum? That is about the most outrageous thing kids did: chew gum. Also disgusting today is the student/teacher sex incidences we hear about in the media.

Changes in the business climate; new businesses and old businesses that cease to exist, neighborhoods and home styles—they are all part of the changing landscape.

My grandparents would be shocked to see the home they built on Ludington Street in 1933, the home where I lived, now the Don Johnson Insurance Agency. On the corner was DeGrand Oil Co.—now Bobaloons; I stop there for an occasional Chicago Dog.

Next door and of course my favorite neighbor Richie's pop shop is where I hung out on their dock like a little beggar until they offered me a bottle of pop.

Stegath's lumber yard was next to Richie's. Across the street was Guay's mom and pop store. You know the kind where they live in the back. A bell rang when you opened the door alerting the Guays that a customer had entered.

At times I was sent there to buy 10 cents worth of baloney and I spent many an hour laboring over choices from the penny candy display with my nose pressed against the glass case. Mrs. Guay was so patient. She would appear from the back wiping her hands on her apron and always a wearing a smile. Wonderful aromas permeated from her kitchen.

Mr. Guay wasn't quite as patient—but then he worked for the city sweeping streets all day. Yup, that's how the streets were cleaned back in the 30's and 40's. Imagine a job of pushing a huge broom all day, everyday; then coming home and waiting on the neighborhood kids while they spent 2-cents on penny candy.

"I'll take a jaw-breaker, no, no make it a licorice stick, no, change that to a nigger-babe." (Believe it or not, that was the name of a popular licorice candy in the body of a babe) In today's society that name would certainly not be politically correct.

Today there is a beauty shop (Total look) where Guay's, an important landmark in my youth, once stood.

Catherine Manley's home was on the corner next to Guays. My brother and I used to shovel Manley's huge corner walk for 10 cents each. Agnes Burke, a Junior High English teacher, lived around the corner on First Avenue South. That is also where George Harvey and his sister Belle resided.

George Harvey, the well-respected city manager of Escanaba for many years, still is the benchmark used to compare all those that followed him. And yes, he is a difficult act to follow.

Pat Baribeau, council member, recently mentioned to me that our present city-manager, "Jim O'toole, just may be another George Harvey."

I have to agree. Mr. O'toole seems to be doing a fantastic job. He wears many hats, balances so many important city issues and is forging ahead with the master plan for the city. He may not be a life-long resident like George Harvey, but his 'life' is all about dedication to the City of Escanaba.

Escanaba is home to his family and he is not going to be looking for greener pastures. It is quite apparent that his affinity for Escanaba is commensurate with the fine job he is doing. We need to support, praise and appreciate him when warranted because God knows we have gone through a host of less than satisfactory city managers. That said, we can't give him a blank check though; we may also have to differ at times.

Even the make-up of city council over the years has changed. In the days of H. George Nelson, a councilperson for many years, education wasn't even a consideration. His followers from North Town loved him. He was a no-nonsense person and dedicated to doing the city business. Today most council members hold degrees; a sharp contrast over the years.

Gone are the days when mom and pop stores dotted the landscape. Gone is the old high school. Gone are many of the people I mentioned. Gone is the innocence and naivety of the times.

I am sure the oldsters will concur with this one: Gone is the respect we were taught to show for our elders. The shocking language and revolting dress of today is for another story.

Ahh—memories! We were the 'babes' of the Depression and may have been poor but what's astounding—we didn't even know it. Hardships and all; those were wholesome, innocent and great years.

## VOLUNTEERS ON A LIFE CHANGING MISSION
### Friday, October 24, 2008

No special talent is needed to serve God's less fortunate. The local volunteers that travel to Central America are on a mission: A mission that is life changing to both the disadvantaged of LaPaz and the volunteers.

Charlene Carlson, pastoral associate, from St. Annes Church visits our home weekly to administer communion. Charlene piqued my interest when she related her experiences and excitement of embarking on her first mission trip to Central America last February. Questions bubbled out of me about the mission; I wanted to know what the mission accomplishes and about the special people from our community that donate, time, money and energy to help the needy in another country. Hence a story was born.

Charlene's trip was for 17 days. "We were allowed one carry-on bag for personal belongings," states Charlene. "I wondered how I would cram everything I needed into one small bag." Each participant is allowed 2-50 pound bags. Among some of the items they pack are electric fans, electrical equipment, school supplies, medical supplies and bedding.

Everyone pays for their own plane fare. Fund raising includes bingo, concession stands and donations before the trip to cover the costs of the materials for the projects. Last year over $5000 was raised.

Housing is set up at Father Abel's complex which houses young seminarians and older disabled men. The accommodations are barracks type. All of the women sleep on cots in one room. The walls, floors and even the sinks and showers are concrete. Charlene smiled when she exclaimed, "there were frogs in the showers that consisted of a metal pipe that dribbled out cold water."

"The sisters were wonderful, feeding us constantly while working at schools. They planned wonderful parties for us." Their system is rather strange. "Anyone can go to school—it's free, but a uniform is required. Sadly, many families are too poor to purchase a uniform."

Teachers are responsible for providing all supplies such as paper, pencils and crayons. Maintaining the classroom (cleaning and painting) is also their responsibility. The government provides only the space for classes.

"People are so appreciative, so happy to see us, so welcoming; they are so poor and don't even know that." says Charlene. "I thought the word 'barrio' meant slums, I found out it meant neighborhood. Conditions aren't a distraction though."

Sandy Thomma, a volunteer nurse from Escanaba witnessed children outside their one room cement block house. Through an interpreter she learned the seven and five year-old cared for the baby while the mother and two boys, age 12 and 21 worked in the fields.

The baby lay in a hammock made out of a feed sack—naked, no clothing and no diaper. Jim and Sandy Thomma literally adopted the family. The bought shoes, socks and uniforms for the children so they could go to school and cloth diapers for the baby. The children were so proud to be able to go to school.

One day Charlene and her son, Art were helping to do wiring at the public school. "A young man stood outside the window all morning just listening and soaking up information. He didn't have a uniform to come into the school." said Charlene.

The schools, convents and boarding house are enclosed by concrete walls with barbed wire on top. The watch dogs are ferocious and chained up in the daytime. The dogs are let loose at night.

The residents can't speak English. The volunteer group has access to two interpreters. Charlene is taking a 6-week Spanish class at Bay College. "I want to be able to understand, but they talk so fast I only catch a word here and there. I am also using CD's to supplement my class learning," says Charlene. "I'm looking forward to joining the group again this coming year for 22 days."

"Our last trip included two high school students. Lacy Klatt, now a student this year at Bay College, is planning a 6 month stay on her next trip leaving in February."

Some local good Samaritans on the last trip included Dennis LaMarch, Art Carlson, Charlene Carlson, Phil and Phillip LaMarch, Bob Gartland, Lacy Klatt, Linda Shumard, Troy Mosier, Ron Vanderlinden, Patrick Berres, Thomas Charon, Dan Mattys, Tim Rodgers, Mark Worm, Kathy Hartlaben, Jeff Cretens, Laura Pottala and Jim and Sandy Thomma.

The group has a growing nucleus of long-term members who travel annually and support the project efforts. Volunteers also come from throughout the Midwest. People from as far away as Florida, California and El Salvador have joined the group. All are welcome to join the effort.

The original mission to Honduras remained for five years. The move to the current mission was made after some persuasion by a retired American priest, Father Brady. In the past five years thousands of dollars have been invested in mission projects around LaPaz as well as recreational and maintenance projects at the former mission.

Projects planned for this year include: wiring in the public school in Flores, painting classrooms, building library shelves, supply miscellaneous medical supplies, purchase food for soup kitchen, distribute school supplies, install ceilings, purchase uniforms for children not able to attend schools, major maintenance and paint, paint and more paint just to name a few.

Ken Garland departs before the rest of the volunteers to purchase supplies needed for the projects. The mission is by no means all work and no play: Several parties are also arranged for the volunteers as well as a sight seeing tour. The cost for this year's 17 day trip that departs in February is $1400 (includes meals). All are welcome.

There is room for 30 volunteers with a few openings left. To be included in a mission that is life changing call Dennis LaMarch at 906-786-3000 for further information. Also call Dennis if you are interested in helping in other ways such as a sponsorship program, buying a uniform for a disadvantaged child or just donating any amount.

## THE UNFORGETTABLE FORTIES
**Friday, October 31, 2008**

Everyone's life holds the key to a best seller. Everyone's life is an individual unique story—like DNA—no two lives are the same. I find interviews so fascinating and engaging; especially exploring the life of older individuals that take you back in time.

Jeanette LeCaptain's story deserved another chapter. Jeanette, the icon of skate and dance, takes us back to the war years that so many of us 'relics' remember.

The United States had declared War on Japan after the bombing of Pearl Harbor on December 7, 1941. Jeanette remembers 1943, when the United States was in the midst of World War 11, and the many exceptions made to help the war effort. Young boys in high school were allowed to graduate in March to enter the military. "My brother was one of them," recalls Jeanette, "he went to Officer's training school to become a navigator."

Jeanette had finished her junior year in May of '43. The previous summer she spent training to be a figure skater in Colorado Springs. "I opted to leave school to audition for Holiday on Ice in Boston. I didn't make it! They instructed me to go home and take off 15 pounds; they encouraged me to try again in NYC two month later. The pounds came off and I was hired."

The troupe traveled by train from city to city. "What an experience!" exclaims Jeanette. "It took us five days to reach San Diego from Toledo, Ohio. Our entire cast was in the caboose, the last train car of a long GI train. I doubt if the GI's were even aware of us being on the train. We weren't allowed to go to the dining car until after the GI's were fed. Most often there was no food left."

"The choice was to go hungry or when the train pulled to a stop we ran to a grocery store. Sometimes we got lucky. When we pulled into a train station there would be a man with a huge coffee urn and bologna sandwiches on the boardwalk. He couldn't work fast enough to feed us all before we heard, 'All aboard.'"

Jeanette recalls a train trip to Canada. "It was a long miserable trip; there were continuous jerky stops to add and drop off train cars— and no sleeping cars! Day by day the train got filthier. The toilets were plugged. I walked through dozens of cars to find a usable toilet. To my surprise when I exited I was in a lone train stopped in the middle of nowhere."

"I felt like a hobo walking amid rows and rows of train tracks. Finally I reached the depot to find that my troupe was on the way to Quebec City. I was put on another train and met up with my troupe in Sault Ste. Marie, Canada." Scary

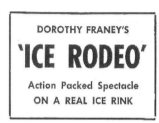

times for a young girl!

"I returned home in March and was allowed to 'catch up' with my school work so I could graduate with my senior class. With the help of a tutor I managed to graduate with honor roll grades."

By then skating was in Jeanette's blood. She wanted to continue but not in a road show. "I joined the Dorothy Franey Tank Show. That's a show held in an upscale hotel where they roll the dance floor back to expose the ice. We were a young cast of 12 teen-agers."

Shocking to Jeanette was the treatment of blacks even as far North as Philadelphia.

In Dallas and other southern cities, blacks had to use separate back entrances, use a separate toilet and drink from a separate water fountain.

"Being from Massachusetts I was unaware of prejudice and discrimination toward blacks," said Jeanette. "Black people were not welcome as hotel guests. The black people who worked at the hotel had to use the back entrance and the special elevators designated for blacks."

*Jeanette LeCaptain and La Maye, performing in "Ice Rodeo" at the Joseph E. Mears Benjamin Franklin Hotel.*

The Tom Harris family lived in Escanaba during the thirties and forties. Tom, a black man, worked at Walker's barber shop where he cleaned, swept up hair and shined shoes. In fact "Big" Bill Bonifas would send five pair of shoes at a time to get shined.

Tom was embraced by the community. Discrimination was unheard of. This was a man loved by all who knew him. He often put up black porters overnight who came in on the train. His son, Tom, graduated from St. Joe High School in the mid-forties. I understand Tom Sr. had one of the largest funerals ever held at St. Joseph's church.

The times also dictated strict conservative standards. "Dallas was a fun place," reminisced Jeanette. "There were always famous people in the audience. One night Errol Fynn, a famous movie star in the forties, was sitting at a table with several men friends. We were all excited because a huge floral bouquet was delivered to our dressing room with an invitation to join their table."

"We were told, 'if any of you go to that table you are fired!' We got the message." A few days later one of the youngest girls in the troop was fired. "When we questioned why," explained Jeanette, "the answer was, 'you don't wear Christian Dior dresses on a line girl's salary.' Later we heard she was spending her spare time at the Baker Hotel across from the Adolphus where we were performing." Sounds like the pay was better in her secret line of work?

Yet, think of the irony of the times: Everybody smoked including the young girls in the ice show. Smoking was considered fashionable in the forties. The health repercussions of smoking were virtually unknown. "In Dallas things were very loose; the hotel employed scantily dressed 'cigarette girls' to sell cigarettes," recalls Jeanette. Photos were taken of patrons holding their cigarettes as a prop that signified sophistication, class and in-the-groove.

I remember the 'cigarette girls' in the movies during the forties. They were dressed like the "Playboy Bunnies" of today: A sharp contrast to the prude thinking of the times when divorce was frowned upon and babies' out-of-wedlock was considered shameful and disgraceful.

Jeanette met her husband Lyle, who was in service at the time, in Dallas. They fell madly in love and weeks later they were married. The plan was to return to Lyle's Midwest Wisconsin roots and begin their married life.

Jeanette scoured the skating trade magazines for a job. George Grenholm, Escanaba's recreation director at the time, had placed an ad for a director of ice shows. Jeanette applied, was hired and the rest is history. Escanaba would become known as the "biggest small town ice revue in the world" under the direction of Jeanette LeCaptain.

Today Jeanette at age 83 is still active in her dance studio, costume making and designing. There is no question she has made a great contribution to our community's history while touching thousands of lives since her arrival in 1946.

## 1939 ESKYMOS UNDEFEATED AND UN-SCORED UPON
### Friday, November 7, 2008

If you have never heard of Ray "Boxcar" or "Pants" Pepin, you're in for a treat. He's a colorful character and was a member of the 1939 Eskymo football team that blew away all records before and since that year. The 1939 Eskymos were not only undefeated but also un-scored upon; an astounding feat that has never been duplicated and perhaps never will.

In August I was at the athletic field viewing the extensive renovations that occurred as a result of a brainchild and dream that took years to reach fruition. Some key players were Rusty Bluse, Fan Club President, Gary Seehafer, Jim and Linda Beauchamp, Tom Nault and Carl Eastman. That's where I first became aware of "Boxcar."

A member of the Jim Davidson family approached me and suggested a column about the '39 team that racked up an almost mythical season. "There are only a couple of members living," she said. "You could contact "Boxcar." Boxcar? Just the name conjures up an image.

I did just that last week. However, "Boxcar" explained he was

*Raymond "Boxcar" Pepin.*

having surgery in Marquette the next day, "so call me back in about three days." Wow! Eighty-eight years old, with health problems galore; yet he was eager to sit down and reminisce about the glory days of his high school football career.

He sat in a huge chair still hurting from the surgery. Out came his scrap books that were meticulously maintained: They documented the feats of his team more than seventy years ago. "Boxcar" is jovial, friendly and uninhibited. Right away I knew I was in for a delightful afternoon and he didn't disappoint me. His wife Corky sat near-by beaming with pride and eager to listen again to stories that she probably heard ten-fold over the years— some perhaps not printable!

There are only two guys still living from the starting line up: Roy Cress, who lives in Scottsdale, Arizona and Ray "Boxcar" Pepin.

I was curious about the names of "pants" and "boxcar." Ray said, "Everyone had a uniform but me in Junior High. I was big and there weren't any football pants that fit me. Two pair of pants was made into one by a tailor and from then on team mates called me "pants." The name "Boxcar" was coined by Coach George Ruwitch in high school. They both stuck!"

"Carl Nordberg was the coach my first two years in high school.

When he left for Saginaw assistant coach Ruwitch took over." The indomitable 1939 team was Ruwitch's first as head coach. History was in the making.

He inherited a team of players that were athletically gifted. What's the probability of a coach topping not only a season that boasted being undefeated, but un-scored upon? Not possible! Ruwitch did follow up with two more UP Championships before their winning streak of 25 straight games was broken in a heart-breaking loss to Marinette in 1941.

Ray reminisces, "I vividly remember when we played Stambaugh. Friday evening I had tipped a few beers. I was sicker than a dog the next day. Still in bed nursing a 'hang-over' a knock came at the door. My mother answered. It was Coach Ruwitch and the bus with the players was parked out side. 'Ray is sick in bed,' my mother told Ruwitch. 'Can I go in the bedroom and see him?' said Ruwitch. Ruwitch entered the bedroom and demanded 'get you're a— out of bed and get on the bus!'" Ray complied.

"I was getting sicker and sicker on the bumpy road to Iron Mountain. George stopped the bus at a corner drug store got a Bromo Seltzer and said, 'Here drink this!' It was a tough game but we won 6-0. I tackled one guy, fell on him and broke his jaw. I felt bad about that. Ruwitch said after the game, 'Boxcar that was the best d—- game you ever played!'"

Ray "Boxcar" Pepin was voted All-UP and All-State (first team) in his senior year. Later he played semi-pro with the Manistique Marines and the Kenosha All-stars. Merle Pfotenhauer made second team All-State and Bob Barron garnered Honorable mention.

I contacted Roy Cress, the only other living member of the starting line-up, who lives in Scottsdale, Arizona. He eagerly reminisced about his participation in athletics at Escanaba High School; in particular his memories of the '39 football team.

His most vivid recollection is, "no team ever moved the ball beyond the Escanaba 40 yard line." That in itself is another remarkable achievement. On a personal note he recalled scoring three touchdowns in the game against Menominee. Roy said, "Coach Nordberg was young and an athlete himself having played football at MSU. He would occasionally don a uniform and practice with us."

Pepin entered the Navy in 1942. Stationed on the island of Maui in the Hawaiian Islands, "Boxcar" had a dream job. He was on shore patrol and transported girls (Hula dancers) to different camps to perform.

Ray remembers one occasion when they transported the girls to a base where 50,000 Marines were ready to ship out. "As I went through the gate in a bus," relates Pepin, "I was asked where I was from.' 'Escanaba!' repeated the gate guard. 'We got two other guys here from Escanaba.' "He got on his walkie-talkie and dredged up George Shomin and John Peltier. We got together and let me tell ya we did more than just talk—we hoisted a few Old Premo beers."

Most of the '39 team served in the Armed Forces during World War 11. Tom Brokaw, author of the *Greatest Generation,* would have had some really interesting stories had he interviewed our hometown Escanaba guys. Roy Cress served with the Army in France.

Two of the most impressionable times in the lives of these men were; their high school athletic careers and their war experiences. Now they are dying off at the rate of 1000 a day and with them the memories that defined what has been called The Greatest Generation.

## A PRESIDENT FOR ALL THE PEOPLE
### Friday, November 14, 2008

Finally after 20 months of hard-fought campaigns by presidential candidates—it's over! Most of us sighed with relief at the end. The debates, the polls, the speeches, the conventions, the pundits, the negativity, the lies; we're all just sick of it.

With the election behind us and serious issues ahead of us, most of the country now seems to be getting behind new President-elect Obama, including those who did not vote for him. Even Republican California Governor Schwartzeneger, who just several days ago stumped for McCain, said over the weekend that he is prepared to do what he can to support America's new President and commented that last weeks election makes him "proud to be an American."

Of course, Republican Schwartzeneger is married to Democrat Maria Shriver, niece to former President John Kennedy. One can only imagine the spirited discussions in that household.

No doubt, many have experienced healthy (or maybe not so healthy) political discussions within their own household this election season. How did the election results affect our family? Well, first consider this: My husband is a die-hard Republican. I, on the other hand, consider myself a kaleidoscope of sorts: A Democrat in youth turned Republican as an adult turned Independent in later life.

A different sort of transformation occurred with my youngest son Jeff. Although he now holds a non-partisan attorney position at the U. S. Treasury Department, he began his career on Capitol Hill working for three Republicans. He also worked for Republican presidential candidates, including Reagan-Bush.

However, after some years of introspection, he shed his conservative leanings and became an Independent. But with this most recent election, he continues to evolve, now leans Democratic, and was a very enthusiastic supporter of Obama. He also had the good fortune to be at the Democratic Convention in Denver to witness Obama accept his party's nomination.

Here is a quip by Winton Churchill: "If you're not liberal at 20, you have no heart, and if you're not conservative at 40, you have no brains." It may be true for some as we are all shaped by our unique experiences, but it certainly is a great over simplification. Certainly neither Republicans nor Democrats have a monopoly on heart or brains.

Unique experiences do mold us. For example, as a child born at the time this country was still paralyzed by the Great Depression, I grew up thinking everyone was Democrat; you just adopt your parent's leanings. People were hurting, jobs were non-existent, food was scarce and President Franklin Roosevelt was the lifeline for hundreds of thousands. He implemented the Public Works program (WPA) that helped to dig our country out of dire circumstances. My Dad worked for the WPA.

By contrast, though we are from the same era, my husband's experience was totally different. His father was a staunch Republican and fortunate to have steady work as an Escanaba city employee during the Depression. Their family never experienced going without like so many families did. Gary naturally adopted his father's leanings—and, wow has it stuck!

I just wanted to set the stage as to our differing political evolutions and more importantly, how we all feel now about our new President-elect Barack Obama. My Republican-turned-Democrat son's sentiments were sent in an e-mail.

"I just have to say that Obama makes me feel good and hopeful as an American...just as much as Reagan did. I have supreme confidence in Obama's intellect, sincerity, and talents. We've dug a deep hole in this country on both the economic and foreign policy/defense fronts. There's no magic cure to either, and some mistakes no doubt will continue to be made, but I am now confident we are headed in the right direction as a nation.

"On a historic note, it truly makes me proud to see that an enormously talented African American (well at least half black, or as Obama said in his first post-election news conference today, 'a mutt') has been elected some 145 years after Lincoln freed the slaves.

"Obama as a role model as well as the symbolism of a black man as President of these United States (and a black family in the White House) will have enormous positive influence on issues of race in this country in so many ways in the years to come.

"It is truly amazing that many people in America have been able to witness—within their own lifetime—both institutional discrimination (e.g., whites-only drinking fountains, etc.) and then, only several decades later, the election of a black U.S. President.

"I am also very pleased that Virginia (Jeff lives in Alexandria), which was the seat of southern Confederate government during the Civil War, helped to place Obama in the White House. Abraham Lincoln is smiling—and I dare say that even Robert E. Lee is looking upon us with admiration."

I can't match Jeff's eloquence but "ditto"—I do share his

sentiments.

Not so much the case for my husband! Of course he wasn't enthralled with McCain either so he voted for himself (as a write-in) in protest. He went so far as to have cards made up and developed a 'tongue-in-cheek platform.

He must perceive me as gloating, although that is not the case, so he continuously reminds me that 48 million people did NOT vote for Obama. I do see signs of him softening when he says, "He is MY president now and I want him to succeed." Still, he continues to vacillate back and forth as he tries to convince himself its okay!

Picking up on what my husband said about the 48 million Americans that did not vote for Obama. That is, of course, not inconsistent with what has become the short-hand of American presidential elections. Approximately 40 percent of us vote Republican and 40 percent vote Democrat based roughly on party allegiance and political philosophy.

The real decision will likely continue to be made by the other 20 percent in the middle—moderates, independents, and those with loose party affiliation. And the decision of the 20 percent often seems to be made largely on the basis of which individual is: 1) perceived to be more up to the task of addressing whatever the hot-button issues are; and 2) whoever is, on an individual basis, more dynamic, likeable, and presidential.

Apparently, America has decided that Obama won out in these categories.

## 1908: Life 100 YEARS AGO
## Friday, November 28, 2008

In just a few months the Daily Press will celebrate its 100th birthday bash. The changes in 100 years, of course, are astronomical. What a difference a century makes! For the many young folks that will find it difficult to believe that life 100 years ago was really *that* archaic—this column is for you. And for most of you (including me) that have lived through the many changes, some good and some not so good, you can say, "Yes! That's the way it was!"

Marilyn Molin Olson (Florida) sent me some interesting facts and statistics from the year 1908:

The average life expectancy was 47 years.

The average wage in 1908 was 22 cents an hour. The average worker made between $200 and $400 a year.

There were only 8000 cars and only 144 miles of paved roads.

Only 8 percent of the homes had telephones.

Only 14 percent of the homes had bathtubs.

Only 6 percent of all Americans had graduated from high school.

Two out of every 10 adults couldn't read or write.

More than 95 percent of all births took place at home.

The population of Las Vegas was only 30.

There was no Mother's Day or Father's Day.

Five leading causes of death were: 1) Pneumonia and influenza 2) Tuberculosis 3) Diarrhea 4) Heart disease 5) Stoke.

Ninety percent of all doctors had NO COLLEGE EDUCATION. Instead, they attended so-called medical schools, many of which were condemned in the press and the government as 'substandard.'

Marijuana, heroin and morphine were all available over the counter at local corner drugstores. Back then pharmacists said, "Heroin clears the complexion, gives buoyancy to the mind, regulates the stomach and bowels, and is, in fact, a perfect guardian of health.

Al Lord (Escanaba) sent me some observations for those born from 1925-1975.

Dedicated to all the kids that survived the 1930's, 40's, 50's and 60's.

First, we survived being born to mothers who smoked and drank while they were pregnant.

Then we were put to sleep on our tummies in baby cribs covered with bright colored lead-based paints.

We had no childproof lids on medicine bottles, doors or cabinets and when we road our bikes, we had no helmets, not to mention the risks we took hitchhiking.

As infants and children, we would ride in the cars with no car seats, booster seats, seat belts or air bags.

We drank water from a garden hose and not from a bottle. We shared one soft drink with four friends, from one bottle and no one actually died from this.

We ate cupcakes, white bread with real butter and drank Kool-aid made with sugar, but we weren't overweight because, WE WERE ALWAYS OUTSIDE PLAYING!

We would leave home in the morning and play all day, as long as we were back when the streetlights came on. No one was able to reach us all day and we were OK. And nobody worried about us.

We did not have Play stations, Nintendo's, X-boxes, no video games at all, no 150 channels on cable, no video movies or DVD's, no surround sound or CD's, no cell phones, no personal computer, no Internet or chat rooms—We had friends and we went outside and found them.

We rode bikes or walked to a friend's house and knocked on the door or rang the bell, or just walked in and talked to them.

We would spend hours building our go-carts out of scraps and then ride down the hill, only to find out we forgot the brakes. After running into the bushes a few times, we learned to solve the problem.

We fell out of trees, got cut, broke bones and teeth and there were no lawsuits from these accidents.

Little League had tryouts and not everyone made the team. Those who didn't had to learn to deal with disappointment. Imagine that!

The idea of a parent bailing us out if we broke the law was unheard of. They actually sided with the law!

These generations have produced some of the best risk takers, problem solvers and inventers ever!

The past 50 years have been an explosion of innovation and new ideas. We had freedom, failure, success and responsibility, and we learned how to deal with it all! We had the good luck to grow up as kids, before the lawyers and the government regulated so much of our lives—and get this—for our own good.

## GEORGE RUSCH: THE REAL DEAL!
## Or... MAN OF DISTINCTION
## Friday, December 5, 2008

George Rusch, at age 83, is a unique and remarkable person. George was the first person to respond when plans to implement the Bonifas Mausoleum Restoration Project was conceived in this column. He has always been civic minded. I remember him as Mayor of Escanaba in the 60's but it is through our work as committee members on the Bonifas Project that I really came to know him.

One day I received a call from Lori Rose at the Historical Society: "Patt, just a suggestion. George Rusch has had an interesting life and would be a great subject for a column." Of course!

George is a dedicated individual with a boundless amount of energy. He works out at the Y several times a week and can be found most mornings having coffee at Rosie's where the "guys" work on solving the problems of the world. And I would venture to guess there's a bit of local color 'talk' and spirited conversation mixed in to stir the pot.

"Where are you from George?" I asked. He shocked me with

VOTE FOR THIS — VOTE FOR THIS
GEORGE RUSCH OR GEORGE RUSCH
But VOTE FOR
GEO. W. RUSCH for CITY COUNCIL

his answer: "Nowhere!" He went on to explain he was born in Chicago but his family moved every three years with his Dad's employment. He graduated from Christian Brothers Academy in Albany, NY garnering honors as an outstanding football player.

Fate so often alters the course of one's life. So it was with George. He joined the Marines right out of high school in 1943. WW11 was front and center. "I was assigned to radio school right out of boot camp," says George. "I flunked out! I had orders to ship out to the Islands." While packing his bag to leave he was informed the CO wanted to see him.

George, a kid of 18, stood at attention while literally shaking in his boots. 'Well, do you want to go to school or not?' said his CO. George answered, "Well, ah-yes sir!" 'Then get the H— out of here,' his CO replied. George's voice cracked with emotion as he pointed upward and told me, "God intervened!"

"After finishing Aviation Machinists School I became aware of an opportunity to be considered for V-12 Program (Marine Officer training). I applied and was fortunate enough to be selected."

The quota was one out of 5000. George was that special 'one' selected. He was allowed to pick a college of his choice for Officer Training. "I picked Dartmouth, just 150 miles from my home. His path in life had been forever altered.

*George and Susan Rusch.*

George eventually graduated from Dartmouth where football dominated his college years. George, a stand-out end in every respect, was voted by Notre Dame Gridsters to their all-opponents team. George also had the distinction of being named Honorable Mention All-American and was invited to try out for the Green Bay Packers and Cleveland Rams.

In a lighter moment George related hitch-hiking in to New York City with a friend right after high school graduation. "We didn't have any money, but wanted to see a ballgame." The two young naive kids went to the ball game then decided they would attempt to see Tommy Dorsey who was playing at the Palace during the era of "big bands."

Apparently the door man was remembering his own youth: He had the kids stand back and wait till he had a moment, and then motioned them to follow him—to a ring side seat, no less! George said, "The music was great. Then some skinny ding-a-ling guy started singing. We were blindsided with girls screaming and fainting in the aisles. We couldn't figure out what was going on. Guess what—the ding-a-ling was Frank Sinatra."

In 1954 George would come to the remote UP. Escanaba, the town he had never heard of before, was destined to become near and dear to his heart. He went to work for Hoyler and Bauer as sales and personnel manager. Many will remember the Hoyler bread company and the famous Hoyler Tea Room right across from the Delft Theatre: the meeting place of the '30s and 40s youth.

George eventually purchased Cloverland Commercial College. Aside from his administration duties, George maintained an active involvement teaching a range of classes. Ironically, it was as a result of class interaction with the many GI's returning home from the Korean conflict that he got involved in politics.

The older Korean Vets urged George to run for a seat on city council. George told the guys, "Look, in order to run for city council a petition has to be signed by 50 residents and turned into the city clerk." George figured that would be the end of it; but the guys, determined, called his bluff and got the necessary signatures needed.

Two seats were open. George ran against incumbents Harland Yelland, an attorney and Ed Cox, who worked for the railroad. He came in third and lost. During the first year Harland Yelland succumbed to a heart attack. George was appointed to finish out the two-year term.

"While a newcomer on the council I remember asking questions maybe too far out of line or even talking too much," reminisces George. "Jacob Bink would kick me under the table! I had only been in town for five years at the time and didn't know many people." The emotional side of George again bubbled up as he recalled how Bink took him under his wing as a mentor and a friend.

He ran for a second 4-year term in 1960 and won. He ran again in 1964, received the high vote, was appointed mayor and served until 1968. During his tenure Harnischfeger came in with 2000 jobs, and natural gas was brought in. George also recalled the state office building, built with Bonifas dollars, was sold to the State of Michigan through the efforts of then city manager George Harvey.

Meanwhile an era came to an end. Cloverland College closed its doors in 1961. A new era was ushered in when Bay College began operations in the old high school.

George had an uncanny ability to recognize a community need and seize upon an opportunity. To that end he continued to unleash his talents by establishing CUPPAD. As executive director in Escanaba; he also organized regional planning commissions in Houghton and the Sault.

In 1976 George moved to Lansing, working for Dominic Jacobetti a short time, eventually retiring as a fiscal analyst from the House Fiscal Agency in 1987.

George's relentless drive and energy continues to keep him involved in civic projects. George's many friends and acquaintances throughout the years will agree that he wears his heart on his sleeve and is passionate about life, family, religion, Escanaba, politics and loves interaction with people—including spirited conversations. Retirement really isn't in his vocabulary.

❦

## STEM CELL ETHICAL CONTROVERSY
### Friday, December 12, 2008

I didn't think it would pass! I am referring to the November election referendum to approve legalizing embryonic stem cell research in Michigan. But it did! Bill Clinton called the measure, "pro-life, pro-health, pro-science and definitely pro-Michigan."

I have followed the national stem cell controversy for years. Efforts by congress to override President Bush's restrictions on federal funding for embryonic stem cell research have fallen short. Granted, I do have an extremely personal interest regarding the hot-button issue of using federal funds for embryonic stem cell research.

Remember, under President George W. Bush federal money for research on human embryonic stem cells was limited to those stem cell lines that were created before August 9, 2001. No federal dollars could be utilized on research with cell lines from embryos destroyed from that day forward. However, federal regulations do not restrict embryonic stem cell research using state or private funds.

President-elect Obama made it quite clear during the campaign that he would overturn Bush's directive. He said, "As President I will lift the current administration's ban on federal funding and ensure that all research on stem cells is conducted ethically and with rigorous oversight." John McCain also indicated he would allow research to resume.

Although I am pro-life, I have sided with proponents and advocates like the late Christopher Reeves and Michael J. Fox to overturn the Bush directive on stem cell research. My reasons are of a personal nature just like Reeves and Fox. Reeves had hoped research would eventually find a cure for spinal cord injuries; not only for him but for the millions of people paralyzed by their injury. Fox, likewise, hopes for the same: A cure for him and the hundreds of thousands afflicted with Parkinson's disease.

My hope is that one day the mysteries of brain-damage will be unlocked and cured with the use of embryonic stem cells. Not only for my son and the millions of people whose lives have been reduced to an unproductive shell of a person in need of 24/7 care; but also the families that care for them.

A quote from my book, *Brain Injury: A Family tragedy:* "While medical technology may have saved my son's life, he is left with the maladies of a severe brain-injury for which medical or rehabilitative treatment has, thus far, proven largely ineffective. More than two million individuals sustain brain injury each year of which 100,000 are left with permanent, severe and multiple impairments requiring long-term care and support." Sadly, today, over 20 percent of our troops in Iraq are coming home with brain-injuries.

In the last six months my son has been hospitalized twice: In the spring with surgery for a broken hip and a few weeks ago he almost died with a bladder infection that evolved into septic shock. I relate this because out of those two tragedies hope was renewed. Of course, the yellow brick road in the *Wizard of Oz* is mythical, but maybe there is a pot of gold at the end of the rainbow.

During both hospitalizations, Gary 'came back.' It sounds impossible, but it happened, not once but twice. He reverted to his normal self, normal intelligent conversation, using big words, acutely aware and tearfully thanking us for caring for him all of these years. He claimed he finally 'woke up.' He talked about getting a job, hopefully getting married and having a normal life again. My husband couldn't stop the tears flowing from joy and exclaimed, "Gary has come home to us!"

It wasn't to last though. Exhausted from talking non-stop after a day and night each time he fell into a deep sleep. When he awoke twelve hours later the 'old Gary' was again lost in the abyss of amnesia, unable to remember yesterday, incapable of anticipating tomorrow.

We lost him again—just like in the movie, *Awakenings,* when people with Parkinson's sprung to life only to eventually return to the world of the living dead. Gary "returned" to us for only a brief time and for that we are eternally grateful. Yet the tears flow when we think of losing Gary again, the essence of who he was. And even sadder is his personal loss of who he was—again.

Dr. Brown, a visiting physician (pulmonologist) from Milwaukee, attended to Gary at St. Francis Hospital. He took a special interest in Gary's case. He is a graduate of Princeton and had heard of such a phenomenon; however he was at a loss to explain it. Could those brain cells connect again—maybe permanently? Or was it divine intervention?

Gary's care at St. Francis was second to none. The nurses and staff displayed extremely good judgment in their appropriate interaction with Gary. Dr. Brown took the time to create grafts to explain Gary's recovery. During the past 20 years we have run the gamut of hospitals throughout the U.S. You can't know how impressed and pleased we were to know that the very best care is right here at home.

The doctors are puzzled and can't account for what happened. What I do know and have witnessed is that apparently connections did occur in the brain for a short time. I cling to the hope that someday stem cells will cure a host of afflictions like brain-injury, Alzheimer's, Parkinson's, diabetes and spinal-cord injury.

Stem cells are the building blocks that turn into different kind of tissue. Embryonic stem cells are blank slates, unlike the mature adult stem cells. If scientists could control them, directing regenerative therapy would be possible.

Dr. Chi Dang, professor of medicine at John Hopkins University School of Medicine, agrees there have been tremendous advances with adult stem cells. He also stated, "It is yet unclear if they have enough flexibility to be utilized in all the ways that an embryonic stem cell could be."

Harvesting stem cells from an embryo a few days old kills the embryo. This outrages opponents of this type of research. Consider this though: Hundreds of thousands of embryos being stored in fertility clinics will be destroyed anyway.

Dr. Chi Dang poses the question, "Is it ethically more acceptable to destroy these embryos by pouring acid on them, or do you deploy these clusters of cells to create new cell lines that could benefit us in the future?" Personally, I have reconciled this powerful ethical dilemma in my own mind.

## A LFETIME OF CHRISTMAS'
**Friday, December 19, 2008**

The excitement and anticipation of Christmas is almost too much to bear for young children awaiting Santa's visit. Each day must seem like a year in their young life. The crescendo grows with the Santa Claus Parade, putting up the Christmas tree with its twinkling lights, the smell of cookies baking; perhaps helping mom decorate them. Images of this season's popular toys on TV grab their attention and are placed on their wish list to Santa.

"Santa Claus is Coming to Town" is heard over and over while the poem, "The Night Before Christmas" tells it all —with the children all snuggled in their beds while visions of (Christmas morning) dance in their heads."

For the adults it is a time of rejoicing and celebrating with family and friends, Christmas parties, decorating the house, shopping and wrapping gifts, religious faith, and delicious food. Stir in the nostalgia and images of past Christmas'—the family traditions and the memories of grandparents. If you are sentimental you will remember the traditional songs of Christmas that warm your heart and tug at it at the same time.

"I'm Dreaming of a White Christmas" and "Have Yourself a Merry Little Christmas" come to mind. The fireplace burning, stockings hanging, children caroling and Christmas programs all add to the warm and fuzzy image of Christmas and the picture-perfect Norman Rockwell vision of happiness.

Bah! Humbug! Some will say. For some the holiday season is a time they would rather skip. For some it conjures up sad feelings of loneliness, obligations, stress and anxiety. And some feel the commercialism of the holiday season has robbed it of its true meaning, therefore taking any joy out of the season.

The name of this phenomenon is so wide-spread that mental-health professionals have tagged it with a name: the holiday syndrome; also known as "the holiday blues." Not everyone is privy to a Christmas that is portrayed in the movies—like, "It's a Wonderful life" or "Miracle on 34th Street".

The reasons for sadness and unhappiness at Christmas take on many forms: The ghost of a past Christmas in childhood could conjure up pain. The loss of a loved one during the holidays or the memories of Christmas' spent with a loved one who is no longer here. A divorce and remembering happier times or remembering abuse from a marriage gone wrong is another reason people are sad at Christmastime.

Christmastime is supposed to be a time when families get together for wonderful dinners and gift giving. At least that is the

Norman Rockwell picture-perfect holiday. When it falls short, the pressures to conform to some ideal of peace and goodwill to all can create guilt—especially true if you feel getting together with family members is really a charade: Or even worse if you are estranged from the family.

Then there are the folks in between, like me, that know about the ghosts of yesteryear Christmas' and also the Normal Rockwell kind of Christmas' I experienced raising a family. ˙

Some experiences when I was very young are too painful to even share. Yet, they are mixed with great memories too. I remember the excitement when the whole town turned out for the arrival of Santa at the coliseum; I remember the nostalgic Christmas show with the talented Ammel's singing and the Christmas song sing-a-long. I remember the huge bag of mixed candy we all received from Santa.

I remember being excited when the Salvation Army delivered a huge basket of goodies to our house in the 30's. I remember our stockings filled with an apple, an orange, a banana, some peanuts and candy. What a treat! I remember helping my mom decorate the tree with the silver tinsel and removing it carefully to save it for the next Christmas.

I remember downtown in the 30's and 40's: The Salvation Army bell-ringers on the corner of the Fair Store and their beautiful window displays. Santa held court in the Fair Store too. There was piped Christmas music and the streets dressed up in colorful lights while scores of people shopped for their treasures in downtown Escanaba. It was busy, bustling and full of excitement.

During my early marriage some years were meager. My husband was in the Air Force stationed at Wright Patterson Air Base. The year was 1951 with a baby due on Christmas Day and another one only 14 months old. We didn't have money for a turkey—come to think of it—I probably wouldn't have known how to cook it. I was barely 19. Instead we had spaghetti and two pumpkin pies. Yet we were happy. Our Christmas present and bundle of joy arrived on December 28: A five pound baby girl!

We had three children and probably my best Christmas' revolved around our little family growing up. I remember the church Christmas pageants the kids were in. Vicki was Mary and Gary was Joseph one year. We tried to shush our youngest,

four-year-old Jeff, during the pageant by telling him, "You have to be quiet. This is God's house." He stood up in the pew, looked all-around and with his arms outstretched exclaimed in a loud voice, "Well, if this is God's house—then where is he?" He brought the house down with laughter. We still talk about that evening 46 years later.

I made the traditional French meat pies my grandmother and mother always made. We had cookie night when I let the kids decorate cookies. Those were very good years. The presents under the tree included the figure skates I never had as a kid. Even better—now I skated with my kids.

The kids grew up and so did the family grow. The kids had children and their children had children. For years our house was where all generations congregated. The years are brimming with great memories and yes, lots of work, but I was up for it then.

Last Christmas 20 family members ascended upon us from D.C. to Milwaukee. We knew this would be our last huge family Christmas. We no longer can handle the kids screaming and running around the house, sticky hands and spilling, meals 24/7, suitcases and beds all-over; the normal stuff that didn't bother us before.

We've turned another page in our lifetime of Christmas'. Less work and stress, but I'm not so sure I like it. Instead of the outdoor decorations, the 10-foot perfectly color-coordinated Christmas tree and a home that permeates with aromas of cookies and meat pies baking; we have meals-on-wheels delivered, a small table tree and two little porch trees lit up outside. And no family visiting us this year.

So what's next? Christmas at the nursing home?

# DIET IN THE MIDST OF THE HOLIDAYS?
## Friday, December 26, 2008

I know! I know! Who wants to think of dieting the day after Christmas? But the showdown is closing in. I hate to play on your guilt as you chow down on delicious cookies, fruit cake, egg nog, Sayklly's candies, a Christmas toddy or two, and plates full of fancy hors d'oeuvres. But the 'reckon with" time is right around the corner.

I know! I have been there, done that—for nearly a lifetime. Two years ago I lost 22# and bought a whole new wardrobe for my size 6 to 8 back to normal body. What fun! I embarked on the path to skinny world the day after New Years. The kids and grandkids left for home after the holidays and I threw out what I didn't want to eat. That left nothing in my refrigerator. No temptations. I had devised a plan.

I had heard about the Slim-fast.com weekly weigh-in; although I didn't use Slim-fast. I recorded what my ultimate goal and weight should be for my 5' 2 inch small frame. I weighed daily and every week I recorded my weight on Slim-fast.com. A graft was displayed to show my progress with little encouragement notes. I was on a roll. Every Sunday when I weighed in I was one week closer to throwing out my fat clothes.

Amen! I was successful. I reached my goal in April. Summer was the best; sporting my new small clothes. Even my clothing style changed (more youthful) and the way I walk changed (sexier at 74?) My energy level soared.

I am guessing you want to know: Did I keep the pounds at bay? Gee, I would have liked to end my column on a great note and tell you, "I never gained back a pound!" However, I am not in that super-human category; less than two percent of the folks are successful at keeping the pounds off permanently.

That's why diet books and diet aids are a multi-million dollar industry. We keep looking for the magic bullet the easy way.

So two years later twelve of the pounds have mysteriously crept back into their comfort zones. Ladies, you know what I mean. The good news is I did manage to keep 10 pounds off for two years. I tell myself I am ahead of the game: I'm not back to the fat clothes.

I am into my in-between clothes. But oh how I yearn for my skinny duds!

Just so you don't feel guilty until you start your next ploy to streamline your body; I found some helpful diet tips on the internet to round out the holidays.

If no one sees you eat it, it has no calories.

If you drink a diet soda with a candy bar, they cancel each other out.

STRESSED is just DESSERTS spelled backwards.

If you eat the food off someone else's plate, it doesn't count.

Cookie pieces contain no calories because the process of breakage causes calorie leakage.

Food used for medicinal purposes have no calories. This includes and chocolate used for energy, brandy, cheesecake and Haagen-Dazs ice cream.

When eating with someone else, calories don't count if you both eat the same amount.

Movie-related foods are much lower in calories simply because they are a part of the entertainment experience and not part of one's personal fuel. This includes: Milk Duds, popcorn with butter, Junior Mints, Snickers, and Gummy Bears.

\*\*\*\*\*\*\*\*\*\*\*\*\*\*\*\*\*\*\*\*\*\*\*\*\*\*\*\*\*\*\*\*\*\*\*\*\*\*\*\*\*\*\*\*\*\*\*\*\*\*\*\*\*\*\*\*\*\*\*\*\*\*\*\*

On a serious note, my New Year's plan is to shave off the 12 pounds and get back into my skinny clothes—not only for appearance, but for health's sake. It isn't healthy to lose and gain, lose and gain, but what are we poor mortals to do?

One of the richest women in the world, Oprah, cannot control her weight. The talk show queen recently revealed she is over 200 pounds again. She has a personal trainer, and can afford dieticians to plan her meals. She has the means to do anything, go anywhere and yet, it is her weight that makes her unhappy.

Oprah declares in her January issue of "O" magazine, "I am mad at myself. I'm embarrassed. I can't believe that after all these years, all the things I know how to do, I am still talking about my weight."

Enjoy your indiscretions until the New Year holiday is over. If your New Year's resolution includes losing a few pounds (and whose doesn't) attack it in a positive manner. Record your progress on a graft and pat yourself on the back as the pounds melt off. You can do it. I did.  E-mail me and let me know your progress in the spring and I will tell the world.

Meanwhile, I wish you a Happy New Year filled with best wishes for good health and many blessings.

## HOLIDAY MEMORIES EVOKE JOY AND SADNESS
## Friday, January 2, 2009

I couldn't possibly let go of the holiday season without sharing a letter I received from Mrs. Ray (Naomi) Morin.  And the thoughts of recent widows experiencing their first Christmas season without their beloved spouses reflected in me a melancholy I couldn't explain.  I just had to share some of those thoughts.

The Morin's owned a Ma and Pa grocery store (Ray's Market) in Rapid River for years.

She writes, "We have never met but I feel like I know you personally after reading your weekly column in the Daily Press. Your last column (Dec. 19th) brought to mind similar memories.

"We too survived the 'Great Depression.' We were married in 1948 after Ray returned from the war in Europe.  We had two boys and seven years later our precious 7# baby girl was born December 11, 1958.  What a wonderful Christmas gift she was.  We will never forget that year with all the happiness and love.

"Now for the sad part of the story.  In 1984, (our daughter) Michele was diagnosed with Multiple Sclerosis."  Naomi told about how Michele graduated from Northern, loved teaching, married and had two beautiful children, a daughter and a son. But the years took a toll on her.

Naomi and Ray moved to Green Bay to help the family for many years. Michele became totally disabled.  "Michele's positive attitude somehow got us through eight more years," wrote Naomi. "She was such an inspiration to so many people.  In 2000 she finally succumbed to the disease.  Our hearts are still heavy."

"Your last question (column Dec. 19th), so what's next? Christmas at the nursing home?, prompted me to write to you. (My husband) Ray has Parkinson's disease and has been at Bishop Noa for four years.  He is cognizant and he is still my "Ray." This has become our "home" now.  I am able to spend every day with him.  That's where we are now, hardly what we expected or wanted, but we are not in charge of our lives so (we) go on each day loving each other and praying for strength  to accept the inevitable...."

Naomi's letter prompted me to call her.  She reminisced about their youth; her husband going to the coliseum to see Santa and receiving the huge bag of candy.  She lived in Harris and remembered Santa coming through on the train with all the kids waiting to see him.  The train didn't even stop, but Santa stood on an outside platform and threw out buttons from the moving train. The kids scrambled to get a button.  They read, 'Meet me at the Fair Store.'  They proudly wore the buttons on their coats long after Christmas.

Naomi's story is a slice of life.  She reflected on memories of her youth and she is handling the adversities in her life with grace, acceptance and faith.

BETTY GOULAIS lost her husband Don in August.  Don had been at the nursing home for over two years.  This is her first Christmas without her beloved Don; her husband of almost 59 years.  Most will remember Don as the state Assistant Attorney General.

"I felt all alone throughout the holidays," relates Betty, "even though family and friends were all around me.  Christmastime is family time and still I had that lost feeling because he wasn't beside me.  Sentimental songs like White Christmas bring tears to my eyes."

"Even now, everyday at 11:45 a.m. and 4:30 p.m. I am reminded that Don would be in the dining room at the nursing home waiting for me to visit.  I brought cross-word puzzles and we worked them together.  If I was a few minutes late he would call and say, 'are you coming?'  Thinking of it causes misty eyes."

"I gave Don a Christmas ornament years ago; it was a little

golfer in a golf cart. So when the Mausoleum (where Don is laid to rest) called and asked if I would like to bring an ornament for their tree I immediately thought of the golfer with special meaning. When I went out there later and eyed the ornament on the tree I almost lost it! Although it was comforting to see something that represents him, I will be glad to see the holidays end. I have been swamped with feelings that are just too painful."

ANGIE HIXSON'S husband Vern was only in the nursing home for a few months. He died the end of November. She says, "After 60 years with your mate it is an almost impossible task to see them suffer so and to say goodbye. He is still here everywhere I turn, everywhere I look, and every song I listen to reminds me of him and when we danced together.

"I miss him, mourn him and cry for him and remember all the good times. Sometimes I see someone on the street and from the back the person resembles Vern or I see someone with blonde hair and blue eyes and they remind me of him. He is really still here with me and always will be.

"People tell me that the first Christmas without him will be the most difficult. They say as the years pass it gets easier. My children do bring me much comfort and I am fortunate that two of them live close by. But still—I miss him!"

I couldn't end this holiday-themed column without mentioning some caring people in our community. NINA JOHNSON has touched countless lives of friends; some in nursing homes, some in the hospital and others who are at home under the weather, with her signature home-made rice pudding. She is well-known for her pudding and her caring nature. At Christmas time she brought us a delicious home-made blueberry pie.

She is what the Christmas spirit is all about and a throw-back to generations long ago when gifts at Christmas consisted of home-made mittens, a scarf, a dish of home-made cookies or a meat pie.

CHARLENE CARLSON, who visits us from St. Annes church, brought us some of her home-made cookies. Betty Goulais baked us an angel food cake. And our neighbors, NICKY AND MIKE WANGRUD, are so caring. Mike clears our drive and walks of snow and Nicky sent over her home-made spaghetti sauce.

I met my cousin, BETTY KELDSEN, for a luncheon just before Christmas.  She brought me a plate of her delicious cookies that she and her daughter, Jo-Annette made.  My gift to her will be an old time photo of our maternal grandparent's wedding in sepia tones with dates and history attached. Meaningful gifts you can't buy.  I love to give my home-made raspberry and strawberry jams (I picked the berries) to the caregivers that help us everyday with our son.

Somewhere along the way we lost that sincere innocence of giving of one's self.  In exchange we have adopted a frenzy of Christmas shopping that literally drives us all crazy.

## A CREED TO LIVE BY
**Friday, January 9, 2009**

Hanging from her neck, near and dear to her heart, was a medal inscribed with the Serenity Prayer: "God grant me the Serenity to accept the things I cannot change, the Courage to change the things I can, and the Wisdom to know the difference." It's the creed Amy lives by.

Amy Chenier, a special-education teacher at Gladstone Middle School was diagnosed with an inoperable brain tumor in 2005. Slightly more than one year earlier Amy had been diagnosed with thyroid cancer and underwent a complete throidectomy at Mayo Clinic.  "Finding out that I had an inoperable brain tumor and needed to go back to Mayo Clinic, this time for six weeks of radiation, was very difficult." said Amy.

Amy's mother, Nancy and her sister, Angela accompanied her during the treatment.  Nancy related how people all over the country offered prayers for Amy.  Even people in other countries were praying for her.

Amy's students wrote her letters of encouragement while she was undergoing treatment at Mayo Clinic.  One of Amy's middle school students wrote: "Someday I hope to have your patience and strength to make it through hard times…You have taught me how

to take care of my body, mind and spirit ...I am never going to forget the way you helped me through hard times and what you said to make me feel better about myself. I am never going to forget you. I hope you will come to my graduation and wedding."

As I read the letters of encouragement the students wrote to Amy it brought home what a powerful and responsible task teachers have; helping to mold a child and knowing that they can make a difference.

Amy's desire to become a teacher became known early on. In Kindergarten, the teacher asked the students what they wanted to be when they grew up. Amy took the microphone and proudly announced, "I want to be a teacher or a nun."

At Mayo Clinic, a mask of plastic was made for Amy's face to keep her head firm. She lay on her stomach while ten radiation beams were shot at cross-angles every day for six weeks. The tumor was flat but about 3 by 6 inches long. It filled one side of the brain and started to encroach over the midline-section to the other side. Treatment would shrink the tumor but never eradicate it.

Amy spent the first two weeks in a hotel. "I was bored and the days were long." she commented. Amy was on a waiting list to stay at Hope Lodge.

Finally Amy's name came to the top of the list. "Hope Lodge," she said, "is the equivalent for adults what Ronald McDonald is for children. The support system I developed, friends I made, fun I had and the festivities I participated in made my stay at Hope Lodge wonderful."

A highlight for Amy was meeting the mayor when she spoke at a kick-off event to raise awareness for the need to expand the American Cancer Society Hope Lodge in Rochester. The mayor later wrote to Amy, "What a joy and inspiration you are for many!"

After Amy's cancer treatment for her thyroid, the Chenier family would visit Rome where Amy's brother was a seminarian at the time. Together they visited the Vatican and attended Midnight Mass to witness Pope John Paul 11 celebrate the mass. Just before Amy embarked on her journey with her family, she swallowed a radio-active pill destined to eradicate any cancer cells that were left. It worked!

Now slightly over a year later (after radiation treatment for her brain tumor) Amy asked Dr. LaChance what she could do to get better faster, "He looked at me and said," 'Amy, be social.' "I must have looked at him quizzically, because then he added," 'Be social. Wake up in the morning and be grateful you have another beautiful day to enjoy. Get out there and live, be with people, and don't sweat the small stuff because it really is just small stuff. Go on with your life, find a guy and get married.'"

Amy did just that! She went home to Gladstone, resumed teaching 'her kids' at Gladstone Middle School and decided to buy a house. In the process of purchasing carpeting for her new home she met Todd Kositzke, an employee, at Heynssens-Selins. A romance blossomed. A relationship grew. And just this past November Todd and Amy were married.

Amy's brother, Michael, now a Deacon performed the ceremony—his first as a Deacon. During the Mass Homily Michael said, "Well, Amy your ambition to become a teacher was met." Then with a twinkle in his eye he looked at Todd, said "but

I guess becoming a nun won't be part of the plan!"

Amy has an MRI every three months to ascertain whether the brain tumor is staying static or growing. In June the test showed a slight increase in size. The doctor pensively said, "Amy, the tumor is growing." Up till then it had continued to shrink. "Do you want to wait a few months or hit it hard now?" "Hit it hard now!" Amy replied. Recent tests show it beginning to shrink again.

"My family has been so supportive," says Amy. Her father, Frank, is a retired geologist and her mother, Nancy, is an accountant at the U.P. State Credit Union. Many local people, including me, know them by the raspberry farm they established more than 22 years ago.

Their kids were raised spending the summers helping with the raspberry business. "It was great," says Amy. "We were able to focus on our studies during the school year. In the summer we worked in our family business and besides earning money learned so much about business and interacting with people."

Her sisters, Angela and Michelle are also college graduates while brother, Michael, is poised to become an ordained priest in June.

Amy has a perpetual smile that lights up the room along with an effervescing personality. She credits her survival to her support system of family and friends, faith, positive attitude, the power of prayer; yet is ever mindful of the role played by today's advancements in technology.

One of Amy's students asked her one day why she is usually so calm and happy. "I had to stop a minute and think," said Amy. "It reminded me of the famous quote," 'Life is 10% what happens to you and 90% how you choose to react to it.' "I'm glad I've chosen to be positive and make the most of it. Yet, there are still days, of course, when it is a struggle to keep that decision."

Amy wrote the following powerful poem:

*Reflecting...*

*Laying here relaxing*
*Not a worry in the world*
*That I'm not strong enough to make it through*

*Having faith that everything really will be okay*

*Waking up in the morning*
*Asking myself, "Who can I help smile today?*
*And make their burden easier to bear?!*

*Believing that everything happens for a reason*
*This can only make me stronger*
*To be the type of person who others are happy to know*

Amy Chenier
28 years old
Thyroid Cancer Survivor and Brain Tumor

Dear Patt,

Thank you so much for taking the time to write the inspiring article. I had no idea how many people it would bring encouragement to until I was approached by so many. Even Todd & our parents are still receiving positive responses to the article. It has helped me to further appreciate each day. Thank you for telling my story.

Sincerely,
Amy Chenier-Kositzke

## AMY AND THE MIRACLE PRAYER
**November 2, 2012**

Amy Chenier at the age of 27 was diagnosed with an inoperable brain tumor in November 2004. After radiation treatment for her brain tumor Dr. LaChance at Mayo Clinic gave her this advice, "Amy, be social. Wake up in the morning and be grateful you have another beautiful day to enjoy. Get on with your life, find a guy and get married." She did just that. She met and married Todd Kositzke on November 29, 2008. They were blissfully happy.

"Never in my entire life had I known anyone with such inner beauty," says Todd. Her radiant smile drew people to her." We always had hope that a miracle would happen. We never accepted that she might die.

However, the tumor had begun to grow again. She began taking a more powerful drug called Temetor. Her mental attitude continued to be upbeat and her perpetual, radiant smile drew people to her like a magnet. Amy and Todd were in love and determined to live every day to the fullest.

They spent many hours in the Euchartistic Adoration Chapel at St. Francis Hospital hoping and praying for a miracle. People all over the world were praying for Amy. "We really believed that she would be healed," said Todd.

They decided to take a trip to Door County for the week-end. While there as they were preparing to retire Amy had a seizure. Again, her meds were increased and the seizures stopped.

Amy was never sad. She decided to go to a Catholic youth conference at Steubenville North to pray with the 3000 plus youth that attended. During the conference the priest leading the conference walked around the group with the Monstrance in his hands. As he surrounded the group of young people and prayed he came upon Amy. He stopped and placed his hands on the left side of her head-the side of her brain tumor. At that moment Amy saw Jesus in the Eucharist. The priest had never met Amy and was unaware of her brain tumor. Months before Amy had seen Jesus during Adoration at the OSF hospital chapel. Every time she went to the chapel she was beaming; she would see Jesus when she received the Eucharist and a glow would come over her.

The tumor was growing. Dr. LaChance informed Amy's husband, Todd, and her mom and dad of the grim news. Still there was hope. Amy's positive attitude allowed her to continue working as a Special Ed teacher at Gladstone Middle School.

Meanwhile the tumor continued to grow. Amy still could read and write until mid-November. Around the 18th of November Amy's mother picked her up from a continuing education class. Amy came out the class excited with her papers and exclaimed, "Look mom, I can do advanced Algebra— with my tumor!

That week-end Amy and Todd went to the Detroit Lions game to celebrate their first anniversary and to visit the Father Solanus Casey Center. During the trip Amy became very ill and thought she may have a touch of the flu. "It got scary on the way home," relates Todd. "Amy's brain had begun to swell." Amy's beautiful smile continued even as she arrived as the hospital ER in Escanaba. She entered the ER singing the Divine Mercy Prayer.

That episode marked the beginning of the end. On December 8th Amy went back to Mayo Clinic with Todd and her mother and dad. After attending Mass, which was the feast of the Immaculate Conception, she became very excited as she related seeing Jesus again in the Eucharist during the elevation at Mass. Dr. LaChance told Amy that she had one to three months to live. The tumor had grown and was encroaching her entire brain. Amy was all bubbly and happy and continued to smile. Dr. LaChance said, See, she doesn't understand what I am saying." Amy turned to him and said, "I know what you are saying— but why would I be sad when I know where I am going?"

When they came home Todd and Amy moved into her mom and dad's house. They would be moral support for one other while caring for Amy.

Amy began to lose strength as she faced her demise. She

continued to be fully aware and offered up the pain of her illness as redemptive suffering for the poor souls in Purgatory. "Amy and I talked about our love for one another and in event she didn't make it-our love wouldn't end here," said Todd between his tears. "Rather we would be together for eternity. The short two and a half years I had with Amy I didn't think I was capable of loving that much."

They laughed and played charades at times when Amy needed help with a word to be understood. Through all of this Amy's beautiful perpetual smile continued. She would stay up all night and didn't want to sleep because angels and saints were visiting her. She even was able to describe her Guardian Angel to her mom. On several occasions she would look upward and would go into a trance like state while being totally unaware of her surroundings for up to a minute or so. When she would come out of the trance, she would be very joyous and tell of seeing angels and name saints that she had seen. She lived off of the Miracle Prayer the last year of her life.

Todd related, "Each day your expectations of what is normal become less. You accept anything; it just happens."

The day before she died she was experiencing terrible headaches. Her last words to her mom were, "Mom, why am I suffering so much? I guess God wants to save a soul in Africa." The morphine no longer controlled the headaches. An ambulance took Amy to the hospital at 6:00pm.

Father Norden performed last rites. At 8:30pm Father Michael, her brother arrived and also administered last rites to Amy. On January 2, 2010 at 2:30 in the morning one month short of her 33rd birthday, Amy passed away. Her loving and devoted husband, Todd, was holding her in his arms when he felt her last breath.

"Amy never lived in fear; she lived off the grace of God. She trusted God implicitly," said Amy's mom, Nancy. Amy's parents, Nancy and Frank, are blessed with strong faith and courage and accepted God's will. But that doesn't make it any easier. They do take comfort in the fact that their beautiful daughter Amy will live on in the minds and hearts of her loved ones and the hundreds of people that were touched by her radiant smile, her goodness, her enduring faith, and her endless hope.

Her brother Fr. Michael Chenier concelebrated her funeral mass with 15 other priests and three deacons present. There was standing-room only in the church.

## The MIRACLE PRAYER:

Lord Jesus, I come before You just as I am. I am sorry for my sins. I repent of my sins. Please forgive me. In Your name, I forgive all others for what they have done against me. I renounce Satan, the evil spirits, and all their works. I give you my entire self, Lord Jesus, now and forever. I invite You into my life, Jesus. I accept You as my Lord, God, and Savior. Heal me, change me, and strengthen me in body, soul, and spirit.

Come Lord Jesus. Cover me with Your Precious Blood and fill me with Your Holy Spirit. I love You Lord Jesus. I praise You Jesus. I thank You, Jesus. I shall follow You every day of my life. Amen.

Mary, my Mother, Queen of Peace, St. Peregrine, the cancer saint, all you Angels and Saints, please help me. Amen.

✺

## CHILDREN SHOULD BE SEEN AND NOT HEARD
## Friday, January 16, 2009

Does the age-old adage, 'Children Should Be Seen and Not Heard,' bring back some bittersweet memories of childhood? According to an article in the New York Times that adage may be due for a comeback. American society may have reached a tolerance level for wild kid behavior.

I can't tell you how many times I heard that adage while growing up. A reader called me recently and said, "When I was a child and would hear adults talking; I yearned for the day I would grow up and be able to talk like them and with them".

I remember sitting on the stairs, hidden from view of course, trying to listen to what the adults were talking about. What was being said? Was it something magical or something sinister? Was I being mentioned? We learned early on that talking must be a privilege. One thing for sure; we learned discipline.

My husband visited his grandparents with his father weekly. He remembers sitting on a chair patiently while his father talked with his parents. They completely ignored him; no kind words, no questions, no cookie—nothing. He never would have dreamed of trying to talk. When they left there was no good-by, no kiss on the cheek, no pat on the back, nothing to show feelings. Every week was the same scenario.

Their harsh treatment was no doubt modeled by their parents in Norway where they were raised. And then—what an about turn in our society!

Today, only nine percent of adults were able to say that the children they saw in public were "respectful toward adults." In 2004, more than one in three teachers told Public Agenda pollsters they had seriously considered leaving their profession because of "intolerable" student behavior.

The rules changed and so have the kids. It was acceptable for teachers to use corporal punishment in our era. I think the consensus was; parents discipline at home and teachers were in control while children were in school.

Granted, some male teachers took advantage of their authority. Kids from our era could tell you a few horror stories; Hair pulling, slapping, grabbing kids by their collar, extreme physical discipline like the 'spanking machine' or shoving a kid against the lockers. I remember one teacher drawing a line on the blackboard and making a student hold his chin above the line the whole period.

In Junior High we were told the principal had a rubber hose and he would use it if you were sent to his office. Fact or fiction? I don't know? I do know that in today's society if these incidents occurred a law suit would probably be initiated.

"Nobody feels entitled to discipline other people's kids anymore. More than half said they ended up being soft on discipline because they can't count on parents or schools to support them" says Dan Kindlon, a Harvard University child psychologist.

He goes on to say, "Rude behavior, particularly toward adults, was something for which children had to be chastised, even punished. Most parents today would like their children to be polite, considerate and well behaved. But they are too tired, worn down by work and personal needs to take up the task of teaching them proper behavior at home."

Another conservative psychologist, John Rosemund, "denounced the increasing presence of 'disruptive urchins' who obviously have yet to be taught the basic rudiments of public behavior." He described a wretched experience he had in a four-star restaurant. "One child roller skating around his table while another watched a movie on a portable DVD player."

He says, "Parents are out of control. We always want to blame the kids, but if there is something wrong with their incivility, it's the way their parents model for them."

Some of my grandchildren interrupt their parent while talking to an adult. And the parents let them! I see so many things that are "quite different" from the way we were raised. Most times I bite my tongue rather than voice my opinion. For sure, my husband and I roll our eyes and mull over in private "the difference" in kids today.

Clark Gable's famous line, "Frankly, I don't give a d—-," was censored in Gone with the Wind. Today, "p—-ed off" is even common use on TV. Girls are as bad as boys. That offensive language is accepted today. The F word is common place. I experienced a young man giving me the finger when I apparently did some minor thing wrong while driving. That disgusting behavior wouldn't have happened in our era.

The threat of a spanking was common place when I was a kid; sometimes we even earned one. Was it fear of discipline that helped us to respect adults? I dare say talking back or being sassy to an adult was nearly unheard of. There were consequences.

I don't agree totally with the concept that, Children Should be Seen and Not Heard. Children are little people. There are times like a trip to Disneyland or a children's birthday party where screaming in delight, climbing, singing and things kids do may be acceptable. By the same token there are times where children are not the *focus*; where children should not be allowed to interrupt adults and they need to be taught the difference. And yes, there are times when adult/children conversations should be encouraged.

While striking a delicate balance, what shouldn't be thrown out the window, is teaching children to respect their elders. That learned courteous behavior should be modeled and taught at home.

"There was a time when there was a certain code of conduct by which you viewed the character of a person," states Alvin, Rosenfeld, a child psychologist, "and you needed that code of conduct to have your place in the community."

He must have been referring to the thirties and forties. Right?

## KARL DICKSON: "HERE'S THE PITCH!"
### Friday, January 23, 2009

If I had to sum up an overview of Karl Dickson in one-sentence; this is what it would be: Karl loved sports, his family, was civic minded, and he and his wife, Winnie, had a life-long love affair that spanned over six decades.

However, anyone who knows Karl is aware that he can't be defined in one sentence; probably not even in a book. Karl has earned the well-deserved distinction of a sports guru in Escanaba. His legacy will follow him for decades.

Karl's daughter, Peggy Pickle, spends every day with her dad at his Portage Point home with a glorious view of the bay. The sun dappled through the huge windows overlooking the bay. It shimmered on a huge table with a puzzle half completed and hundreds of pieces scattered about. It illuminated sports memorabilia that defined every nook and corner. Most notably was Karl and Winnie's 1944 wedding photo: Karl in his Air Force uniform and Winnie in her tailored suit and hat with a veil so indicative of the 40's.

I remarked what a handsome couple they were! Peggy brought the photo closer. Karl stared at the photo and with a far-away pained look of profound sadness you could tell he was mentally reviewing their life together. Tears welled up and spilled over, "I don't know what she ever saw in me," said Karl. "She was so special." Winnie passed away in 1998.

Indeed, Winnie Royce was special. She hailed from a special pioneer family. We can thank her great-great uncle, Eli Royce, a surveyor who platted the city of Escanaba (1862/1864), for his foresight.

Escanaba is the envy of every city in the U.P. with its generously wide main street and great immense park area. Harrison Ludington's instructions to Royce were: "Lay it out as to your best judgment leads you, and be liberal to the railroad and to the people." For that the inhabitants of our community can be grateful.

My husband, Gary, came along for the interview since he

*Karl and Winnie Dickson, married 1944.*

delights in talking with Karl, whom he considers a walking sports encyclopedia. Karl had sent us his treasured book, "All I ever Wanted to be was a Jock," when we wintered in Florida. What a historical gem; it is brimming with sports and local history.

By Karl's own admission he didn't have the talent to be a "jock" so the next best thing was writing about sports. He became a writer for the *Escanaban* in high school. His love of sports and his desire to become a sports writer lead him to the University of Missouri, one of the best journalism schools in the country. "I couldn't type and I couldn't spell—so I gave it up." said Karl with a grin and a hint of his self-depreciating humor.

Karl may not have scored any points as a "jock;" but as a patriot, an officer and navigator during World War 11 his compelling experiences of flights over Guam and Tokyo—one time with five Japanese prisoners huddled in the back of the plane—give pause for the case of heroism.

He and Winnie were married in 1944 and two days later Karl left on a mission—not to return for some 450 days. Karl would return home to run Office Service, the business his father established in 1921.

Baseball is, no doubt, Karl's first love. It has been sixty years since he teamed up with Al Ness to build a baseball dynasty. Their ten year record is phenomenal and still stands: Three Little League State championships, a Little Bigger League State Title, high school teams that made Ripley's "Believe it or Not" news for winning 43 consecutive games, the only Upper Peninsula American Legion Team to win a state championship and defended their U.P. Title for the next 13 years.

In 1957 the Escanaba Little League team represented the North Region of the U.S. and participated in the Williamsport World Series. Karl was quick to point out that "credit is due John Chylek, Ed Gauthier, Paul Vardigan and Mark Olson and a host of others as part of that great baseball legacy."

Another great contribution by Karl: In 1954 after Esky had won only two football games in two years which resulted in poor attendance, Karl approached Al Mathison, the athletic director about forming a fan club as a morale booster.

Neither the school board nor the faculty was in favor of the idea of a fan club. That didn't deter Karl. He held a meeting at the old high school to gauge the interest. 25 people showed up. He enlisted the help of Lawrence Erickson and Gump Olson and they sold the idea. Karl says, "Other than a dues paying member I can't take credit for its success as I was busy meddling in other affairs such as getting the school board to hire Bob Gernand as football coach after John Lemmer had turned him down earlier that day."

Inducted into the U.P. Sports hall of Fame in 1992; Karl has been a member of the council since 1982. He was voted J.C. Man of the year circa 1952. He also held the office Lions Club President and manager of the American Legion baseball team.

Karl's appreciation of his daughter, Peggy, can't even be measured in words. His eyes blurred with tears and he choked up as he pointed to Peggy and said, "She is the person you should be writing about." Peggy cooks his meals, maintains his house and yard, drives him to appointments and social events, assists him in activities of daily living and makes it possible for Karl to continue to live in his comfortable home. Their relationship is almost story book.

Karl also has a son, Blaine, a retired educator who resides in Portland, Oregon. "He's a good boy and writes to me every week," says Karl. "He also helps me with all of my writing research."

"What do you attribute your longevity to?" I asked Karl, expecting to hear the usual; genes, diet or lifestyle. Instead he said, "This will get you. Although I tried exercising, brown nosing (and other avenues), my failure to become a "jock" is probably the reason (for my longevity). There are less than a dozen surviving boys in my class; none of them were "jocks." So much for being a "jock!"

Over the years Karl has written many articles for the Historical Society. Karl, like Grandma Moses who painted into her nineties, is busy writing his second book at age 92. He has already selected a befitting title: "Here's the Pitch."

# A HOLY MAN IN OUR MIDST
## Friday, January 30, 2009

Hundreds of people mourned the recent passing of an Escanaba man, Irving "Francis" Houle. Walking among us was a true holy man. Francis bore and suffered the wounds of the stigmata. Throughout history the Catholic Church has recorded approximately 300 "stigmatists."

The first known and documented stigmatic was St. Francis of Assisi (1224). Stigmata are primarily associated with the Roman Catholic faith. According to Wikipedia stigmata are bodily marks, sores, or sensation of pain in locations corresponding to the bloody wounds on the hands, feet, forehead and back similar to the wounds of the crucified Jesus.

Francis received the stigmata on Good Friday, April 8, 1993. A priest, Father Robert J. Fox from South Dakota heard about "Francis" and contacted him for an interview. Father Fox, a prolific author, subsequently wrote a book, "A man Called Francis" in the mid-nineties. According to Francis the Lord first appeared to him on Ash Wednesday; Francis was bleeding profusely and was told to get ready. He was unaware of what that meant at the time.

From that day forward Francis underwent the suffering and Passion of Jesus Christ every night between midnight and 3a.m. Head pains would start similar to pain from a crowning; then the pain would move to the hands and feet similar to being crucified.

I first heard of "Francis" years ago when a friend told me we should seek him out to pray over our son, Gary, who has a brain injury. Eventually we took Gary to a healing mass where "Francis" laid hands on his head. It was so moving to Gary who responded with tears and in such an appropriate manner—that was a miracle in itself.

Walter Casey, my husband's friend and classmate, traveled with "Francis" as a companion and assistant. He informed us about the prayer meetings that Sandy Boucher hosted at her home every Tuesday for years. People would come from all over—even other countries as the word of "Francis" became known. We also attended a few prayer meetings. Each time he prayed over Gary.

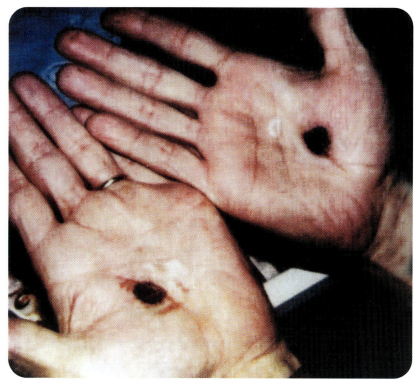

Each time Gary was completely appropriate.

Two weeks later (after a prayer meeting) we were driving to Florida when Gary had his first episode of reverting back to normal. He said he woke up after being in a fog for years. It was to last only an hour—if it was a coincidence—it had never happened before. Three more times he would return to normal; each time it would last for a longer time. Doctors cannot explain what has caused the phenomena.

"Francis" was a very ordinary humble man. Yet, my husband was so in awe of a man that actually spoke to Jesus and Mary that he didn't quite know how to relate to him. Think of that! A man of God actually talks with our creator. Gayle, his wife, told my husband that he wasn't alone—most were in such awe and felt the same way. Francis's main focus was to bring people back to prayer and the church. But many a miracle can be attested to as a result of being prayed over by Francis.

He never claimed any extraordinary powers. He was so unpretentious. All credit for healings as a result of prayer went to

God. His greatest mission was the healing of souls.

Amy Chenier, who has an inoperable brain tumor, went to "Francis." He prayed over her and she attributes her positive outcome to the power of prayer. The blood from the wounds is said, in some cases, to have a pleasant, perfumed odor, known as the Odour of Sanctity. Both Amy and her mother said they smelled the significant sweet rose aroma.

Even as Francis's health failed, he continued to pray over people. A friend of ours, Dick Wiles, lay in a coma dying at Christian Park Nursing Home. We visited him daily and he had been in a coma for over a month. He body was reduced to 128 pounds; he had trouble breathing and was congested, his oxygen level fell and at times he was curled up in a fetal state. There was virtually no chance that he would come out of it. His brother, Jerry, said doctors told him if he did survive he would never be

the same.

My husband contacted Walter Casey to have him set up a meeting for "Francis" to pray over Dick. It was his last hope. A few days later while I was talking to Dick and rubbing his head and hands (he was still in a coma); I witnessed a fluttering of his eyes and a slight smile on his lips. I knew then that he was "in there" and just maybe he will wake up.

Well, in my opinion, a miracle did take place! Dick did wake up and is now living on his own in the Senior High Rise. He has no memory of all that took place, but he was made aware that "Francis" prayed for him. He attended Francis's funeral and told his wife, Gayle that he believed he is here because of Francis.

Many of the people Francis prayed with have reported spiritual and physical healing. People who knew Francis described him as an ordinary man; a man who tried his best to practice his faith.

I can't imagine what it must be like to wake up one day and find out your husband is now a holy man; he had received the stigmata and speaks to Jesus and Mary. According to Gayle (from book excerpts) the first couple of years it was very difficult to figure out how to relate to one another with this special charism. She read books on stigmata to try and gain some understanding. Father Fox had not known of any married man with the bleeding wound marks.

The book, A Man Called Francis, is powerful and profound. It is available at Sayklly's and also from Sandy Boucher at My Mother's House (786-2116). It contains photos of "Francis" bleeding from his palms. Over 30 thousand copies have been sold. Father Fox said in 2005 it was estimated that "Francis" had prayed individually over 100,000 people.

Sadly, we have lost a humbled servant of God with the passing of "Francis" Truly he was a holy man that walked amongst us.

## CABIN FEVER REARS ITS UGLY HEAD
**Friday, February 6, 2009**

February is the shortest month of the year—yet seems the longest. It right smack in the middle of winter, freezing weather, piled up snow and more blowing snow. I look out the window in the morning and it's still dark. I think of Siberia and try to reconcile that we are in the bowels of winter.

I haven't enjoyed winter activities since grade school. No wonder I spent the winter months in Florida for the past 20 years. In Florida I walked, ran, played tennis, and enjoyed dancing, swimming or just basking in the sun by the pool. We went to concerts, theatrical productions, ballgames and a favorite pastime was viewing multi-million dollar open-houses and absorbing decorating ideas. Visiting countless malls, trips to Naples and Venice and outdoor eateries were all fun activities.

My garage is a filthy mess here in the winter whereas in Florida a finished garage floor was always shiny and clean. All around the caged pool area 40 beautiful peach hibiscus plants bloomed continuously, palm trees swayed in the breeze and a small lake in front of the pool area was home to a myriad of wildlife.

The white egrets with their slender long necks and little families of ducks putting around in the lake were fun to watch. On the walking path a stream of seniors began at 7:00 am either exercising or walking their precious dogs and stopping occasionally with their little pooper scoopers. Many were beyond old; yet they seemed energized by the delightful weather.

Now we take separate short vacations. My husband is going to Phoenix in March for the Cubs Spring Training. My son, Jeff and grandson, Zach will join him and I am sure the guys will have a great time. I am planning a spring trip to visit my son and granddaughters in Washington when the cherry trees are in bloom.

Enough day-dreaming! How do I spend my free time here in the winter? Reading, writing and disagreeing over TV channels head the list.

I have read some great books lately. I read mostly non-fiction. *Loving Frank* was a favorite. Frank Lloyd Wright, the renowned architect, had quite a scandalous personal life. His tumultuous years in Chicago almost ruined his career.

Married and the father of 6 children; he was commissioned to design a house for the Cheney's in 1903. He fell in love with Mamah Cheney, the mother of two and thus began a clandestine affair. Ultimately, they left their spouses and children to spend a year in Europe. Upon their return, they were scorned and hounded by the Chicago media.

They bought property in Wisconsin where Frank was raised and built a mansion. Frank traveled back and forth to his Chicago offices. In his absence one of his domestic workers (insane) axed Mamah and her two children (who were visiting her) and set fire to the home. Seven people died.

Frank went on to marry two more times and father another child. His son, Frank Jr. invented Lincoln logs in 1918.

Another great read was *The Glass Castle*. Jeanette Walls memoir was on the New York Times best seller list for over a year. It is a remarkable story of resilience and a revealing look at a dysfunctional family.

The educated mother of six was a free spirit who didn't want the responsibility of raising a family. The father was brilliant, but when he drank he was destructive and dishonest. The children basically raised themselves and eventually found their way to New York. The parents followed them and as their children prospered they chose to be homeless eating out of garbage cans. An astonishing true story.

*To Love What Is* could be considered a new kind of love story. It's about the power of a loving relationship in the face of devastating brain damage. The couple, who met in college, fell in love and then went their separate ways. Thirty years later they found one another again, married and enjoyed an ideal relationship that many people dream about; then he fell 12 feet out of a loft bed and defied death. It's about the durability of love.

Most recently I read *Revolutionary Road*—now a movie. It's about a 1950's couple with two children living in the suburbs. Maybe married too young and started a family too early—laying out their foibles, trials and tribulations. "A powerful treatment of a characteristically American theme...moving and absorbing," declares the Atlantic Monthly.

Come to think of it; all of these books were about love; true love, forbidden love, unconditional love. Guess I am a romantic at heart. Remember February is Valentine's Day month and it's been said that, "love is what makes the world go around."

Gary and I have some differences as far as watching TV. We both like the Evening News, Jeopardy, House and depending on the guest; sometimes Larry King—that's where we diverge. I wonder if all men insist on controlling the remote?

He likes sports, the History Channel, the Discovery Channel and more sports. Right now I am interested in everything that is going on in the Casey Anthony case: The tot mom that allegedly murdered her adorable little girl, Caylee, and dumped her body like trash in the woods near her home. It is beyond bizarre and seeing that personality-plus little girl in videos is heart-wrenching. The case has gripped the nation and the world. I get the updates from the Nancy Grace Show.

My memories of winter weather in youth are a far-cry from how I feel about winter today. There is no doubt my perception today may be skewed looking through the eyes of a 75 year-old compared to those of a 7 year-old. As a youth I remember only traces left of snow in March. I remember embracing windy days so we could fly our home-made kites. Early spring we played jacks, marbles, jump rope and hop scotch.

I don't remember school EVER being cancelled because of snow. Yet, we did have some real Russian-like snowstorms. I remember one year (around 1940) that banks were so high you could look into second story windows.

High school games were never cancelled due to weather. Gary reminisces about the 1949 basketball game with Ishpeming. "There was an enormous snow storm; the team took the Greyhound bus to Ishpeming, stayed at the Mather Inn, and rode the Streamliner home the next day."

At any rate the famous groundhog has seen his shadow (Feb. 2) and legend has it that this already long winter is sure to last six more weeks.

Meanwhile, I guess I will read more love stories, continue to concentrate on getting my body in shape for my skinny clothes and eagerly look forward to my favorite three seasons coming up.

## THE DEPRESSION ERA
**Friday, February 13, 2009**

Our economy is hurting. Our people are hurting. Everyday we hear the doom and gloom from the media of the recession we are in. The Great Depression has been a topic of conversation on many tongues.

Research shows we have endured 13 recessions since the crash of 1929-late 1930's. The Great Depression was precipitated by the Wall Street crash of October, 1929 when millions of dollars were wiped off U.S. share values in a matter of hours affecting world wide markets and economy. It wasn't until World War 11 that the U.S. really began to recover.

No recession could even be remotely compared to the Great Depression. Most recessions were short-lived. Only three lasted more than a year. Most were followed by years of prosperity.

During the Great Depression unemployment reached 25 per cent. Many were forced to seek charities for food and shelter. Some people had to send their children off to be boarded with other family members. I remember first hand some of the effects of the Great Depression.

My sister and I pulled our wagon to the Relief Office to receive surplus foods like raisins, prunes, grapefruit, oranges, flour and a variety of commodities. We were fitted with dresses made of feed sacks. It wasn't unusual for a family to be without a car. A phone for us would have been unheard of.

We were raised during that era and never knew any different—only in retrospect. For us those times were normal. Both my mother and father must have had a difficult time during the depression. Both came from above average families. They had experienced a better lifestyle. They were 18 and 19 when I was born in 1933 and depended on their families.

Their rent was four dollars a month and they ate their meals with their families. They couldn't afford groceries. The Depression would have a life long-lasting impression on my mother.

I remember her frustration when I asked for something I needed for school. "Money doesn't grow on trees. I just don't have it," she would say with a pained look. I went to a couple of Senior and Holiday Balls during high school. I wouldn't have been able to attend if I couldn't borrow a dress.

The Depression would affect my mom's thinking as far as money for the rest of her life. In later years she had means; yet she was frugal with herself. Her brother who once owned a resort in Rhinelander, WI eventually left her an inheritance. They were childless and my brother was farmed out to him during the depression for a school year. He was only six and became so homesick he had to come home.

A memory of my mother a few years before she died stands out. She showed me a beautiful winter coat she bought for herself and wanted my opinion. The next time I seen her she had on a cheap looking coat. "Why aren't you wearing your new coat?" I asked. "Oh, it was too expensive and I didn't really need it. I returned it and found this one at a rummage sale for three dollars." She was so proud of her thriftiness. She even bought me three bras in my size at the rummage sale. No, I didn't wear them. I just thanked her and threw them away. Perhaps her frugalness

*A soup line during the depression era. The sign reads "FREE COFFEE AND DOUGHNUTS FOR THE UNEMPLOYED".*

made me extravagant.

She returned just about any gift I bought her. She wasn't able to enjoy anything she conceived of as a luxury; even a toaster oven I bought for her. She found fault with everything so she could return it. She wasn't alone in her thinking. For many people that experienced the depression frugality became a way of life. Even in times of prosperity saving money was very important; so much so, they wouldn't ever allow themselves anything they deemed a luxury.

Then all Hell broke loose! Our generation of children grew up thinking that indeed, "money does grow on trees!" There wasn't any delayed gratification. Credit cards gave them what they wanted instantly. Most have not just one credit card but three, four, five or six. "Charge it!" became a way of life.

They bought expensive homes with little money down. The thinking was: property is always a good investment. And they were right—until now. Never in our lifetime had property values eroded.

The bubble burst and people were left with homes they couldn't afford because of job losses. Thousands have just abandoned their homes because they were paying high payments on a property now worth thousands less that what was owed. They just walked away—hence the present multitude of foreclosures.

God help the President to lead us out of this mess!

Consumers are getting a duel message to save, cut back, don't purchase unless it is necessary. On the other hand, give them money so they can spend and get the economy rolling again. Talk about a message in dichotomy. The job loss is rising every week. People are worried what will they do when their unemployment ends. Is it any wonder that consumers are wary of spending? And what will they do if jobs are not forthcoming?

The government just can't afford to sit back and do nothing. A stimulus plan should be in the works by the time this article is in print. But the scary thing is: Our government is like two different countries working against one another—Democrat and Republican. When are they going to act in the best interest of the people—you and I?

If one side proposes it, the other side predicts doom and

gloom. Either side does not want the other to get credit for anything—even if it is in the best interest of the people. We, the people get fed up and throw the "bums" out through our election process and the same scenario begins all over.

The government is not part of the problem—it is the problem! And the people have to share in some of the blame.

I shutter to think of a full-fledged depression—and it is a real possibility. How will the generations of folks that don't have a clue about hard times function? They don't know about the soup lines, begging for charity, boarding your children out, searching for jobs that are non-existent—or the countless suicides of people who just couldn't cope with their financial losses or mental depression.

I quote Jack and Suzy Welch, "Business Week" to end on a positive note: "It is human to view your own difficulties as "the worst of times." But this painful necessary correction will result in a healthier deleveraged society with a renewed focus on productivity, innovation, and better governance. The end is not here. A new beginning awaits."

Let's pray they are right!

**FACTS ABOUT WOMEN'S HEART HEALTH**
**Friday, February 20, 2009**

Since February is the month of the heart; romance, love, Valentine's day, so is it the month to bring awareness regarding the leading cause of death: heart disease.

Heart disease is not just a man's disease. Heart attack, stroke and other cardiovascular diseases are devastating to women too. Women may not be aware that coronary heart disease, which causes heart attack, is also the leading cause of death for women.

Many women believe that cancer is more of a threat, but they're wrong. Experts estimate that one in two women will die of heart disease or stroke and statistics reveal significant differences between men and women in survival following a heart attack.

Some of the reasons according to research are that women may not be diagnosed or treated as aggressively as men, and their symptoms may be very different from those of men having a heart attack.

Here's an example:  42 percent of women who have heart attacks die within one year compared with 24 percent of men.

The American Heart Association has identified several factors that increase the risk of heart disease and stroke.  Some of these risk factors you can't control such as increasing age, gender and family health history.  But most risk factors you can modify, treat or control to lower your risk.

Being knowledgeable and of course, taking action, will more than likely increase your life span.  We are very fortunate to live at a time when there have been leaps and bounds in medical technology: the direct reason for such an amazing increase in life-span.

My father died at age 33 of a heart attack; my brother at age 45.  My husband's father died of a heart attack at age 53.  My husband had by-pass surgery at age 44, so you can see the double whammy my children have regarding genetics.  My son, Gary was 37 when he dropped dead while jogging: he was resuscitated but suffered a severe brain-injury from the prolonged lack of oxygen.

My youngest son is 50 and totally on top of heart health.  No doubt what has happened to his brother has had an impact on his awareness and dedication to control any risk factor he can.  He has regular check-ups and scans to determine if there is plaque build-up and he controls his cholesterol numbers and ratio with medications.

My husband's father, who died in 1951, had heart disease.  In that era there wasn't general knowledge of how your diet might affect heart disease; no knowledge of cholesterol levels; no correlation of the heart and exercise; no operation such as by-pass surgery; really, the only known help was putting a nitroglycerin tablet under your tongue.

And that's what Gary's father did:  Placed a tablet under his tongue with a pained look when he took his son, Gary, to Chicago to see a ballgame and had to walk any distance; or when he ate a heavy meal and experienced discomfort.

## RISK FACTORS YOU CAN'T CONTROL

Increasing age—as women grow older their risk of heart disease and stroke begins to rise and keeps rising with age.

Sex (Gender)—Men have a greater risk of heart attack than women, and they have attacks earlier in life. Each year about 60,000 more women than men have strokes, and about 60 percent of total stroke deaths occur in women.

Heredity (family history)—both men and women are more likely to develop heart disease or stroke if close blood relatives have had them. Race is also a factor.

## RICK FACTORS THAT CAN BE MODIFIED, TREATED OR CONTROLLED BY FOCUSING ON LIFESTYLE HABITS AND TAKING MEDICINE. (If needed)

- Tobacco smoke—Smoking is the single most preventable cause of death in the United States. Smoking is a major cause of cardiovascular heart disease among women. Constant exposure to others' tobacco smoke (secondhand smoke) at work or at home also increases the risk, even for nonsmokers.

- High blood cholesterol—High blood cholesterol is a major risk for heart disease and increases the risk for stroke. Studies show that women's cholesterol is higher than men's from age 55 on.

- High blood pressure—high blood pressure is a major risk factor for heart attack and the most important risk factor for stroke.

- Physical activity—various studies have shown that lack of physical activity is a risk factor for heart disease and indirectly increases the risk for stroke. Overall, they found that heart disease is almost twice more likely to develop in inactive people than in those who are more active. The American Heart Association recommends accumulating at least 30 minutes of physical activity on most of all days of the week.

- Obesity and overweight—if you have too much fat—especially if a lot of it is located in your weight area—you're at high risk for health problems, including high blood pressure, high blood cholesterol, high triglycerides, diabetes, heart disease and stroke.

Often, women's symptoms differ from men. Women's major symptoms prior to a heart attack included:

- Unusual fatigue – 70%

- Sleep disturbance – 48%

- Shortness of breath – 42%

- Indigestion – 39%

- Anxiety – 35%

- Women can also experience discomfort /pain between the shoulder blades.

Classic symptoms can occur in men and women:

- Squeezing chest pain or pressure

- Shortness of breath

- Sweating

- Tightness in chest

- Pain spreading to shoulders, neck or arm

- Feeling of heartburn or indigestion with or without nausea and vomiting

- Sudden dizziness or brief loss of consciousness

Being aware of these symptoms could save your life. Don't delay if you experience symptoms—get medical attention immediately.

# MOVIE STAR ASPIRATIONS OF YOUTH
## Friday, February 27, 2009

I couldn't wait to grow up—my childhood friend of 70 years, Joan DeGrand and I lived in a real dream world during the early 1940's. We dreamed of being movie stars. We were two kids from Escanaba who had barely been outside of the city limits.

Joan's father owned DeGrand Motors and coming off of the Great Depression didn't seem to alter their lifestyle. Through my youthful eyes: I thought they were rich because they took Joan and me to almost every movie change at the theatres; they lived in a big home, had a car and a phone. The movie admission price for teens was 12 cents.

We always sat in the front row and both of us fell in love with Van Johnson, America's heart-throb, in the 40's. We were so impressionable at that tender age. I'm sure the theatre was also a major escape from reality for adults during the 30's and 40's. Movie stars were bigger than life. Musicals, the Road Shows and Saturday afternoon serials (the week to week cliff hangers) were the rage.

I revered Betty Grable: her legs were reportedly insured for a million dollars. Some of the other female greats were Heddy Lamar, Shirley Temple, June Allison, Katherine Hepburn, Betty Davis, Joan Crawford, Jennifer Jones, Ingrid Bergman; Ann Miller, Judy Garland, Greer Garson, Barbara Stanwick, Lana Turner (the sweater girl), Jane Wyman (Reagan's first wife), Virginia Mayo and Dorothy Lamour (the sarong girl with long brown hair) who teamed with Tarzan in the jungle serials and Bob Hope and Bing Crosby in the Road shows.

Male greats were Errol Flynn, Tyrone Power, John Wayne, Spenser Tracy, Jimmy Stewart, Pat O'Brien, Bob Hope, Bing Crosby, Mickey Rooney, Dick Powell, John Payne, James Cagney, Gary Cooper, Humphrey Bogart, Donald O'Connor, Joseph Cotton, Edward G. Robinson, Caesar Romero, Ray Miland, Cary Grant and host of others.

At age 13 I was in demand as an experienced baby-sitter. My mom had two baby boys and I was 13 going on 20. I had a burning desire to earn money. 25 cents was great pay for the entire evening. I was going to save money to go to Hollywood.

I worked as a waitress each summer at the U.P. State Fair at a very young age. I also cleaned houses for people. I worked for Donn Olin's family and remember ironing all of the starched white shirts he wore to school.

When I was fourteen I applied for a social security number. I was fortunate to have landed a job at Vagn's Bakery Bar (located where Swedish Pantry is today). I made sodas, sundaes and sandwiches; a plus included all I could eat. Those were the days you could eat all you wanted and still weigh 90 pounds dripping wet.

Then I had to make a choice: work after school or be involved in school activities. I chose being a majorette. For the time being that was the closest I could get to being a movie star. Wow! We really were dreamers with big ideas; in those days some movie stars were discovered in soda fountains (Lana Turner) or running an elevator in Chicago's Marshall Fields (Dorothy Lamour).

I wanted to be like Dorothy Lamour. She had long dark hair

and wore a signature tropical flower in it. I was 14 when I had a photo taken trying to look like Dorothy. Hollywood was like a million miles away to a kid from Escanaba.

Who would discover us in Escanaba? In Vagn's Bakery Bar or the Fair store elevator? Or perhaps a talent scout would be lurking around Sayklly's soda fountain, the City Drug Store, or the Boston Sweet Shoppe? As naïve young girls we believed it could happen. Dream on!

Then boys entered the picture. My interests changed! I was no longer obsessed about Hollywood. I had entered the boy-crazy stage. And there was no shortage of boyfriends. I fell in love every week—with someone new, of course.

Ultimately, the closest I ever got to Hollywood was to visit Grumman's Chinese Theatre where movie stars were immortalized by hand prints in the sidewalk.

My husband, Gary, has confessed some of the same aspirations he had as a youth. Gary loved movies too. Remember TV wasn't available yet. He liked cowboy shows and would gallop home after the show as if he were Hop-A-Long Cassidy or Gene Autry on his horse. Popular with kids in that era was playing cowboys and Indians.

World War 11 in 1941 brought with it a myriad of war movies. He had aspirations of joining the military and was fascinated with uniforms. He always wore a sailor hat. His two brothers brought home war memorabilia: a German Lugar and a Japanese soldier's helmet. They added to his mystique.

He was also drawn to movies portraying athletes. His big dream was to play football and basketball for the U.S. Military Academy (West Point). His youthful and perhaps unrealistic aspiration lured him to visit his dream, West Point, a few years ago with our son, Jeff.

I suspect almost everybody had way-out dreams when they were young; some have fulfilled them. Yes, some were unrealistic, but the fun of youth is to dream big. And sometimes dreams do come true.

A quote by a young Marilyn Monroe when she was Norma Jean: I am going to be a great movie star someday.

I suppose kids today have big-time dreams too. And there are definitely more opportunities. Looking back at a year book from 1949; girls aspired to be secretaries, teachers and nurses. Not much more was available to them. It had been only 30 years since 1919 when women gained the right to vote.

Who would have ever dreamed of men going to the moon in a space ship? That would have been a science fiction story in our day. Movies do record our history.

And what would life be like without movies? I can't even imagine!

## THE DIONNE QUINTUPLETS AND OCTOMOM
## Friday, March 6, 2009

Octomom? My computer didn't recognize that word when I did a spell check. No wonder. It's a media invention. It starts out like octo-pus, meaning eight arms, but eight babies in one womb?

Most mothers could not even phantom such a happening: First, to carry eight babies to term; second, nursing eight babies and raising them. No wonder Nadya Suleman, whose octuplets (even that word is not in the dictionary) were born in January, has been dubbed unstable; if she isn't she will be. A total of 14 kids! No husband! And no means of support!

For the sake of the children I hope someone comes to her rescue. That's probably what she had in mind all along when she had eight embryos implanted in her womb. All I can say is when you think you heard it all even stranger things happen. What in the heck is this world coming to?

14 kids on food stamps! No place to live! How is this mother going to take care of eight babies, diapering, feeding and nursing besides caring for the six she already has! My granddaughter has twin boys plus two other children and their care is overwhelming.

Octomom has suffered from depression and suicide ideation in the past. She needs the help of a Good Samaritan to help her through this. Both she and the babies are at risk. The devil-may-care media aren't helping; they are doing a good job of demonizing her.

Now here I go again, reminiscing about the 1930's and 40's. My peers will smile when I remind them of the Dionne Quintuplets born May 28, 1934 in Ontario, Canada.

Today it is not uncommon for sets of quintuplets or sextuplets to occur with fertility drugs and sophisticated neonatal care. Yet the survival of the Dionne's—identical quintuplets is unique. Twice before their birth (in 1786 and 1849) and four times since (in 1936, 1959, 2004 and 2007) *identical* quintuplets have been born, but the Dionne Quintuplets still remain the only instance where all five survived.

They were considered miracle babies of their time. In the depth of the Depression they brought with them wonderment, excitement and a light-hearted story of five babies that would become darlings to the world. Yvonne, Marie, Emile, Annette and Cecile would be a source of fascination for years following their birth.

I remember them in the newsreels (Movietone News) and in movies. They were adored by the public who just couldn't get enough of them. They were used to publicize products like Quaker Oats and Karo syrup. They were in magazines with their Shirley Temple curls and starred in four Hollywood films. And remember the Dionne Quintuplet paper dolls?

The babies were born to poor, French-speaking Catholic parents. Together they weighed less than 14 pounds. They were put by an open stove to keep them warm and mothers from surrounding villages brought breast milk for them.

To protect the infants from germs, kidnappers and a father that wanted to make money from their birth; they were taken from the family and placed under the government's guardianship. They were "exhibited" three times a day from a gauze-covered corridor. Between 1934 and 1943 about 3 million people visited "Quintland." They became the nation's biggest attraction—bigger than Niagra Falls. Even their mother had to stand in line to see them.

The Canadian encyclopedia called them a, "500 million dollar asset to the province."

However, their story is a tragedy; their lives became a circus.

They were exploited by the government. In 1943 a bitter custody fight brought the girls home to live with their parents and other siblings. They lived there until they were eighteen and then broke off almost all contact with their parents.

Emilie died of a seizure at age 20 while she was a nun at a convent. Marie died at age 35. She was living alone and had not been heard from in days. Her brother-in-law broke down the window and found her dead. It was determined she had a blood clot in the brain. Yvonne died at age 67 of cancer.

Marie married and had the only multiple births: twins. Annette and Cecile went on to marry and have children, but both eventually divorced.

In 1995 three of the then surviving sisters revealed they were sexually abused by their father for years. The revelations were made public in their book, "The Dionne Quintuplets: Family secrets."

They claimed the incidents of sexual abuse occurred when they went for car rides with their father. He took them for rides one at a time and touched them in a sexual way. The sisters never told their mother, but did try to discuss the abuse with a school chaplain. Annette said they were told, "to continue to love our parents and wear a thick coat when we went for car rides."

In 1998, the Ontario government reached a settlement ($4,000,000) with the three surviving sisters for ruining their childhood.

Today, the two surviving sisters live near Montreal.

## KING DAD CHANGES THROUGH THE YEARS
**Friday, March 13, 2009**

A wife's roll was considerably different when I was a young housewife. Even the term "housewife" seems to fit with the era I am referring to. Perhaps we took our cue from our mothers who catered and waited on Dad hand and foot.

King Dad had his special chair. If anyone sat in it, they knew to vacate it as soon as Dad was ready to sit on his perch demanding peace and quiet while he read his newspaper (The Daily press, of course). Ala Archie Bunker.

My mom would set a lovely dinner table and the aroma of a roast and apple pie in the oven was mouth watering. However, if my step-dad was late getting home, we all had to wait to sit down to dinner. God forbid if he stopped for a beer! We waited and waited!

Moms were our role model and we married with the idea that Man was the bread winner and Woman did everything she could to make Man comfortable. I have a mental image of Edith (Archie called her Dingbat) scurrying around trying to make Archie comfortable. That's just the way it was.

Not many women worked outside the home in those days. They worked at home washing, cooking, canning, cleaning and taking care of babies. Plus waiting on Dad!

Gary's dad woke at 5 a.m. to go to work for the City of Escanaba; he was superintendent of the steam and gas plant. He had a really gross saying of anyone he deemed lazy—that is, if they slept beyond six a.m. he would say, "They slept with the sunshine in their a—. Not only gross, but very descriptive.

I will admit I did spoil my husband like so many of my generation did. In our younger years I met him at the door when he came home from work. I would change into something sexy; no house dress or apron for me. I would do up my hair (no curlers), splash on a hint of perfume, a little lipstick and greet him with a kiss. He was the breadwinner and came home to his castle where he reigned. I baked him special things and made his favorite meals.

Of course the years left that little girl with stars in her eyes behind. Every now and then he asks, "What happened to that little girl I met over 60 years ago?" Guess she grew up and developed a mind of her own! Fairly normal—hey ladies!

At times I did work outside of the home—mostly part-time. In those days if you worked outside the home, you were still responsible for your motherly and wifely duties. No help from your husband; nor did you expect it.

Fast forward to my son Jeff's generation. He and his wife both worked in demanding jobs on Capitol Hill for the US Government; he an attorney for the Treasury Department, she a speech writer for the Department of Energy. Her income matched his.

I was amazed when I visited them in Washington. They shared all of the chores and they were so organized. A schedule hung on their kitchen wall listing their duties. They each had special days when they were responsible to prepare the meals. They had a cleaning lady to change the bedding, clean the house and do the washing. And they took turns taking their daughters to dancing, baby-sitters and pre-school.

When they visited us in Florida, Jeff sat on the floor packing their suitcases to leave. He claimed packing wasn't Peggy's strong suit. And he was good at it. Wow! I can't even fathom his dad packing a suitcase. My husband recently joined our son and grandson Zach in Phoenix for Cubs Spring Training and to soak up some rays.

He said, "I'll get the suitcase up from storage so you can pack for me." As I brought shirts out of his closet and questioned him, "what do you want to take?" He was shocked to see some shirts he forgot he had and of course wanted me to coordinate the colors with pants.

Then he said, "Oh ya, my pants are all too big since I have lost weight. You need to buy me some new pants." "Do you really need them now—the day before you leave?" I sighed. Yes, he needed new pants now! He proceeded to tell me about a recent incident when he ran some errands. "I got out of the car and my pants fell to my ankles at the post office." Good Grief! Zikes! If anyone witnessed this, please know he is not a pervert.

So the day before he left I scrambled to purchase new pants and wash some of the shirts he had hung back in his closet –dirty. I fixed him a folder with his e-ticket, Hampton Inn information where he would be staying in Scottsdale, and other pertinent information he needed. He had written his departure date on the calendar for Friday instead of Thursday. Good thing our son called him to discuss the trip. It's not altogether his fault. I always took care of those incidentals when we traveled.

Of course much of this is tongue-in-cheek. Let me tell you, he saved the best of him for the last. He is such a wonderful Dad to our son, Gary. He asked me 50 times a day, "when is my Dad coming home?"

He really has become another Mom; he changes his diaper, he fixes his cereal, he sings with him and his playful sense of humor brings a delightful chuckle to our son. If Gary cries when he hears a song that jogs his memory of how life was before his injury; my husband cries with him. Once in a while Gary Jr. will say with a twinkle in his eye, "Dad, you are such an idiot!" He hugs and kisses his son and sometimes weeps early in the morning when he is alone and feels so helpless regarding his condition.

So if he can't fix a sandwich for himself because he says it tastes better if I make it, if he can't keep his clothes straight, if he can't pack a suitcase or if he loses his pants in public, he has attributes that are so much more important.

He's got to be the best dad ever!

## TODAY'S TECHNOLOGY
## Friday, March 20, 2009

Today's technology has left the majority of seniors in the dark. Many of my peers don't want anything to do with a computer. Those of us that have adapted to computers really feel out of the loop when we realize our grandkids are more proficient than we are.

Seniors today are faced with technology they can't understand or even use as it is too complicated for them to deal with. Life is just too fast for the average senior today.

Seniors, are you familiar with Twitter? I surely am not. How about Facebook, YouTube, Yahoo, Blackberry, Bluetooth and MySpace? It seems everyday there's some new gadget coming out that is designed to make our lives easier and more fun. As seniors we balk at the idea of learning how to use some of these new things.

My experience in college as a senior speaks to our reluctance to something new: In one class we had to take our final exam on a computer. I was 56 years old in 1989 and terrified of the word computer. I knew the material but the thought of using a computer freaked me out.

In a writing class I adamantly refused to use the computer to write a story. Instead I did it the old-fashioned way; I hand wrote it. At Northern I experienced the same fear of using the computer. I was forced to send information to an instructor via the computer. It made me feel so inadequate to have to ask the young kids for help. They were so helpful and understanding though.

Clearly, many of the kids were just as much a novice at computers as I was in the early nineties. The difference is they were open and eager to learn. I was rigid. Guess you could apply the old adage, "you can't teach old dogs new tricks."

I came away from college hating computers.

It wasn't until ten years ago my daughter, Vicki, came to visit and insisted that I consider buying a computer. That was her expertise. I finally relented and became frustrated when she left and I didn't even know basics. For one year I never did anything but e-mail. Now I wonder how I could have ever managed without one.

My computer is like a member of the family. It has its own room and personality. Even my husband has adapted. It took a bit longer for him though. Now I'm thinking we need a second computer to accommodate both our needs.

I finally relented and have a cell phone now. However, I am trying to learn by myself and it is complicated even to load more minutes and retrieve messages. I detest feeling amateurish with all of this stuff.

We have a navigation system in our car that I insisted on— never used it. And perhaps never will. My husband realized it worth during a recent trip to Phoenix. Our grandson brought his portable navigation system along and it was invaluable getting them around to their destinations. They punched in restaurants, ballparks, golf courses and hotels. The information was at their fingertips.

I realize these new fangled electronic gadgets are the thing of the future. You can't imagine what new inventions will be on the market ten or fifteen years from now. Most seniors are utterly lost—and frustrated.

Gary's grandmother born during the Civil War (1862) was afraid of a telephone when the family insisted she have one. What would our ancestors think of today's lifestyle and technology?

My grandmother wouldn't leave her house overnight without unplugging all of the electrical cords in the house. She was certain there would be a fire.

They grew up when most of the United States were rural. My grandmother traveled around Shaffer and Bark River on a horse. She was only twenty when she stopped at a railroad track crossing and a train whistle spooked her horse, throwing her into a telephone pole and leaving her with injuries that caused her to be deaf.

New technology can also lead to unscrupulous criminal behavior. For example I was shocked recently when we received a letter from our credit card company to call them regarding suspicious activity. Someone at sometime copied our credit card and charged 200 dollars at a Wal-Mart in Boynton Beach, Fl.

I was amazed that could happen. I only used my card once on

the internet; I bought gift certificates from Outback for family members at Christmas. Could that have been how our identity was compromised? That just happened in February. Subsequently we have been issued a new card.

I remember a time in 1981 we didn't even own a credit card. We were on vacation and wanted to rent a car. We had cash. They wouldn't rent the car to us without a credit card. That was the primary reason we finally applied for one. Now credit cards are used for everything.

I didn't touch on the incredible advancements in health technology. My husband or son wouldn't be alive without it. That's fodder for another article.

The era of the on and off switch that our generation was familiar with is over. Survival in our society means adapting to all of the new technology now and in the future. Just like our grandparents had to adapt to phones, cars and electricity.

## WHAT WILL I WRITE ABOUT?
**Friday, March 27, 2009**

I rather think most columnists experience a time when they have to dig deep to come up with a column. That has never been the case for me—until this week. My problem is I didn't have time to research or conduct an interview this week. Thanks to my readers who call me with great suggestions I have a huge list of local people to profile.

Amazingly, everyone has a life story that could be a best seller. Our community is filled with wonderful stories just waiting to be written. I enjoy researching; it's a learning experience for me too. But what I really enjoy is interviewing people.

It could be a sports story (Boxcar Pants Pepin) or an inspirational health story (Amy Chenier Kositzki) or a beloved member of our community that has contributed so much in so many ways (Karl Dickson). It may be a generational or historical story about a family (Pa Karas and Clara Embs) or an inspirational and awesome religious story (Irving "Francis" Houle).

Whatever the focus I certainly feel blessed to be able to bring some of these amazing stories to the readers. It does entail more time to set up an interview and write their special stories and since time was of essence this week I will have to write about what's happening in my life. No research and no interview needed.

This past year has been a traumatic one regarding my son Gary who lives with us. Last May he fell out of bed and broke his hip requiring surgery. He spent three months in the nursing home for physical therapy. This winter he was hospitalized with a serious bladder infection and sepsis (blood infection).

Just three weeks ago he was vomiting profusely. An ambulance again took him to St. Francis Hospital. He tested positive for a blood clot. Tests revealed a huge gall stone. Further testing, a cat scan, revealed a much more insidious problem. Gary has an abdominal aortic aneurism that needs surgery as soon as possible or game is over.

We began a whirlwind of tests traveling back and forth to Marquette General. Some were serious and posed risks. The pre-op testing was required to go forward with the surgery to take place in Houston.

Dr. Coselli who specializes in aortic aneurism surgery at Baylor College of Medicine (Texas heart Institute) is world-renown and number one in his field having performed over 4000 surgeries of this type.

So that is where my priorities have been focused. We are thankful the problem accidentally came to light.

Meanwhile we have a host of healthcare visitor's everyday. Marquette General provides a nurse to oversee Gary's needs and aides to bathe Gary. Community action provides a companion 7 hours a week to give Gary a break from us and likewise give us some respite time. In between, either the priest from St. Anne's or Charlene Carlson visits Gary weekly. We do have many light and humorous moments too.

One day when Father Mike came in the door. Gary questioned him, "Are you Catholic?" "Oh yes," said Father. "I'm here to give you communion." Gary was sitting on the sofa and said in all seriousness, "Well, hurry up and give it to me—I'm starving!" As if the communion would satisfy his hunger. Father Mike laughed and said he might have to use that story in a sermon.

Just yesterday, Gary's dad was hugging Gary and kissing his neck. Gary said, "Dad I have a very important message for you!" "What is it?" asked his dad. "Your breath stinks like sh—!"

Or like when we were in Marquette; Gary demanded to know why one nurse had a fat stomach. Not in the least bit offended she told him, "I have a baby growing in there." "Who put it there?" Gary asked in a slightly cruder and more direct way. They all got a laugh and now you know why wherever we go, Gary gets special attention and the three of us are always remembered.

Yet, he can play chess, spell almost any word, knows the words to almost every song over the last 40 years and seriously questions why he takes any pill. He is so with-it in so many spheres. He is uninhibited though and says what he thinks; whatever comes to mind—just like a kid.

And there are times when the realization of what has happened to him penetrates and he sheds tears keenly aware of what he has lost. We are both powerless to fix it. That's when I cry too. He certainly is a mixed bag.

Well, this seems like a long-winded way to tell you I won't be doing a column article during the month of April. And maybe beyond. We welcome your prayers for a good outcome. For now we can only take one day at a time and rely on our faith.

Gary absolutely loves and appreciates cards. He keeps them on his dresser and reads them over and over. If you want to send him a card; send it to our Escanaba address. To be sure he will enjoy it.

Happy Easter and Hasta la vista for now!

## THE BONIFAS STORY: FROM RAGS TO RICHES
### Friday, May 22, 2009

If ever there was a story of rags to riches the Bonifas story qualifies. The legend begins in Luxembourg in 1864, the birth year of William "Big Bill" Bonifas. As a young man "Big Bill" was one of thousands of immigrants to land on the shores of America in search of a better life. He arrived in New York, eager to make his mark in this wonderful new world, with a paltry few dollars to his name and wearing a suit that was several sizes too small for him.

His plan was to board a train in Chicago that would take him to North Dakota to work in the wheat fields. That plan didn't materialize because "Big Bill" boarded the wrong train and ended up in Green Bay. He forged his way to the Upper Peninsula and went to work cutting timber into railroad ties and fence posts for a contractor.

He worked for starvation pay. He was strong and cut and carried two logs to the other men's one. Finally, he was able to buy a cheap horse to haul the stuff down to the dock. When the horse proved weak Big Bill strapped himself into the harness and teamed with the horse to help pull the logs.

Big Bill was frugal and knew how to pinch a penny. He saved enough money to send for his seven brothers and sisters from the old country. He soon set up his own camp and his sisters did the cooking. Big Bill eventually branched out into big timber and bought pinelands for 65 cents an acre.

Timber was in demand. The railroads bought millions of ties and growing cities in the Midwest demanded lumber. The city of Chicago was rebuilding bigger and better after being desecrated by the Chicago fire in 1871.

Big Bill was in the right place at the right time; but it took more than that. He was eternally industrious, very canny and had to be lucky too. Remember in those days there was no income tax; so amassing a fortune was possible.

Catherine "Katie" Nolan was a beautiful Irish girl of sixteen when her family sent her to America to escape the wretched poverty in Ireland. America was thought of the land of opportunity and the Upper Peninsula was one its great frontiers.

Kate worked as a waitress at a lumberjack boarding house in Garden. The Irish lass caught the eye of Big Bill. The strapping, broad-shouldered, six-foot Bill asked Kate for her hand in marriage. They were married in August of 1894. It has been decreed that Kate was Big Bill's greatest find and asset.

The Timber King invested in automobile manufacturing, paper and oil which further contributed to his sizable fortune.

They built an opulent home on Escanaba's shoreline overlooking Ludington Park. Kate was never comfortable with their wealth. She still scrubbed her own floors. Unlike Bill who was outgoing; she was shy. The couple never had any children.

Even as millionaires, Bill and Kate were thrifty. When big Bill traveled on business, Kate packed his lunch. She darned his socks and had her bloomers made out of feed sacks. Bill's millions went to Catherine when he died in 1936.

The community stepped up to the plate when attention of the Bonifas Mausoleum and burial site was brought to light. 60 years of neglect resulted in marble tumbling inside; the bronze door turning black and the outside granite had never been cleaned. The sight was eerie.

The Bonifas legacy is unprecedented in Escanaba history. Anyone who has ever lived here has been touched in some way by the Bonifas gifts to the community. Yet, until now, their full legacy

*"Big Bill" Bonifas*

*Catherine "Katie" Nolan*

and history has not been fully disclosed—other than a couple of buildings they financed and carry their name.

Last year the Bonifas Committee petitioned the City of Escanaba to rename a short street in the park "Bonifas Drive" in their honor. Mission accomplished.

The last phase consists of funding an endowment to ensure the Bonifas burial site will never fall into disrepair. Equally important is the historical and educational value of the Bonifas legacy. A granite memorial is planned to educate the public about their lives, their legacy and their importance as pioneers in this community.

The memorial will have a

*Kate feeding the chickens in Garden, Michigan.*

home in a dominate place in the community—accessible to all. Recently the recreational advisory board approved and recognized the historical and educational value of such a memorial to be located at a site to be determined –the Municipal Dock or near the Karas Band shell. Incidentally, the Bonifas home overlooked the band shell.

A funding drive to complete the last phase is in progress. All donors will be remembered with their names inscribed on the back of the Memorial. Please consider a contribution to this worthy cause.

Checks can be made out to Pat Baribeau, treasurer for the Bonifas Memorial Committee. Mail checks to: Bonifas Memorial Fund, Delta County Community Foundation, 2500 7<sup>th</sup> Avenue south.

## MEMORIES OF YOUTH WHEN
## WE WERE BRAND NEW
### Friday, May 29, 2009

Recently I sat in my dining room sipping on a cup of coffee and looking out a huge window at Spring in all its glory: the sun glistening on the budding leaves of the stately red maples; some students running by from the high school; early walkers; a couple of pigeons hopping and picking in the grass and suddenly my mind regressed into years gone by. Call it daydreaming if you like, but it happens more often as the years fly by.

Take the pigeons for example. I thought back to my youth when the city was home to hundreds of Robin red breasts hopping in yards and stopping now and then with their heads cocked to the ground listening for worms. Where have all the robins and their morning chirping songs gone? We had fertilized the day before those poor pigeons were picking in the grass. Is the fertilizer we use today the culprit? Could it be implicated in the kill off of birds?

When we were kids Ludington Park was like the land of OZ. It was indeed magical—a wonderland of birds and majestic trees sprinkled with slides, teeter-totters and swings. It was home to the Red-headed Woodpecker. Often we heard their familiar peck, peck, peck and looked for them in the giant trees. Other familiar birds sighted often in the park were Red-winged Blackbirds, Blue Jays and Baltimore Orioles.

And frogs! Any kid from our era remembers the thousands of frogs in and around Ludington Park. The boys would ride their bikes down the lake shore after a rain storm and hear the clicking of frogs as their wheels ran over them. Where have all the frogs gone?

Remember the old green bath house located where the Lagoon is today? The drinking fountain across the road would be our last stop before we began our trek home. We were so small that someone had to push the water pedal at the base while another kid boosted us up to get a drink. Near the fountain was a wringer where we rang out our bathing suits after swishing them in the water.

As we skipped out of the park, of course, we were obliged to stop at the slides, the teeter-totter and swings before we hiked up the hill tired and hungry to arrive home just in time for supper—as we called it.

My husband, Gary, remembers his grade-school days at Barr School. The class marched double-file down to Ludington Park with the teacher on the last day of school for a picnic. A sack lunch from home included a baloney sandwich and Twinkie. The teacher provided Dixie cups. What an exciting day!

Needless to say anyone who grew up in Escanaba would have a truckload of memories at our enchanted park—because it was enchanted in our young minds.

No, we weren't couch potatoes watching TV—there was no TV. We were in perpetual motion from the minute we got out of bed in the morning. We walked everywhere. No wonder we were all so skinny. No fast foods either.

In the spring our mothers beat rugs on the clothes line with a wire whip. Wall to wall carpeting was unheard of— nor was there such a business that offered carpet cleaning. Linoleums could be bought at the dime store for five dollars. They were light-weight and could be transported rolled up and tied with a string. They didn't last long before the pattern started to wear off. Many homes had wood floors and scatter rugs. The wall paper in our rented flat made me dizzy.

You would have to be a certain age to appreciate this. I remember cleaning the clothesline with a wet rag before I could help my mother hang clothes. Coal soot and other dirt filled the air. "Whites" were always hung first. You never hung a shirt by the shoulders—always by the tail. What would the neighbors think?

Wash day was on Monday. You didn't dare hang clothes on the week-end—especially on Sunday. A reader sent me a spiel on washing clothes. "You always hung the sheets and towels on the outside lines so you could hide your "unmentionables" in the middle (perverts and busybodies, ya'know!)"

A poem from a reader claimed the clothesline was like a newscast. There weren't any secrets kept from the neighbors when the clothes were hung out to dry. Neighbors knew when company stopped by from the fancy sheets and towels on the line. Fancy tablecloths were another dead give-away.

The clothesline also announced a baby's birth with scads of diapers and baby clothes. As the children grew so did the sizes of clothes on the line.

When illness struck the lines were full of sheets and nightclothes. It also announced the family was "gone on vacation" when the lines were limp and bare. Neighbors raised eyebrows if a wash was dingy and gray.

Clotheslines are a thing of the past. We welcome the dryers of today; but now what goes on inside the home is anyone's guess! Those were the good old days when neighbors knew each other best by what hung on the line.

Everyone had a Victory garden in the early forties. I still recall the great tasting tomatoes. They just don't have that "garden" flavor today. Meat, coffee, sugar, and gas were just a few items that were rationed. You were allowed two gallons of gas a week unless it was considered work related. My mother gave our gas stamps to my aunt; we didn't have a car.

We helped in the war effort by collecting scrap iron and bundling paper to be recycled. I remember hauling a couple of pieces of iron or copper in a wagon to Coplan's junk yard located at the corner of 14th Street and Second Avenue North. How excited we would be to get a few nickels or pennies.

On Friday my mother gave us a dime to buy a defense stamp at the school. You pasted them in a book until you had $18.75— enough to buy a defense bond.

When I think about the war I remember the sad story of the Sullivan brothers. Five boys were all on the same ship during the war. All five lost their lives when the ship was blown up by a Japanese torpedo in the Pacific. I remember the movie about the Sullivans. After that tragedy the war department made a ruling that two members from the same family could not be assigned to the same ship.

As you can imagine many of my memories of youth have to do with the war. We were so much more affected and involved by the war than people are today. The depot bustled with boys in military uniforms coming home or leaving for overseas on the Streamliner;

families hugging and crying in grief or joy.

Seems my memory of childhood is jogged even more as the years fly by. I think so often about the cherished years of youth when we were brand new and oh, how innocent!

## Researching Our Family Tree Roots
## Friday, June 5, 2009

A popular past time, especially in the last few decades, is researching our ancestors. Many local resources are available to delve into family background. The Mormon Family History Center staffed with volunteers is eager to help and guide you. The Delta County Court House (clerk's office and register of deeds) can reveal vital information and get you started on the project. Cemeteries, churches, obituaries and the internet are all good resources.

In retrospect I wish I would have had the foresight and interest to question the senior members of my family while they were still here. What gems they would have told us. Well, maybe! Those were also the days of skeletons locked in the closet—hopefully forever.

About ten years ago my interest piqued. I took the basic facts I knew about my background and like a "babe in the woods" went to the Mormon Family History Center. Little did I realize that decision would propel me on a course that would take over my life.

We ate, slept and talked constantly about all the revelations being discovered—both interesting and shocking! I wrote stories about the ancestors of both my husband and I. Eventually I put them into book form and distributed them to my children and other family members. Really, the reason I first became interested in a computer was to document my research.

The research is still ongoing. My French-Canadian research on my mother's side dates back to the 1600's in the Province of Quebec. They came to the Schaffer area in the 1880's. Six generations ago.

My research on my father's side took me to Ireland. My great-grandfather, Charles Kidd and his two brothers, James and Alexander came to Escanaba as teens circa 1878. All three went to work on the railroad. That was seven generations ago and still counting in this area.

My husband's paternal grandfather, Hans Abrahamson, came here from Norway at the tender age of 17 in 1882. His maternal grandfather, James Elliott (first cousin to Thomas Alva Edison) was born in Ontario and came to Escanaba circa 1879. He eventually owned a grocery store in the 400 block of Ludington Street. Thomas Alva Edison and my husband both have a common grandfather: Ebenezer Mathews Elliott. The Edison blood runs through his family and that's another story—one that I have done in the past.

By now you probably get the idea why my husband and I have such a passion for the history of our community. Both of our family ancestors were immigrants and among the earliest pioneers.

My focus of interest today is on one of my ancestors. My great-grandfather Charles Kidd arrived here from Ireland as a teen-ager in 1878 to work on the railroad. He must have been aware of the Bonifas family. Perhaps their paths even crossed in some minor way.

Charles Kidd, like many immigrants, had a hard life. Still, circumstances were probably better than they would have been in Ireland. One wonders if he was trying to populate Escanaba all by himself; he was father to 18 children. WOW!

Charles was a trimmer for the Chicago and Northwestern Railroad. He met Ellen Connahan who hailed from Wisconsin and they married in 1882. Escanaba was home to Charles and Ellen. Soon babies were on the way. I was able to piece together some information from court house papers: In 1888 a warranty deed; in 1893 his citizenship papers.

Life had to be one big hardship for Charles and Ellen. Their ninth child was born in 1896. Ellen died of childbirth fever three weeks after she delivered her ninth child. She was just 35 years old.

At the time of Ellen's death the children's ages were; 3 weeks.

1 year, 2 years, 3 years, 6 years, 8 years, 11 years and 13 years. One child died at 19 months in 1888. The 11-year-old was my grandfather, Frank Kidd.

My grandfather left school to care for and help raise his brothers and sisters. The oldest boy James, age 13, helped his dad earn a living.

One can only imagine the hardships the family endured. In 1902, six years after Ellen's death Charles met and married Sarah Weber Jorgensen, a young widow with a child, from Wisconsin. Eventually her son Palmer Jorgensen owned a bar (The Tavern)

*Charles Kidd and Ellen Connahan married in 1882*

for years in the 900 block of Ludington Street.

More babies started to come—nine more in all. Sarah was inundated with raising her children, her step-children and having more babies in-between. She sent for her young sister Martha (Mattie), age 16, to help her.

Now here is the strange part of this story. My grandfather, 19 at the time, fell in love with young Mattie. They married and his step-mother also became his sister-in-law. Charles was Mattie's brother-in-law and now also her father-in-law. My grandfather and his father became brother-in-laws. Really weird! Just like the hill-billy song, "I'm my own grandpa."

Charles died at age 65 in 1924. At the time Roach, his youngest child, was 5-years-old. Another interesting story that old-timers may remember: Roach gained notoriety when he was just 18 and teamed up with a friend in the 1930's to go to Spain and fight in the Spanish Civil War.

The impetus for this story is the wedding photo of Charles and Ellen recently given to me by Lawrence "Lug" Kidd, also a descendent. I was unaware of its existence. How exciting –now I could put a face on our great-grandfather and grandmother.

New family revelations continue to unfold. Just recently I found out that Charles' mother, Mary, born in Ireland in 1826 was buried in Holy Cross Cemetery in 1891. Perhaps she came to America as a widow so her sons could care for her. Some things we can only guess at.

My dad's sister, Dorothy, told me before she died that the notorious pirate, Captain Kidd, was an ancestor. I haven't verified that yet. Sounds like more colorful discoveries ahead.

My son, Jeff, and I are in the talking stages of a trip to Dublin, Ireland. I hope that materializes. For anyone interested in researching their roots the Family History Center is a great place to start. Be prepared for an adventure of revelations while documenting and preserving the history for future generations.

## THE PEARSON STORY:
## GIVING BACK TO THE COMMUNITY
**Friday, June 12, 2009**

Harold and Mary Pearson are an exemplary example of former Escanaba residents "giving back" to the community where they were born and spent their formative years. The Pearson story— not exactly a "rags to riches" story; but rather about a local couple from meager beginnings who have been blessed with enormous success. Yet, they have not forgotten their roots.

The Pearson's retired in 1990 to Harlingen, Texas (near the Mexican border) where they enjoy warm weather, lots of golf and the beautiful beaches of nearby South Padre Island.

"We take great pleasure in returning to Escanaba during the summer months," says Mary. "We have come to appreciate that which we took for granted all of the years we were growing up. I didn't know that not everyone had a beautiful park and marina and access to hunting, fishing, skiing and a State Fair."

Harold's father, Fred Pearson, was born in Sweden. He immigrated to the USA in 1915 and worked in the lumber industry as a camp cook. In 1917 he entered the Air Force and served his new country during World War I. He returned to Escanaba where he worked for the Birds Eye Veneer Co. until his retirement.

His mother, daughter of Swedish immigrants, was born in Escanaba in 1892. She died in 1992 shortly after celebrating her 100th birthday at the Bishop Noa home with her family present.

Mary's father was born in Lower Michigan. Her mother died when Mary was age three. She was sent to live with her father's parents in Ford River. Mary graduated in 1951, fifth in her class, and was always disappointed that she wasn't awarded a scholarship. There weren't that many available then.

In 1995, with the assistance of Jim Hansen, former Escanaba High School Principal, they instituted the Harold and Mary Noyes Pearson Scholarship. "This would be our way to 'give back' to the community." says Mary. "Since that time," relates Harold, "we have provided four year scholarships each year to fifteen outstanding graduating seniors including the 2009 winner, Megan Markham."

The Pearson's are benefactors of the largest scholarship award at EHS.

Harold graduated in 1949 and enlisted in the Air Force during the Korean War after working various jobs in Milwaukee. Mary, meanwhile attended the Milwaukee Institute where she honed her secretarial skills and returned home to work for Mead Corporation.

They knew one another vaguely from high school. In 1953, Harold was home on leave from Korea when Mary, now a blossoming beauty, caught his eye big time one evening at a popular Escanaba watering hole. They dated while he was on-leave and their love affair continued. Wedding bells were ringing soon after Harold's discharge from service.

Thus they began their life together. The couple moved to Milwaukee where Harold attended college while working four part-time jobs. Mary worked full-time until the babies start coming—five in all. Mary was a stay-at-home mom while the children were young. She dappled in fun things like interior decorating after the children were raised.

Harold advanced rapidly throughout his working years. They

*Harold and Mary Pearson.*

moved to different locations as he garnered experience and respect while climbing the latter of success. Eventually he held high-powered corporate and executive positions with several large corporations.

During their summer visits the Pearson's especially love attending band concerts like so many people that visit the area. Mary explained, "two years ago we took notice of the fact that the (Karas) band shell was in dire need of new landscaping and also the stone needed to be cleaned."

"We talked with Jim O'Toole about perhaps providing funds for the work and discovered that landscaping and cleaning was only the tip of the iceberg, so to speak. The band shell needed electrical upgrades as well as new siding and a new paint job. We agreed to fund this work and are looking forward to seeing the finished product this summer."

The Pearson's have also contributed to the athletic field restoration project. They belong to the Historical Society and read the press on-line everyday to keep abreast of local happenings.

Just recently, they contacted the Bonifas Memorial Committee with a wish to contribute to the current project regarding the endowment fund set up by the Community Foundation to ensure the Bonifas resting place will never again fall into disrepair and the historic memorial planned for the park.

Their lifelong interest in their hometown and their desire to "give back" is more than admirable. As adults they have carved out a charmed life, have deservingly enjoyed the fruits of success from hard work, and have traveled the world. From my point of view, as a friend and former schoolmate, they are quite the cosmopolitan couple.

It is no surprise that the Escanaba area has a way of creating an indelible lifelong mark on its inhabitants and beckons you back. So it is with Harold and Mary.

The passion for their family ties and childhood hometown find the Pearson's eager to return in July for their summer visit: the band concerts; the art exhibits; breakfast at the Swedish Pantry; dining with old friends; visiting the local library; visiting golf courses and old haunts while just enjoying the local color and culture; A step back in time filled with many memories.

# AN OPEN LETTER TO PRESIDENT OBAMA
## Friday, June 19, 2009

Dear Mr. President,

First, I voted for you as an Independent and also contributed to your Inauguration. I am age 76 and just naïve enough to think you will answer my concerns and just maybe do something about them.

When you proposed a stimulus package to create jobs and build infrastructure under the American Recovery and Reinvestment Act; I thought what a great idea. It reminded me of the Roosevelt Era when public works programs were so evident in our community. I was born in 1933 and remember the fruits of those government projects like paving the streets, dredging in the bay and enlarging our park.

My father worked for the Works Progress Administration (WPA). The WPA was a God-sent and provided food and utilities for my family. I recall pulling our wagon to the Relief Office to receive surplus commodities. Millions of people limped through the Great Depression with the help of Roosevelt's programs—especially in rural areas of the US.

I was pleased about your proposed stimulus package and felt certain our community would be a high priority since we are considered a depressed rural area. However, when our city government sent you the required "wish list" we were by-passed. Our community received no consideration—absolutely nothing.

Our small community of Escanaba, in the Upper Peninsula of Michigan, has again been overlooked. We have a population of just under 14,000 and our Delta County unemployment rate is 13.1 (March 2009). Shouldn't we have had some consideration?

Jim O'Toole, Escanaba City Manager, and a number of local officials recently attended a meeting with the Governor in Marquette. They were told by the Governor that the items on the wish list were not eligible and "thank you for your trouble." Thank you for your trouble? That's it?

According to Jim O'Toole, responsible for diligently compiling and submitting our community wish list:

"From what I understand and heard the Governor say

personally, all the projects (99.9%) that were submitted for the "Wish List" in Michigan were not eligible. It appears the State was going to run all of Michigan Stimulus Funds through their existing state programs.

"For that reason and a few others, I asked Council to pass a resolution that would be sent directly to the Vice President (he is overseeing stimulus) asking that the feds do direct stimulus allocations to local units of government (vs. the state) so that the money can be directed to projects on a local level, implemented and completed on a local level and done faster on a local level (federal revenue sharing if you will)."

Our community is getting hurt right and left. Just recently, Governor Jennifer Granholm and the state legislature in a budget-balancing effort voted to eliminate all state funding for Alzheimer's patients effective June 15. What on earth can they be thinking? Is this fiscally or morally responsible?

By providing service to this population helps keep people in their homes and will certainly forestall nursing home placement which saves millions in Medicaid dollars.

Locally, the day-care center provides care to people with Alzheimer's and other forms of dementia. The respite for family members who are trying to "hang on" and care for their beloved family member is invaluable.

The center serves 20 to 25 people with activities and a nutritious meal plus the all-important respite needed for caregivers. It operates on a budget of 80,600 per year. Three people will lose their jobs.

Where is the humanity? These cruel cuts for the Alzheimer's programming and critical programs for senior citizens should be priority.

In short, our ailing community has not been helped in any way by the stimulus. Lansing has control and we are orphans in the U.P.—always overlooked, always side-stepped and always by-passed.

In a nut-shell, our community not only has been by-passed regarding stimulus allocations, but the dichotomy here is, cuts in services and programs essential to maintaining quality of life are also being eliminated with a promise of more in the works  Where is the justice?

Better yet, what happened to the billions of dollars in stimulus funds that were to be used to relieve fiscal stress at local levels?

My questions to you President Obama are:

1. Can you review our city's "wish list" and allocate stimulus dollars on a local level? Our community is bleeding and our streets are crumbling.

2. On a federal level what can you do to help our community reinstate service for our Alzheimer's local program which in turn provides respite to family members needed to keep them strong and to help protect their sanity?

The program cost: 80,600 per year and retains three jobs.

Perhaps providing stimulus monies directly to our community is the answer.

I should tell you I have a 58-year-old son with an acquired brain-injury. My husband and I have cared for him for 22 years. He requires 24-hour care. Without a daily respite time we could not have survived as a family.

Like I mentioned; I am just naïve enough to think you will have a solution for the problems besetting our depressed community in the UP of Michigan. I would be more than happy to come to Washington to personally discuss them with you.

# WHY HUSBANDS KILL THEIR WIVES
**Friday, June 26, 2009**

Is murder becoming a divorce substitute? It seems that men murdering their spouses has become more rampant –or is it just more sensationalized and followed blow by blow on news magazine shows and Larry King Live because it is so bizarre? God forbid that men murdering their partner become so commonplace it isn't news anymore. The public is shocked beyond belief but yet find the heinous acts titillating

Till "Death do us Part" seems to have taken on a new meaning. One of the most notorious cases in recent history that riveted the country was the televised court proceedings of OJ Simpson. Another case that captured the American people was Scott Peterson killing his beautiful pregnant wife, Laci.

Too close to home was Tom Richardson, the husband that pushed his wife over the spectacular cliff at the Pictured Rocks in Munising and the Tara Grant case: Tara, born in the UP was murdered by her husband who cut up her body into pieces in Lower Michigan. The 1988 Escanaba case of Vincent Loonsfoot who murdered his estranged wife.

I remember an Escanaba case in the 40's when the wife gassed herself by putting her head in the oven. She was depressed over her husband's blatant affair. Surely he killed her by taking away her will to live.

75 per cent of domestic homicides occur just after or during abandonment. Often the wife has a restraining order at the time of the murder.

New cases present constantly—the reasons never cease—but are just as heinous and bizarre. Most recently the alleged case of Christopher Coleman killing both his wife, Sherry, and their two boys by strangulation is just beyond the pale.

Then there is the case of Drew Peterson now in jail for the alleged murder of his third wife. He is also a suspect in the disappearance of wife number four who has gone missing. His televised arrogance has made him a hated man.

The first time I ever heard of a shocking murder was in the 1950's while living in Chicago. Vincent Ciocchi shot his wife and five children; then burned their house down to cover his crime for the affections of 20 year-old Carol Amora.

Most of those cited cases were about husbands who were having affairs. But reasons to shed their wives are many and

*O.J. Simpson with his wife Nicole Brown.*

varied. Sex, philandering, money (either insurance or an unwillingness to split assets) and jealousy are just a few of the motives.

More dads are taking out their entire families. They don't want to split their money and possessions; nor do they want to pay child support; as in the case of Scott Peterson. What kind of a man could strangle his children in their beds or burn the house down to get rid of them? On the other side of the coin some dads kill their wives over custody battles. And of course there is the crime of passion—or rage—that is not-premeditated.

The convicted murderers are incarcerated for life or waiting on death-row. Isn't it interesting that none of them are guilty according to them. They spend their days working on appeals and trying to find loop-holes in the law.

Even more bizarre are the crazy women that write to convicted murderers and want to marry them—in jail. What makes them tick? It's a crazy mixed-up dangerous world if you stop and think about it.

Women are not only victims of domestic violence; but are stalked and prey to the crazies. They just have to be in the wrong place at the wrong time. In urban areas just going out jogging can be dangerous.

Men hire a surrogate to kill. Other men will kill for as little as a thousand dollars. Hiding and mutilating the bodies happens more often than you can imagine. For years it was thought: no body, no conviction. Circumstantial evidence is more difficult to prove beyond a reasonable doubt.

Today, with DNA and the sophistication regarding forensic evidence, there are many more convictions. I remember an Escanaba case where a woman's body washed up, I believe, in the area of the municipal dock. Her purse was found on land. She had been seen in local bars the night before her purse was discovered. Murder or suicide? We'll never know. In the late 40's police and detectives weren't sophisticated enough. As I remember, people that should have been questioned were not. A person could probably get away with murder much more easily back then.

When you think about it: Two people meet, fall in love and join in the sacrament of matrimony; they promise to love and honor one another. How could those attending the wedding ever imagine the union would end up in murder?

Over time, day to day life gets in the way. But how could a man who once professed undying love for his wife end up eventually taking her life and quite often leaving his children motherless. And yet have the audacity to think he can get away with murder?

Most of us will never understand how such a beautiful beginning can have such a tragic ending. After all, divorce is an option.

✿

## IT CAN HAPPEN "ONLY IN AMERICA"
**Friday, July 3, 2009**

We, as a society, are always intrigued by celebrities and the rich and famous. People seek them out to get their autograph, want to shake their hands or have a photo taken with them.

I specifically recall the television series, *Lifestlyes of the Rich and Famous,* which ran from 1984 to 1995. The show featured the usually extravagant lifestyles of wealthy athletes, business moguls or entertainers. The host, Robin Leach, ended each episode with his signature phrase, "champagne wishes and caviar dreams."

Last week I talked at length to a millionaire 150 times over. Yes, that's right—150 million! He lives in Florida and was leaving the following day to fly his private jet to his cabin on the lake in Minnesota for an extended week-end fishing trip. Accompanying him were friends: Urban Meyer, head football coach of the Florida Gators, and Billy Donovan, head basketball coach of the Gators.

You are probably wondering by now: WHO IS HE? He is L. Gale Lemerand and Escanaba can proudly lay claim to him. Born and bred in Escanaba, Gale was a year behind me in high school.

His caring mom, Della, took me under her wing and taught me how to read electrical blueprints when I worked at Harnischfeger years ago. I also visited Della at their modest family home on Washington Avenue. Gale hadn't quite reached the pinnacle of success he enjoys today before his mom died; however, he took her all over the world and was very generous to her. She was extremely proud of him.

As a tribute to his beloved mom, Gale was the major contributor to the Escanaba High School field house addition/renovation. It is aptly named for Della Lemerand. He also provided a 250,000 trust for an Escanaba High School scholarship to honor his parents, Clarence and Della Lemerand. In addition he was the major contributor for the construction of Lemerand Field, a softball diamond.

The Lemerand family was like most in Escanaba after the Great Depression; struggling to put food on the table and provide essentials. Gale grew up during the 30's and 40's and didn't realize they lacked the finer things in life. "If you don't have something, you don't miss it," says Gale. "I didn't realize how bad we had it until I saw the other side."

Gale graduated seventh in his graduating class of 200 but at that time higher education didn't penetrate his radar screen; neither Gale nor his parents were interested and coupled with the fact there wasn't any money for additional schooling.

As a present day philanthropist Gale explains, "Education, that's one thing that was missing—a formal education. I feel I could have been more successful with a formal education. Education is very, very important. I do think common sense and experience are more important, but if you have common sense, experience, and a formal education, it's wonderful. Because of that, I really support higher education now."

Gale succeeded in business beyond his wildest dreams. After a stint in the Air Force he began a career at Williams Insulation in Chicago in 1968. Lemerand bought out his partner and renamed the business Gale Industries at the age of 40.

"Only in America," can someone start from virtually nothing; work from a barn in Illinois, and not only build a multi-million dollar company but also change the face of the entire industry. Gale was not reluctant to take risks or borrow money.

He has given millions of dollars to universities, colleges and other education related issues. Lemerand became a Bull Gator and major contributor to the University of Florida athletic program. He funded a 46,000 square-foot facility that opened in 1995 and houses multiple athletic teams. He followed with a generous donation for the construction of Florida's 47,500 square-foot basketball complex—one of the finest in collegiate sports.

In honor of Gale's major contributions to the University of Florida; the North-South Drive in front of the stadium has been renamed Gale Lemerand Drive. The University has also awarded Gale an honorary Doctorate.

Gale's holdings are too numerous to mention. For starters, he is also the co-founder of Stonewood Grill and Restaurants (the brilliant idea was hatched with a friend on a golf course), and Peach Valley Café—another concept. He owns three Perkins Family Restaurant franchises and the list goes on—and on. He is also involved in real estate.

To his credit Gale has written the book, To Win in Business...Bet on the 'Jockey'. A remarkable story that starts with his humble beginnings in Escanaba: working at the carnival (U.P. Fair), harvesting beans, Hoyler's Ice Cream Store and even delivering papers for the Daily Press. Gale lectures all over the country. His book includes: "Lemerand Lessons" You Can Use In Your Business.

In Gale's words on the cover of his book: "Employees are probably the most important aspect of a business...I would try to hire the very best people. To win the Kentucky derby, you don't start with a jackass and try to train him to win. You start with a thoroughbred because a trained jackass is still a jackass."

A 2006 article in the New York times, "For a Price, Final Resting Places that even Tut Could Appreciate" states, "The most grandiose niche in Paramus is humble compared to the granite extravaganza erected at Daytona Memorial Park to house the mortal remains of L. Gale Lemerand, a Florida philanthropist, who founded a residential insulation company that sold for an estimated $150 million."

"Two $4000 Medjool date palms shade Mr. Lemerand's red granite mausoleum, which costs $650,000..."

When asked, "If you had to do one or two things over again in your business career, what would they be?"

Gale's reply, "Not work quite so many hours as I did, so that I could enjoy a better family life." Gale has been married several times and claims his business success did not carry over in his private life—but added his wives have been well-taken care of and we are best friends. Presently, he is single and enjoys time with his lady friend that lives near him on the water in Florida.

Gale recently set up his son in an insulation business in Florida. He also has two daughters; one sits on the board of Stonewood Grill and Tavern Enterprises.

And what are your plans for the 4th of July? Watching a parade; enjoying a family gathering or perhaps a picnic in the park?

Contrast that with Gale's holiday itinerary. He is flying his jet to New York for the gala quadricentennial celebration of the Hudson River—400 years since English explorer Henry Hudson sailed the river while trying to find the passage to Asia.

Gale's $10 million 124 foot yacht is moored there with his crew of five ready to cruise up the Hudson River and partake of the historic activities. Six barges will fire 40,000 shells in tune with patriotic songs. The show attracts millions of spectators and is televised nationwide.

Like Paul Harvey used to say, "And now you know the rest of the story."

"Only in America"

# PRESCRIPTION DRUGS: LIFE-SAVING OR LETHAL?
## Friday, July 10, 2009

Just because a drug is prescribed doesn't mean it can't be lethal. The likelihood of a drug becoming lethal has to do with overdosing or mixing other non-compatible prescription drugs with it—or even an allergic reaction.

Just last week I brought my son to the cardiologist who changed his heart medication to an extended release medication concluding the dose he was taking was too much. Being a strong advocate I felt comfortable with the new script. But he awoke at 4:00 am—five hours after taking his first dose. He was cool to touch, clammy all over and anxious. He had a glazed-over look, was disoriented and said he was going to jump out the window.

He, no doubt, didn't know how to relate his distress. I knew it was serious—at least needed some evaluation. Immediately, I suspected the change in medication. I also realized that those could be signs of a heart attack. I read on the internet that the same generic medicine he was given had been recalled (2008) without much public awareness. Could this be the problem again? Cases reported an unusual jump in blood pressure after taking the drug. His blood pressure had soared. We were off to the ER.

After a battery of tests my suspicions were confirmed. Gary is sensitive to drugs and the new dosage was too great for his height and weight. He was switched back to what he had previously been taking—only half the dose. It's a delicate balance and can be a dangerous game. He's Ok now.

I talked to the druggist and we essentially agreed that there are risks with every drug; that's why you have to weigh the risks versus benefits. How scary can that be? My husband is on 14 medications a day. In his case the benefits outweigh the risks. Without the drugs he wouldn't be here.

Years ago, there wasn't the array of drugs that are available now. You went to the doctor or he came to the house; you just never thought to question his expertise. Really, drugs were limited. It is so different today. You have to take charge of your own health and be a partner in the decision –making. The capabilities are available to investigate on the internet. Be prepared and ask questions. But what are the elderly or those with dementia to do? They need a strong advocate!

Almost everyday you can hear of a drug that some have been taking for years; and now the industry is taking a second look at. Premarin once touted as a miracle drug for women is one. Likewise, the risks with taking cholesterol-lowering drugs are real and you need to calculate the risks versus benefits. Tylenol is a drug we all think is safe, however a warning came out today about people dying from liver failure due to overuse of the drug. Today a person must be informed and vigilant.

How unbelievably ironic—just now as I write I received a phone call from Colorado. A grieving woman, a former resident, had just received word that her 23 year-old nephew in Escanaba died of a drug overdose. Why? A bewildered, grieving family is wondering, how can this happen?

I think back to when our generation was young; no one ever heard of recreational drugs. Believe me; we didn't need drugs to get high. Everyday was a high, going to school, seeing our friends and going to dances. There might have been a few guys that drank beer—that's about the extent of drugs in our time.

I don't think Elvis Presley meant to die, nor did Anna Nicole Smith. There is still speculation about Marilyn Monroe, suicide or accident? Ultimately they all died from drug overdoses.

And now Michael Jackson! He has abused prescription drugs for years. At one time he left his tour to go into a drug treatment facility. Surely he was aware of the risks. Evidently the drugs and how they make you feel are so powerful that either they don't think it can happen to them or the urge is so great they don't care. Michael suffered from insomnia.

Former Jackson attorney Brian Oxman told CBS, "But the plain fact of the matter is that Michael Jackson had prescription drugs at his disposal at all times."

More troubling, a Jackson family member told TMZ.com that Michael had been receiving daily injections of Demerol, an additive painkiller. Demerol can slow respiration to the point of suffocation, which can deprive the heart of oxygen and lead to sudden death. Reports say that Jackson was fascinated with Demerol.

On his 1997 track "Morphine"—an unusually discordant Jackson song—he sings, "Close your eyes and drift away Demerol." An article in Time magazine states, "His death may well be accidental, but investigators and journalists will spend months determining whether it could have been prevented if those around him weren't so often using him as an ATM."

Of course being from an entirely different generation I wasn't a Michael Jackson fan; in fact that wild kind of music gives me a headache. I'll take the easy-listening of Frank Sinatra or Dean Martin any day. Perhaps drugs were needed to "get high" to perform at the level Michael did—just like Johnny Cash and umpteen other musicians. Entertainers are certainly a different breed.

I did like the classic ballad, "I'll Be There," performed when Michael was twelve. However, he has a world of fans—they're probably just not from my generation. I was in awe, though, as I watched the memorial tribute on TV. The consensus is that he is the greatest entertainer that ever lived. His "Thriller" track has never been surpassed.

I would speculate that drugs to induce sleep will probably be the culprit that took Michael's life—an accident waiting to happen. He never would have wanted to leave his children.

It makes me wonder: When a young person dies of an overdose; you would think that would frighten others imbibing dangerous drugs. It doesn't though. Is it that young people just don't think such a fate can happen to them?

Their reckless disregard to get "high" and perhaps even succumbing to a drug leaves family members devastated and mourning for the rest of their life—wondering what could I had done to prevent this terrible tragedy?

A message to young people taking drugs today: If you don't care about your precious life; think about your family and how your demise will affect the rest of their days. Get professional help. Drugs are a tragedy waiting to happen.

## MORE GEMS FROM THE PAST
## Friday, July 17, 2009

I receive lots of letters and e-mails from readers sharing their early childhood experiences. Many write about the impressionable Depression years and reminisce about the "way it was."

Life was simple and less complicated in the old days. We didn't worry about balancing a check book—no one had one. We didn't struggle with computers—there were none. We didn't get frustrated operating the TV and VCR—they didn't exist. Our parents were concerned with a roof overhead, food on the table and clothes on our backs.

A recent letter from Lorraine Srock: "Being 90 years old all your memories are a part of mine. I love it. Sometimes I sit and dream about my life. Living through the Depression I think is a part of the reason I am living so long. We weren't allowed a second piece of meat till Daddy was through eating and if there was any left. Soda pop and ice cream cones were a luxury and a treat."

Yes Lorraine, I remember when "Dad was King." He brought home the bacon. Dad expected and received preferential treatment. That's just the way it was. During the war when many food items were rationed my job was to mix that awful lard-looking margarine with a yellow dye that came packaged with it. Trying to make it look like butter did nothing for the taste. As a result I hate margarine today.

We weren't allowed to have the "real butter." That was reserved for the "King." So when Mom and Dad went out on Saturday night to the bar for a beer—that was their entertainment—I baby-sat and used the opportunity to have a home-made bread toast and sneak some real butter. Then I tried to smooth it out to cover my tracks so it didn't look like any was missing. I also made fudge for the little ones. That was a big treat. Sugar was rationed but we had lots of kids so we had an abundance of ration stamps.

I laughed when I asked my husband if his Dad was "King" in his household. He recalled the small oscillating fan some folks had to keep cool in the summer. The fan was positioned in front of Dad and oscillated only around him. Don't you just have a mental picture of that? Also the Sunday paper was off limits to anyone until Dad read it. Nobody dared to touch it.

I witnessed an elderly couple that could barely walk at the casino. The wife was patiently waiting for her husband who was engrossed with a slot-machine. He said, "why don't you run over to the soda machine and get me a drink—not too much ice? She could barely walk. And hobble over there she did. Perhaps a today's woman might say, get it yourself—I'm not your slave!
We had a big family and one small bathroom. Sometimes there was a line-up to get in there. Dad always stepped to the head of the line. Maybe he was smart. Girls take a long time with curlers and their hair. No blow dryers or curling irons back then.

I also remember I had only two pair of bobby-socks. I washed them out and hung them by the register, but if the furnace went out as it often did, my socks would be damp in the morning. Many a morning I donned wet socks and trudged the two miles to high school in a snow storm

Another letter from Dorothy Lang Lande: "I graduated in 1945—end of World War 11. I frequented the "Boston Sweet Shoppe" for their olive and nut sandwiches with a cherry coke—or their ham salad. In 1945 the boys would meet us there, but it was all "Dutch" and then they would walk us home. Bring us some more good memories. The Dell's Supper Club would be nice."

Ah Yes! Memories! The Dells holds many. Before our local boys left to engage in battle on the front lines during World War 11 they enjoyed a last evening dancing and dining at the Dells. In those days everyone dressed up in suits—very formal. It was customary for the boys to take off their tie and hang it over a huge beam suspended over the bar. Literally hundreds of colorful ties were displayed on the beam. The idea was for the boys to come home and retrieve their ties after the war—a joyous moment suspended in time.

No one can forget the Dells when the Flath family ran it. There was something magical about it; the sounds of the big band (Ivan Kobasic) drifting outside got your feet moving and your heart dancing even before you opened the door. Huge peacocks spreading their familiar fan of vibrant jewel-like colors; deer prancing leisurely were seen from the dining-room windows. It was different from any place I have ever been. And the sad part is—you can never go back.

Where can you go now to dance and hear the easy-listening music we loved? Well, let's be realistic. If there was a place like that it would go broke. The younger generation wouldn't frequent a place with our brand of music. And when you think of it; us old fogies would hobble in with canes and wheelchairs or perhaps out-of-breath and unable to dance. But we can still day-dream and reminisce about those wonderful days of youth.

Another reader (unidentified) wrote: "I would like some history on the cemetery in Rose Park. When was the first burial and when was the cemetery removed?" That question stymied me. I don't recall the cemetery there. Perhaps a reader could shed some light on the Rose Park cemetery history.

I probably have repeated some tidbits; that's what the elderly do—repeat. But then they forget too, so maybe some of the older readers will think they are reading some of this stuff for the first time. For the younger generations; don't laugh. Your time will come.

## 66 YEARS BETWEEN KISSES:
## A TIMELESS LOVE STORY
**Friday, July 24, 2009**

I watched this dapper-looking couple who belied their 85 years as they approached my door holding hands. Elaine was youthfully dressed with a smart white fedora perkily cocked on her head. White stylish earrings adorned her youthful face. A hint of mascara brightened her wide eyes. Bill was dressed quite sporty in dashing summer colors with a head of hair a young man would die for.

I couldn't wait to hear their unusual and delightful love story that spanned 66 years between kisses. They were in Escanaba for

Bill's yearly family reunion at the pavilion in Ludington Park. Elaine, animated and bubbling over with personality and enthusiasm, recalled how she and Bill met. Bill lovingly watched her every move as he listened to their uncommon lives replayed.

Elaine Lavelle was a junior and Bill Haring was a senior at Escanaba High in 1942. Elaine, not at all bashful, had her sights set on handsome Bill. So when she met up with him on the squeaky running track at the old high school, Elaine introduced herself and asked him, "Hey, how would you like to take me to the basketball game this Friday?"

Bill had been forewarned by other guys, 'watch out for her – she's a big flirt.' Shy Bill replied, "Sure, if I can get my Dad's car (an old Nash)." Bill needed wheels living in Schafer. After the game they went to Hoyler's Tea Room where they shared a soda. Elaine remembers asking Bill for a kiss on their first of many dates.

Their romance slowly faded away when Bill sent a note to Elaine telling her he would be a Baptist minister one day and he needed a Baptist wife. Elaine was Methodist.

They lost touch after graduation and embarked on separate happy lives raising their families and building careers. Elaine married Frank Hanrath and had four children. Frank was superintendent of schools in several Wisconsin communities spending 22 years in Marshfield. Vivacious Elaine even had a bit part in a movie while visiting in London.

After graduation and serving in the Marines, Bill went to college on the GI Bill and became a Baptist minister. Bill said God had spoken to him at age seven. He really didn't want to be a minister. At age 14 he didn't think he was smart enough but finally relented and said, "OK God—you win; but I'll need your help and guidance." Bill's two brother's Bob and Ken are also ministers.

Bill married Esther, a God-driven woman, and they had 5 children—two are now deceased. As a Baptist minister he led congregations in Minnesota, Iowa, and Wisconsin and in the South. He and his family also spent 17 years in Mexico doing Missionary work.

Fast-forward to 2004: Elaine lost her husband. In 2006 her daughter found Bill's address in Alabama on the internet. Elaine sent him a Christmas card—no answer. She sent him another card in 2007. Finally in March of 2008 Bill answered.

He had also lost his wife in 2004. He grieved and didn't care if he lived any longer. He asked Elaine how her health was and told her if she called him not to call after 10pm. She wrote him a ten page letter about her life and her children. Then the daily talks on the phone began. They fell in love again through those phone calls. Yet, they hadn't seen one another in 66 years.

"I felt a real love rise up for Elaine," Bill explained. "We hadn't seen each other for 66 years but I wanted to get together."

Bill told Elaine he was attending a family reunion in Escanaba in July. "I could stop by and say hello," he said. Elaine eagerly waited for Bill and his daughter to arrive. The big moment came. She opened the screen door and according to Elaine, Bill gave her a Baptist peck for a kiss. "I can do better than that." she thought. "I grabbed Bill and gave him a big-time Methodist smacker on the lips." Zowie!

Bill's daughter left for a short time so they could talk.

*Elaine LaVelle and Bill Haring in 1942.*

*66 years later.*

The sat in the sunroom overlooking the lake and both felt like they had been together forever. At this stage of life they had discovered something rarer than gold—a soul-mate!

Bill invited Elaine to attend their family reunion with him. The next day at Ludington Park Elaine met his family and Bill gave a little sermon. The he reached in his pocket and surprised (shocked) Elaine with a diamond ring. She was speechless as he asked her, "Will you be my wife?"

Later that afternoon they found a quiet place in the park and got into the back seat. The hugged and kissed. And hugged and kissed. And hugged and kissed.

After dinner that evening they went for a drive and again parked on a quiet street. Again they climbed into the backseat. They kissed and necked (as we use to call it) from 11pm until 3am. "The windows would steam up—so occasionally we opened them," says Elaine. "At one point a jogger ran by and embarrassed Bill told me to duck down." They were suspended in time—just a couple of 85 year-old teen-agers—necking in the back seat.

They married a few months later on September 13, 2008

surrounded by their children and family members. In the summer they live in Bailey's Harbor (Elaine's home) and they winter in Bill's home in Fairhope, Alabama.

Bill says, "When you're in love, you really know you're in love. We get to talking, and have so much fun being together. One thing Elaine and I have in common is we both come from The Depression (era) and World War 11. I don't care if we go to a Methodist or a Baptist church. We love God."

Before they departed Elaine studied my eyes and said, "I see you wear eye-liner.  Look at me; I had mine tattooed on so I can look good all the time." Then she took off her fedora and proudly displayed her hair extensions.  Tattooed eye liner and hair extensions!?   So you see; never give up and as Yogi Berra once said, "The game ain't over till it's over!"

How fortunate they are to have found a soul-mate again—66 years between kisses.

## SUMMERTIME MOMENTS—MUSIC TO MY EARS
**Friday, July 31, 2009**

"Summertime and the living is easy," just like the song says. Summertime and visitors go together like a "horse and carriage" just like the song says.  And summertime brings many visitors; people we have met from wintering in Florida, old-time friends from school days and of course family members: children, grandchildren and great-grandchildren.

My son Jeff and his two daughters, Mary Pat (age 19) and Kelly (age 8) usually plan a visit during the strawberry harvesting time just before the 4th of July.  He usually helps me make jam to take back to Washington D.C.   This year was different.   The strawberries were late in the UP; so he picked strawberries in Virginia, made jam and brought some to us.

He and the girls did get quite a surprise when my husband answered the door upon their arrival.  Gary, with his playful, weird and wild sense of humor, decided to dress-up for the occasion—a spoof on today's youth of course.

What they saw left them speechless with mouths widely agape; And just maybe a smirk of delight in their eyes.

My husband gave some real thought to his get-up.  His baseball hat was cocked on his head backwards with a curly wig underneath, a large hoop erring hung from one ear.  In one hand he held a cell-phone; in the other he had a bottle of water.  Perched over the cap turned backward was an earphone.

He wore a large baggy pair of shorts that one of the grandchildren had left behind. They hung to mid-calf and exposed his backside. His tee-shirt was short to further expose his lower backside and one of the many removable tattoos he adorned himself with.   Printed on the tee was a huge nut with the inscription, "Most of the people that drive me NUTS are in my FAMILY."

They were completely mesmerized as he jumped around and sang to the loud music playing in his ears. Yes, he created quite a hoopla when they arrived. When things settled down we retreated to the deck for hours—still laughing about their unusual greeting.

Mary Pat, who has completed her first year of college in Virginia, is working toward a marketing degree and was fortunate enough to acquire a summer job as a marketing intern. She has many other interests too; gourmet food preparation is one of them. She and her father insisted on preparing dinner. I didn't argue. Besides it was fun to watch them (father and daughter) preparing dinner in the kitchen in complete harmony.

They purchased fresh whitefish and Mary Pat placed a brown paper bag in the bottom of the pan. She explained the skin would stay on paper when broiled. How ingenious!

Her instructions:  place skin down on paper bag in pan; turn broiler on; drizzle olive oil and lemon on fish; sprinkle seasoned salt, pepper, onion powder and dill; broil for approximately 10 minutes. (Check periodically)

Top whitefish with Mango Salsa: Dice one whole mango and a half red onion; dice a bush of cilantro; add diced ingredients with a can of sweet corn and a can of black beans; squeeze one lime onto ingredients; salt and pepper to taste; refrigerate before serving.

Jeff made a unique salad with strawberries and slivered almonds. A bottle of Asti-Spumanti was just the right compliment to a gourmet dinner you would find in a five-star restaurant similar to the Fairmont Hotel at the top of Nob Hill in San Francisco. I mention the Fairmont because years ago while on vacation we stayed there and fresh Lake Superior whitefish, a real delicacy, was featured on their marquee—at an exorbitant price.

We just may have another Rachel Ray or Julia Child in our own

Mary Pat. Julia's 1961 best seller, "Mastering the Art of French Cooking" is presently in its 47th printing. When I obtain a "difficult to come by" copy of her famed book it will go to Mary Pat. It is French cooking in terms Americans would understand and Julia's way of talking about France and its values which are so different from ours.

Vanity Fair states, "The centuries-old techniques that the French learn like a language could now be learned step-by-step by Americans."

In her memoir, "My Life in France" she states, "I fell in love with French food—the tastes, the processes, the history, the endless variations, the rigorous discipline, the creativity, the wonderful people, the equipment, the rituals."

The true story of her life, "Julie & Julia" with Meryl Streep at her best, debuts in theatres on August 7th. For me it's a must see.

And then there is Kelly. At age 8 her interests were consumed with Ludington Park and the beach. Jeff kept marveling how wonderful our park is—after going for a run in the park/beach area, he noted that is every bit as scenic and beautiful as his usual run on the national mall, between the U.S. Capitol and the Washington Monument. Like most, he took things for granted while growing up here. Now he visits as a father and realizes the beauty and worth of our area.

My life is like an open book through this column. Sometimes I share a sad time in our life with you—perhaps a medical emergency; today's story had a humorous and playful element coupled with some precious family moments.

I guess I am trying to say that "into each life some rain must fall" like the song says. But when the clouds clear and the sun shines through; it is important to cherish those special moments. And when there are clouds "look for the silver lining"—just like the song says.

# SO MUCH FOR TRANSPARENCY IN WASHINGTON
## Friday, August 7, 2009

My column, "An open letter to Obama" (June 19), inspired me to actually send the letter to President Obama. To refresh your memory my chief complaint centered on our community being by-passed by the stimulus distribution. While I was at it, I thought; why not send letters to Joe Biden, Michelle Obama and Jill Biden?

I sent all four letters (including autographed books to the ladies) on June 22. Kind of an experiment—now let's see what happens. Remember the transparency the current administration has promised?

I used the 2-3 day mail guaranteed by the post office and mail tracking. Seven days later on June 30 my correspondence reached Washington D. C. —but the White House did not accept delivery. The letters were held at the post office with an attempted delivery notice. The notice said they would hold the mail for 15 days; if not picked up by the White House, the Post Office would return to sender.

I checked daily; status remained not picked-up. After 10 days I visited Representative Bart Stupak's office. "I'll call the White House and check on it" his aide said. "If your mail is returned bring it down to our office and we will see that it is delivered from our Washington office."

I am not an investigative reporter but: At the same time I complained to Stupak's office that the wish list submitted by our city government (Jim O'Toole) was virtually ignored—no awards. "Not so," she said.

The office manager printed a copy of the multi-million dollar stimulus awards for Stupak's district including Delta County and explained that the projects needed to be "shovel-ready with an end-completion date of no longer than 12 to 18 months." She pointed out that, "Mr. O'Toole's request did not meet the required guidelines because he had some completion dates of 2011 and 2014 which didn't qualify.

She said the guideline information was accessible on the web-site or could have been obtained from Stupak's office. She also indicated Stupak's office conducted meetings to explain and city government apparently chose not to attend.

Mr. O'Toole's failure to check on the guidelines may have cost our community a stimulus award for our badly needed street repairs. We'll never know.

I delivered a copy of the Delta County Stimulus awards to O'Toole (he didn't have one) and also informed him why our city government was not considered. He viewed the report and commented he didn't have much regard for the stimulus. Really?!

Yet, the City of Escanaba sent Vice-President Joe Biden a resolution (June10) "demanding federal recovery funds (be) used to assist local budgets." To date, according to O'Toole, a reply has not been received.

A further inquiry with Congressman Stupak's Legislative Director, Nick Choate, from the Washington D.C. office revealed, "so far Delta County has received a little over $17 million out of the $284 million awarded in the 1st District (which includes 31 counties)."

He also said the state of MI received $1 billion dollars in stimulus funds; 80 to 85 percent earmarked for education while 15 to 20 percent was to be used for discretionary fiscal stabilization. Instead the billion dollars were used 100% for education.

However, he forwarded me "The Recovery Act at Work in Your Community" print-out which listed a Community Services Block Grant for Menominee-Delta-Schoolcraft Community Action Agency and Human Resource Authority in the amount of $3,368,642.

A good share of that money is earmarked for the weatherization of 492 homes in Menominee, Delta and Schoolcraft counties. The Alzheimer and dementia day care program has also benefited from the stimulus award.

The press and constituents are the watchdogs; that's why we have free-press which makes for a better society than a dictatorship. Recently, Obama made an incorrect observation about the racial profiling incident and called the police "stupid." He was "out-of-line" and had to do a lot "backpedaling." If you are a public servant you understand that criticism is a fact of life. It may not always be warranted.

The White House finally picked up my letters to Joe Biden,

Michelle Obama and Jill Biden just before the 15-day expiration date. I am puzzled as to what happened to the letter to President Obama. To my knowledge he didn't receive it and it was never returned. As I said, "so much for transparency."

To date I have received one reply: a letter from Vice-President Joe Biden.

An excerpt of my letter to Vice President Joe Biden: In order not to be repetitious, I am sending you my weekly column article, "An Open Letter to President Obama" (June 19) to address my concerns regarding our small community in the Upper Peninsula of MI. I love my community and I am especially troubled regarding the absence of any stimulus funds.

Vice-President Joe Biden's letter dated July 9, 2009 follows:

*Dear Patt,*

*Thank you for sharing your article, "An open letter to President Obama" with me.*

*President Obama and I understand that our country currently faces many challenges, but we know these challenges bring about new opportunities for all of us. While this Administration will work tirelessly to address these issues, we all must become more accountable in shaping our collective future. I encourage you to remain active in your government, because America needs your voice and dedication at a time of crucial importance.*

*Please know I appreciate your article and thank you for writing me.*

*Sincerely,*

*Joe R. Biden, Jr.*
*Vice president of the United States*

The letter was somewhat generic but at the very least I received an answer. Did he address my real concern about the distribution of stimulus money? NO.

The two chief complaints in my correspondence to Washington centered on the lack of local stimulus awards coupled with cuts for critical local programs such as serving the Alzheimer's and dementia population and their families; plus the lack of any stimulus distribution to shore up our badly needed infrastructure repairs.

I'll keep you posted on any other replies I may receive from the White House. In the meantime I repeat, "So much for the administration's promised transparency." Meanwhile keep informed and voice your opinions in the local forum provided: Letters to the Editor. Your voices are needed to effect change.

Biden's advice: "Remain active in your government because America needs your voice..." That also rings true with local level government—closer to home; making it easier to effect change.

## CITY DECISIONS AND CHANGES AFFECT ALL OF US
**Friday, August 21, 2009**

Sometime seniors have more problems with change than younger folks. And rightfully so! On a broad spectrum: Years of living experiences and witnessing so many changes that have been really detrimental to society as a whole makes us glad and proud we were a part of an era that was so special.

On a local level I would be the first to admit I was wrong when I was against the garbage collection change. I worried that if I survived my husband I would not physically be able to handle those huge trash cans. Like most seniors one of our biggest concerns is losing our independence.

Then I remember when I was no more that age five in the late 30's. The town was infested by huge rats in the alleys where raw garbage was a feast. Remember plastic bags had not yet been invented. The city had an all-out campaign to place poison in the alleys and rid the city of rats.

Boca Raton in Florida got its name (big rats) from the city being overrun with rats and no doubt many cities had the same problem.

In the 30's I remember my mother jumping on top of a table screaming that a rat was in the toilet bowl and I yelled for my grandfather who lived in the big house in front. He came running with an ax. Apparently, rats were in the sewer system. Is it any wonder for years I was paranoid to use the toilet before a thorough examination of the bowl?

Now as I look down 32$^{nd}$ Street and see the neat green trash cans all lined up in front yards—no alleys—I am pleased with the change. Less seagulls hanging around.

The Ludington Street change from 14$^{th}$ Street to 10$^{th}$ Street is a different story. I have seen it change back and forth from angle parking to curb parking over the years. I liked the wide open look of the main drag as we called it years ago. As you enter the city you still get that feel—that is, until you reach 14$^{th}$ street.

As I approach 14$^{th}$ Street I have often seen unaware drivers in the right-turn lane trying to veer over to the small cloistered one-lane. It is downright dangerous for drivers to have to make that decision at the last minute. The same thing happens going west when you reach Ninth Street. Unaware drivers end up driving in the angled parking spaces.

In my opinion the wide-open street ascetically beats the two-lane old-fashioned look hands-down. And who could look at the newly renovated store fronts when you are so busy watching and worried about someone pulling out of angle parking.

Accidents are up 61% since the change. That alone gives credence to change the street back to parallel parking. We have an opportunity to make our community safer and that should be our number one priority. Snow removal is another thing—all piled up in the middle of the street.

Safety is a concern for me. As I try to back-out of a parking place in front of Wickerts or the Morrison Shoppe; all of the sudden cars whip around the corner from South 10$^{th}$ when the light changes. I have nearly gotten clipped on more than one occasion. A member of the DDA says it is better to park in the middle of the block to avoid that occurring. Really?!

And the handicapped parking are on the ends! What a hazard for them. And how about winter time if they want to go to a store in the middle of the block? Another concern is backing up into traffic when a truck or larger vehicle is parked next to you obscuring your view. It's almost like hit and miss.

The city council received hundreds of people complaining about the proposed change. Rosie's diner had a petition with over 600 names alone. Our smart seasoned Mayor Leo Evans voted against it. Why? Because he had a steady stream of folks voicing their objection with the proposed change and he had insight from years past—something our new council didn't have. But council changed it anyway.

The vote was three to one with the Mayor's vote being the only dissenting vote. Pat Baribeau was not on the council at that time. My guess is: it never would have been changed with a public vote.

The jury is still out with the North Shore Plan. Yes, it is good to have a vision and a plan. But was this the time to spend 47,000 dollars on a plan given the present economy? Streets are crumbling—-that plan could have waited for the time being. Talk about the government spending money like a drunken sailor—it's happening right here.

As a heavy tax-payer of this city I am convinced I will never see any development in that area in my lifetime. So now they have a plan—what next?

The same with the Port study in the past. Thousands of tax-payer dollars down the drain—a real fiasco.

Now I understand the City Manager is working on an ordinance for monuments or memorials to be placed in a special area in the park. What is that going to be like? A grave yard in the park? According to O'Toole he has received many requests from people wanting a memorial to a loved one in the park. I wonder!

Remember how our government works. The city-manager's boss is the city council and the council works for the people. We need to keep that in mind.

We, as a community, need to stand up to things we don't want to see happen. Our option is to vote people on city council that have the passion about our city and most importantly listen to their constituent's voice.

Being a public servant is not an easy job. I am sure our present council members are inundated with e-mails, letters and phone calls. It can take over their life with all the meetings they are required to attend. But they are there because they want to be.

We, as a community, need to get involved and not stand by and let things happen in our city that the majority is not in-tune with—by doing so we can make a difference. Remember the council is supposed to work for us!

---

And now the sad news! I will no longer be writing a column on Friday. As much as I enjoyed writing and connecting with readers; I have some personal issues requiring attention: Surgery on a torn rotator cuff and a long rehabilitation in the fall are on my radar screen.

I will still write an occasional piece from time to time as well as work on my new book of memoirs similar to Frank McCourt's Angela's Ashes. Thank you for your great support for the past four years. It's been a great trip!

## GARY ABRAHAMSON TROPHY AWARD

Gary Abrahamson was the 25th recipient of the 1949 prestigious Herman Gessner trophy. Escanaba High School sports played a tremendous part in Gary's life. He set his sights on winning the Gessner Award in the 7th grade.

Gary's love of EHS sports was the impetus that made The Gary Abrahamson trophy become a reality. The trophy was initiated in 2007

Gary died in 2011, yet his memory will live on when the Abrahamson trophy is presented annually at the EHS sports banquet. His son delivered the following 2011 award after his father's death. It encapsulated Gary's deep love of EHS sports.

## Remarks by Jeff Abrahamson
### May 24, 2011

Good Morning Eskymos! We are here this morning to honor members of the senior class for their many accomplishments in the classroom, arts, and athletics.

And I have the great honor and privilege this morning of awarding the Gary Abrahamson Trophy to two deserving individuals. But, before I do that, let me take a moment to talk about the trophy as well as Gary Abrahamson, the benefactor of the trophy.

The Gary Abrahamson Trophy Award is presented each year to the senior female and male athlete who has been awarded the most athletic letters during four years of high school. In the case of a tie, the person with the highest grade point average is awarded the trophy.

But, before I award the trophy, let me say a few things about the trophy's benefactor and namesake. Gary Abrahamson was the 1949 recipient of the Herman-Gessner Trophy (now called the Gessner-Photenhauer trophy). In 1949, Escanaba High School consisted of only three grades (10th through 12th), and Gary Abrahamson won eight of a possible nine letters in three sports (football, basketball, and track). He knew first-hand the dedication, perseverance, and drive that it takes to qualify for an athletic letter.

I am sorry to say that Gary Abrahamson, who is my father, passed away last month from causes related to heart failure. But if he was here today, he would tell you how exceedingly proud he was to grow up in Escanaba and play for the Escanaba Eskymos.

He would probably be able to tell you -- if you cared to listen – in detail about what it was like to play six-man football at the Escanaba Junior High under Bill Pucklewartz. Or how the 1948 Escanaba Eskymo football team won every game -- except one -- and outscored its opponents 206 to 47 that year. Ironically, though, the most vivid memory and most talked about game was – not the wins – but that one loss ... by one point ... to the

Menominee Maroons. Over fifty years later, his classmates (and Coach Ruwich) still talked about that game ... "if only we would have run a different play on that last drive."

It's a testament to how impressionable and important your years in high school truly are. And with that introduction, let me now turn to the winners of the Gary Abrahamson Trophy.

--in 2007, the winners were Allison Harvey & Derek Saari
--in 2008, the winners were Gianna Nardi & Garrick Fisher
--in 2009, the winners were Jennie Mokszycke & Doug Beattie
--in 2010, the winners were Olivia Barron and Mitch VanEffen

This year's male winner of the Gary Abrahamson Trophy is Jared Dagenais. Jared received a total of 10 letters:

--2 letters were in Football. During his senior year, Jared started as a wide-receiver and was an All Great Northern Conference Pick in Football.

--4 letters were in Hockey. Jared was the leading scorer on the hockey team during his senior year and was also a second team all-conference selection and was named team MVP.

--and 4 letters were in Baseball. Jared has been a three-year starter in baseball since his sophomore year.

--in addition to his athletic accomplishments, Jared was a four-year member of the band and a very well rounded student at the Escanaba High School. Let's offer Jared a round of applause.

This year's female winner of the Gary Abrahamson Trophy is Sherri Berube. Sherri received a total of 12 letters:

*Patt Abrahamson, 2009 winners of the Gary Abrahamson Trophy and Jeff Abrahamson.*

--4 letters were in Cross Country.  Sherri was a captain on the cross country team her senior year.

--2 letters were in Girls Track during her Freshman and Sophomore years and 2 other letters were earned as a manager of the boy's tennis team during her junior and senior years.

--4 of Sherri's letters were in Wrestling.   Sherri was the first female in Escanaba history and one of only eight girls to become a Regional Qualifier in the Michigan High School Athletic Association Post Season Tournament. Sherri was an All-American during her senior year and a National Champion.   She has accepted a Wrestling Scholarship to Cumberland College in Kentucky.  Let's offer Sherri a round of applause.

Congratulations to this year's winners of the Gary Abrahamson Trophy.   And I'd like to let you know that although Gary Abrahamson is no longer here, you undergraduates should keep working toward earning letters because the Abrahamson family will continue to fund the trophy.  Thank you.

2012 Winners of the Gary Abrahamson Trophy; Jennie Mokszycke, with 10 letters and Doug Beattie with 9 letters.

# A WIDOW'S GRIEF

Many of my friends became widows long before I was plunged into the depths of despair and devastation after the recent loss of my husband of sixty years. I realize now that I couldn't even fathom the pain and anguish widows experienced until I would unwillingly join them.

I was only 15 when Gary and I began our lifelong love affair. He was 17. We were just kids; the jock and the majorette. But our love endured for 63 years. We raised three children and yes, there were times that life didn't seem perfect. As in any long term marriage it takes work and dedication to overcome the trials and tribulations of raising a family coupled with detours from the road of perfection. Yet our love endured and grew stronger.

We spent hours talking about anything or everything: There was even a comfort in silence; just the presence of one another was soothing. I liked to read upon retiring and he lay next to me with a face that beamed with contentment. He woke early and loved the early morning to just gaze out the window, mediate, pray and count his blessings. In his later years he became very spiritual. When I arose in the morning the coffee was ready and we both loved our special breakfast time talks. He knew everything that was happening in the neighborhood. Most things I was oblivious to. When I jumped up from breakfast table to start my daily chores; he would say, "Come back and sit with me; that can wait."

We met in high school through our love of dance and danced our way through life almost until the end. We went out to dine every Friday. Some would say we acted like lovers. We delighted in the company of one another.

I realize that death, loss and grief are realities of life. Yet I wonder how I will survive the devastating loss of my husband, father of my children, my lover and best friend. Laughing happy people seem out of place in my world. Normal and routine for me is to feel half crazy.

He managed heart problems from the time he had heart surgery at age 45. In later years he was in and out of the hospital with heart failure. Because he was so resilient and always rallied

I guess I never let myself contemplate a time when I might be without him. I didn't allow myself to think that a day will come when everything would change and life as I knew it would spin out of control and never be the same.

I punished myself with guilt. Should I have sent him to a different hospital? Could I have done something different? I blamed myself for hospital errors; the hospital standard of care that was breached; the doctor that lacerated his liver and didn't tell me. I still am besieged with what I could have done differently. Would it have made a difference? There were unresolved issues we had planned to talk about. Now I talk to myself.

There have been days I thought I really was going insane. I would talk out loud to him and scream and cry. I even thought his spirit was listening to me. I couldn't eat and felt dizzy. My heart and chest ached. I wondered how I would ever survive this profound grief. More over I didn't want to survive. At times I felt shaky. I had to get in the car and go somewhere. My breathing was deep sighs. I turned on the radio for distraction only to hear a song we loved to dance to. I screamed and cried in the car.

I see photos of him around the house. The tears flow and memories of good times come flooding back. I flick through the channels and his beloved Cubs are playing. It is like I am being tortured. I picture him engaged in the game and so content. I wonder if they have ballgames in Heaven.

I feel like half a person, going crazy, not at all in charge, and full of rage and anger at times. I forget to sign checks. I misplace things. I feel hopeless, loneliness, guilt, bitterness, sorrow, regret and fear. Three months later I am trying to make peace with the unwelcome status of being a widow. I keep telling myself that other widows have lived through the grief and mourning. They survived. Yet the promise that time will heal doesn't register.

I started to empty his dresser drawers and found valentine cards with loving notes. The last one he gave me played the Unchained Melody: "Oh my love, my darling I hunger for your touch." I listened to it and was tearful all day. I attempted to clean out his closet. I had to leave it go. His closet smells like him. His drawers smell like him. I felt anger that he is no longer with me and fear of being alone. Maybe the beginning numbness was a

*Patt and Gary Abrahamson's 50th anniversary on a Princess Cruise.*

protective shield that helped me through the funeral details and burial mass. The kids left shortly after the funeral and now the reality has set in.

I have flash backs of the suffering he went through. I cling to faith; faith that he is in a better place and someday we will be together again. I read everything I can about Heaven and meeting our loved ones in the after-life. I pray for peace. I am attending counseling to help me deal with the all-consuming grief. In September St. Anne's Church in Escanaba will hold weekly grief sessions. Believe me I'll be there.

## AND...LIFE GOES ON

Life experiences "THROUGH THE YEARS" help to define who we are. And we like to think as the years accumulate so does our wisdom. And darn...so do the wrinkles. But let's face it, the most important attribute of any human being is having a good heart and genuinely caring about people.

Our life experience regarding feelings and the heart take us through a realm of emotions. If we live long enough we complete a life cycle that ultimately may include marriage, divorce, births, deaths, happiness, excitement, sadness, grief and much more. For many the end of life is a loneliness that takes away the zest for life.

John and I experienced extreme grief associated with losing a life partner after 60 years of marriage. Our spouses, Gary and Melissa died within two months of one another. So grief was the element that brought us together. Ironically I had written a love story about John and Melissa a few years ago. (Page 65) Who would have ever thought that our grief meeting over lunch would evolve into such a beautiful relationship? We believe that perhaps there was a divine intervention. John wanted to take care of my son, Gary too. For me that was huge. A few months later we were married in a wonderful ceremony with our children present in Naples. FL,

We really thank God every day for having the opportunity to

have such a wonderful loving relationship at our advanced age. We enjoy the simple things in life and no doubt shock people when we hold hands in restaurants at our age. Oh! We had a few problems in adjustment to begin with. We were both the "heavy" in our first marriage. John took care of everything in his household and I was "in charge" in my household—-mostly because Gary wanted it that way. Sooo—-you guessed it. We both thought we were "boss" in our new relationship. Well we finally resolved that with a compromise. We both agreed that John would be "boss" one day a month...problem solved! End of story!

*Patt and John Besse, married March 3rd, 2012.*